The Cinema Makers

The Cinema Makers
Public life and the exhibition of difference in south-eastern and central Europe since the 1960s

Anna Schober

intellect Bristol, UK / Chicago, USA

First published in the UK in 2013 by
Intellect, The Mill, Parnall Road, Fishponds, Bristol, BS16 3JG, UK

First published in the USA in 2013 by
Intellect, The University of Chicago Press, 1427 E. 60th Street,
Chicago, IL 60637, USA

Cover photos: © xscreen, xscreen archive Berlin, courtesy Wilhelm Hein and
© Živojin Pavlović, courtesy Jugoslovenska Kinoteka, Belgrade.

A catalogue record for this book is available from the
British Library.

The printing of this book was kindly supported by the Austrian Ministry
for Science and Research and the Department 7 - Cultural Affairs of the
city of Vienna.

Cover designer: Holly Rose
Production manager: Tim Mitchell
Copy-editor: MPS Technologies
Typesetting: Planman Technologies

ISBN 978-1-84150-515-2

Printed and bound by Charlesworth Press, UK

Contents

List of Illustrations

Acknowledgements

The research upon which this book is based was funded in large part by the FWF Austrian Science Fund (ref. P18774-G08). Many thanks to them for their support. Smaller and, to some extent, preparatory research projects were funded by the Austrian Ministry of Science, Cultural Studies Fund and the City of Vienna Science Group (MA 7 Wissenschafts- und Forschungsförderung). The final chapters were written during a research project at Verona University that was funded by the European Union, Seventh Framework Programme, Marie Curie Actions, Grant Agreement No. PIEF-GA-2009-234990. Again, thanks to all of them.

While researching and writing this book, I taught at various universities in Austria, Italy and Germany and held several courses on this as well as related topics. I would like to thank my students for the sometimes challenging, often inspiring discussions. I also presented theses and individual chapters from this book at a range of conferences, workshops and lecture series, sometimes held at the institutions where I was working, other times abroad. I would like to thank all the people who contributed through remarks, debate or by questioning some of my theses and who in this way helped me develop my arguments and ideas further.

I would like to thank Tim Mitchell from Intellect Books for his patience and assistance and Kimi Lum and David Westacott for their aid with the English manuscript. Special thanks go to Willem A. de Graaf who was a first reader of most of the chapters and with whom I shared many of the films in this book.

Finally, thanks to all the activists, fans, cinema-makers, film-makers and artists who allowed me to interview them and in doing so often managed to redirect my reflections along unexpected paths. It is the web of initiatives and judgments you have contributed to as well as the passion for cinema we share that I have sought to foreground and make more lasting by writing this book.

Abbreviations

m. t.   my translation
A. S.   Anna Schober
n. d.   no date
n. p.   no pagination

Introduction

O rhan Pamuk describes the cinema as an urban space where it is possible to meet the other – which from the perspective of his youth in Turkey is 'the West' – face to face. Here it is possible to get acquainted with the everyday life of others down to the smallest detail and to enter into their world: the folding of a handkerchief or a gesture of greeting. The darkness in the cinema space acts like a frame for this relationship with the other, transforming it into a rapport of observation and identification. Everything the cinema presents and whatever the story is, he says, becomes in the same instant 'the other'. And for this reason, in the cinema our own desire invoked by the existence of the other usually also comes up: friendship, the pleasures of daily life, happiness, power and sex, as well as the opposite of all these things and their absence.[1] At the same time, however, while watching a film we usually do not notice that we are observing the other, because we become involved in various sensuous experiences, enter different viewpoints and are carried along by the narration.

In the decades after the Second World War, in cities in pluralist democratic as well as socialist one-party societies in central and south-eastern Europe cinema adaptations in the form of ciné clubs, film museums, film archives or film venues in art spaces spread and became important places for seeing a variety of films from different countries. Marko Babac, a member of the kino club 'Beograd' and protagonist of the Yugoslav novi film movement, for example, reports how he watched mostly foreign films every Friday evening in the Kinoteka Yugoslav Film Archive: 'The first contact for me, very important, was with Leni Riefenstahl and [with] Soviet directors, communist directors from the Soviet revolution: Eisenstein, Pudovkin, Dziga Vertov, Alexandrov, [the] famous directors of the Soviet Union at the beginning of this golden era of the Soviet cinema. Films of the real' (I MB).[2] In addition, he mentions having occasionally seen American films. 'In the beginning it was not allowed. It started really slowly,' he says. But he especially remembers seeing the Japanese film *Rashomon* (Akira Kurosawa, 1950) (I MB).

In a quite similar way, the German film-maker Harun Farocki speaks about a 'different trend in film history' in connection with the experience of watching films in the early 1960s at the Akademie der Künste (Academy of Fine Arts) in Berlin. This highlighted the importance 'that one does not only know what is shown on TV or what one's parents watched, but also the undiscovered, the French or German pre-war cinema, or the American cinema. Humphrey Bogart was not known at that time, it was a sensation when this or the Marx Brothers was shown. And this meant that a space like the *Akademie der*

Künste [emerged in a new way, A. S.] [...] this led to there being events with more than 1,000 spectators for one obscure avant-garde film' (I HF). Hence both Babac and Farocki describe certain urban places for viewing film as spaces where the public was exposed to the unfamiliar, that is, temporarily or regionally distant or previously 'undiscovered' worlds, and enjoyed the stimuli that such encounters provided.

This book deals with the potential the cinema has as such a space for encountering the other and – through himself or herself – also oneself as the other and the effects this has on the level of urban civil society. The examples chosen for the investigation are initiatives created by film consumers who in this way turned into cinema-makers and sometimes also into artists and film-makers, that is, they managed to gain a public presence by organizing cinema situations or by squatting in already existing cinema spaces, but also by presenting and discussing film, by writing about film or by engaging in aesthetic production.

In the chapters that follow I will concentrate on the comparison between narrations, deeds and films made by cinema activists and film-makers in central and south-eastern European cities such as Vienna, Cologne, Hamburg, Munich, Ljubljana, Zagreb and Belgrade since the 1960s. In doing so I will especially focus on the differences and similarities in the constitution of politically relevant non-conformist movements in pluralist democratic and socialist one-party systems and will relate this to the follow-up phenomena their activities acquired in the following decades. I will refer to a corpus of interviews with individual film-makers as well as members of cinema initiatives such as the communal cinema, the ciné club and the Expanded Cinema movement in Germany and Austria since the late 1960s and protagonists of the Yugoslav novi film movement (also called 'open cinema' or Crni Talas, approx. 1963–1973) and the follow-up groups they triggered.

These cinema initiatives are a good starting point and suited to a comparative study because they happened approximately in the same time span and mutually influenced each other and – what is even more important – indicate also a historic change in the overall history of politicization processes related to cinema situations. Unlike previous social movements that also focus on the cinema spaces as a place of politicization – such as the working-class cinema clubs or the newsreel movement of the 1920s – the communal and ciné club movement, the Expanded Cinema or the Yugoslav novi film movement are no longer bound to relatively stable class formations and party organizations, even if they remain related to the 'older' movements and sometimes reconstruct a relationship with them in a very active and pronounced way. In contrast to their precursors, however, these cinema activist groups emerging since the 1960s expose aesthetic tactics, media and styles of aesthetic expression as well as of self-presentation in a more pronounced way. They exhibit a 'difference' in the public sphere that can no longer be interpreted in categories set up by the working-class movements – such as 'class' or 'right' or 'false consciousness' – but demands the acknowledgement of other authoritative frames of reference.

Hence these initiatives are situated at the transition between the movements that emerged in the years between the First and the Second World War, which (by eradicating ambivalence and suppressing a variety of cultural differences) focused on the universal dimension of a certain difference – be it 'the worker' or 'the nation'– and the movements that emerged after 1968, which often programmatically rediscovered and exhibited a plurality of differences (such as gender, sexual, ethnic and cultural differences).[3] The research on this book was therefore based on the consideration that a more detailed analysis of the ways in which such movements come into existence, of how they inhabit the city, of the kind of films or artworks they produce and the reception history they inspire, is able to provide insight into how the public management of difference, which is linked to ways of expressing and staging oneself in public and of deploying sense, changes. At the same time it also aims to show that throughout these various contexts, the cinema repeatedly acted – similar to cities or certain urban districts – as a place of ambivalent identification and a non-univocal attribution of identity.

In recent years, films have been investigated in differentiated ways with regard to their cultural, historical implications. Most of these investigations, as differentiated and rich as they may have been in some other aspects, have not focused on the production, presentation or reception of film, nor on the adaptation of films through consumer practice or the wider environment of the city and the multiple relations between cities, nations and transnational processes. Even works pertaining to the political dimension of cinema often do not focus on the creativity of the spectators and the broader public dimension of cinema but rather conceive the spectator as a function of formal film codes (on this tradition, see Schober 2009b: 165f.). Contrary to such approaches, the investigation carried out in this book conceives the cinema as a spatial arrangement within the wider context of (smaller or bigger) cities and the viewing of films not only as a subject-constituting process, but also as a space-creating activity. Furthermore, it concentrates on mostly urban groups and movements that have used films, projectors, screens and seats or artistic action in order to intervene in a space they themselves have usually viewed as a social and political sphere.

In order to tell the stories of cinema initiatives and of the transformation of the public sphere their interventions and productions triggered, I will move into the middle of things, *in medias res* and will investigate the circulation processes around cinema and film in which people become involved (Latour 2005: 196). I will track the traces that activism in and around cinema spaces has left behind as well as, conversely, reconstruct the spatial dissemination of the various deeds, judgments and representations this activism triggered. Part of this is to foreground controversy and conflicts that come up in such processes as well as delineations between the various initiatives and reception and adaptation processes. In doing so, the meaning and sense of stories, actions, spaces or things are not treated as 'matters of fact' but as 'matters of concern', which means that they are perceived, lived and represented differently by the various actors and forces operating in social space.

Part of this approach is developing theses by working 'with' the historical sources (public interventions, films, interviews, photographs or media documentation) rather than by presenting a mere 'bird's-eye view' on the phenomena examined. I also do not claim to tell the whole story in one piece, that is, chapters in which I apply the above-mentioned comparative view alternate with other ones that examine single case studies and in this way elucidate the overall story from a different angle.

The first chapter presents the methodological approach adopted in the present study in detail and clarifies key concepts such as 'social space', 'contentious terrain', 'public sphere', 'aesthetic events' and 'subject in process'. It does not outline a theoretical framework in a careful systematic way that can be applied rigidly for empirical investigation, but rather seeks to propose some initial reflections on such key notions that will later be taken up and developed further.

The second chapter constitutes the core piece of the book. It compares cinema activist groups in central and south-eastern European cities since the 1960s and shows how they originated, the kind of films they present or produce, the discourses they relate to, the kind of audience they manage to attract and the conflicts or fan communities they set in motion. In doing so, the chapter focuses on how the pluralist democratic and socialist one-party context shapes these movements differently, in addition to all the similarities that can also be detected. It shows that the various cinema initiatives investigated all participate in the constitution of a conflictual public sphere in the FRG and Austria and an 'informal public sphere' in former Yugoslavia, and carves out how the particular public sphere emerging since the 1960s in both political systems can be further characterized.

Moreover, this chapter also develops the thesis that the rediscovery of difference that we encounter with these cinema movements emerging around 1968 needs to be understood as a reaction to modern tendencies to eliminate ambivalence and to strongly control difference. The analysis of films that were screened and discussed in these circles shows that the aesthetic statements brought into circulation by these movements managed to exceed the rigid East-West, Cold War frame of reference and to replace it with a new one highlighting the discrepancies between 'first world' and 'third world'.

The third chapter presents close readings of films produced in these contexts. In the process, an alternating gaze on cinema cultures in central and south-eastern Europe is not practised in the form of a comparative analysis constantly switching between these two contexts – as in the second chapter – but in the form of two essays. One analyses works by the German director Rainer Werner Fassbinder, who started his film-making activity in Munich within the frameworks of the student movement but soon started to cast a critical eye on these frameworks themselves. It focuses mainly on Fassbinder's 'migrant guest-worker films' that deal with the very imaginations and projections regarding the other through which people unite as groups and discusses them in the context of the FRG in the years following '1968'.[4]

The second essay takes films made by the Yugoslav film-maker Dušan Makavejev in the 1960s and early 1970s as a starting point. It shows that by representing what was officially excluded or seen as a taboo and by employing an unconventional aesthetic style Makavejev contributed to the emergence of an (informal) public sphere that maintained relations of conflict with the one-party regime. These films, which mainly engage in a figuration of difference as an aesthetic and sexual difference (often merged with ethnic features), are juxtaposed with the work of a film-maker of the next generation, Srdjan

Karanović. Shortly before the wars of the 1990s, he also staged a story that deals with the rediscovery of sexual difference, but was then – again involuntarily but much more insistently than the films by novi film authors such as Makavejev – incorporated into 'ethnic' or 'national' readings and renegotiations of difference.

The last chapter investigates, again in the form of two essays, cinema initiatives in the 1990s and the new millennium that adopt the cinema practices of the 1968 movements, even if they sometimes distinguish their activities clearly from those of their forerunners. One of these essays analyses the revival of a pronouncedly humorous and 'trashy' cinema practice that emerged – as cinema activism but also as a feature film – in former Yugoslavia in the context of the wars of the 1990s. It discusses various ways of judging these methods of gaining humorous pleasure out of (and of trying to master) difficult, violent and painful situations.

The second essay contains examples of cinema initiatives emerging in cities such as Hamburg or Vienna in the 1990s that present themselves either as flash-mob-like events in urban space, as a harbourage for other initiatives or as festivals or artworks. They are again investigated in their relationship to their urban and political environments that have in these decades, too, undergone strong transformations. The affection of enthusiasm that – in conjunction with critique – usually emerges as part of these initiatives is discussed in its role of providing passages and stimulating translations which we need to create a common world.

Notes

1 Because of the enormous differences between the translations of the Turkish text into German and into English and since the German is the one I originally worked with and seems to me to be the more precise and richer, I am referring here to the German translation (Pamuk 2008: 180f.).

2 The interviews were conducted between 2000 and 2011 in the course of several research projects. The most important of these are *Picturing Gender* at Verona University, funded by the EU, Seventh Framework Programme, Marie Curie Actions, Grant Agreement No. PIEF-GA-2009-234990; *City-Squats: The Cinema as a Space for Political Action*, financed by the FWF. Austrian Science Fund, 2006–2009; *Aesthetic Tricks as a Means of Political Emancipation*, financed by the FWF. Austrian Science Fund, 2003–2006, and the fellowship *The Cinema as Political Utopia* (2001) as well as the project *Cinema: Transformations of a Social Space. Vienna 1945–2000* (2000, together with Werner Schwarz and Siegfried Mattl), both financed by the FS Cultural Studies, Ministry of Science, Austria. All interviews explicitly quoted are listed at the end of the book. In the text they are referred to as '(I XX)', where 'I' stands for interview and 'XX' stands for the initials of the interviewee. I conducted all interviews myself (a few times in collaboration with colleagues); the interviews in Austria and in Germany were conducted in German, those in former Yugoslavia in English; all translations are by myself in collaboration with Kimi Lum and David Westacott.

3 In relation to 'difference' and in particular 'sexual difference' see the discussion between Rosi Braidotti and Judith Butler (Braidotti and Butler 1994: 39ff.).

4 I use '1968' for the historic event that goes beyond the year itself.

—

Chapter 1

In the middle of things: city, cinema and the public sphere

The photograph *Le Reflet* from the photo series *Périphérique* by Mohamed Bourouissa (2007, Figure 1) shows old computer monitors and TV sets stacked on top of each other on a low concrete base amid a suburban housing area. At the front edge of the pile but somehow also part of it, there is a human figure in a light-coloured tracksuit sitting on an upturned monitor with his back towards us. He is leaning slightly forward and gazing into the pile. Even if the ensemble of the monitors and the figure seem to be carefully cast, the whole scene gives the impression of a garbage site. The human figure could be an inhabitant of one of the tower blocks of his surroundings, yet his soft, roundish forms and his self-absorption also make him seem like an estranged element in the arrangement. We only see the back of the person and a pronounced unisex outfit, but the broad shoulders and the open position of the legs suggest that the person amid the pile of monitors is a man – probably young or middle-aged since old people usually do not go around in tracksuits like the one depicted here.

This image poses the question of how to create connectivity in contemporary living areas that are heavily interspersed with mass media. In addition, it links this question to a contemporary urban scene that seems to transcend national boundaries. Because even if the series title *Périphérique* suggests that the photograph was probably taken in one of the French *banlieus*, it could in fact also have been shot in parts of Berlin, Vienna, Warsaw or Novi Sad.

Furthermore, various other questions concerning our contemporary urban dwelling condition also come up. For instance, how can public connectivity be created in an environment in which individuals are increasingly thrown back onto themselves, in which one can no longer hark back to the lines of tradition and convention handed on from birth in order to make sense of things and in which affiliations usually change quickly and often? Then there is the question of how to deal with the fact that urban landscapes are increasingly segregated nowadays: there are dormitory suburbs, such as the one depicted in the photograph, as well as office areas and amusement miles. The superposition of various functions in one place, which Richard Sennett (2003: 297) presented as an important precondition for the emergence of a public sphere, is often missing.

At the same time the photograph also highlights the importance media channels assume in such segregated urban environments. These channels are detached from the local setting and at the same time offer a stream of globally organized images and information. One can enter this stream any time in order to find quickly changing material for identification and for a confrontation about sense and belonging – which tends to be expressed in the form

Figure 1: *Le Reflet* from the series *Périphérique,* Mohamed Bourouissa, 2007–2008 © Mohamed Bourouissa, courtesy the artist and Kamel Mennour, Paris.

of direct action (or inaction) and is no longer re-inserted into complicated procedures of (public) representation (Hobsbawm 2007: 106).

Hence, the question arises as to the transnational and global processes that are becoming dominant today and are replacing the older national ones in providing the frame of reference for today's acting and perceiving. Connected to this, we are also confronted with the loss of attractiveness of classical 'modern' institutionalized arenas for creating a public sphere, for example associations, unions, clubs, parties or state-run institutions. What again suggests a corresponding tendency: the importance that cultural phenomena acquire in a struggle over the shape of the common world. This involves new media, film, Internet, music, fashion or sports, and the highly media-dependent arenas connected with them – such as cinemas, multimedia or party spaces, concert halls or stadiums. And in turn, this points to the fact that the struggle about a visible presence of cultural difference is increasingly appearing alongside those about social equality and the redistribution of wealth.

Le Reflet by Mohamed Bourouissa draws attention to the relation of the individual vis-à-vis the global flow of images. It highlights the alienating and isolating dimensions of these changes in contemporary city landscapes. In order not to fall into the trap of narrating a mere history of decay in respect to these transformations, I will confront this photograph with another artwork that exposes and interrogates the community-creating force linked to contemporary media and the role of cinema in constructing a public sphere in particular.

1.1. Cinema's potential for creating a public sphere

The Thai artist Rirkrit Tiravanija created the installation *Community cinema for a quiet intersection (against Oldenburg)* as part of the City of Architecture Festival in Glasgow, Scotland, in September 1999 (Figure 2a–b). He created a temporary outdoor cinema composed of four screens and accompanied by a Thai café right on a traffic intersection in

Figure 2a–b: *Community cinema for a quiet intersection (against Oldenburg),* Rirkrit Tiravanija, installation at the City of Architecture Festival in Glasgow, Scotland, September 1999
© Rirkrit Tiravanija, courtesy The Modern Institute, Glasgow.

a residential neighbourhood in Glasgow and after dusk showed films that had been chosen by the local community: *Casablanca*, *A Bug's Life*, *The Jungle Book* and *It's a Wonderful Life* were shown in parallel on the four screens.

This installation accommodated various references: to open-air cinema or drive-in cinemas, to ciné clubs and community cinemas, but also to management strategies of the Hollywood film industry and multiplex cinemas as well as to newly invented, local 'traditions'. The most striking of these references is that of community cinemas and open-air cinemas.

Already in its title, but also with the amateur-like conglomerate of screens, street kitchen and loosely distributed seats, the installation quotes the practice now widespread in many countries of setting up cinema situations using a bare minimum of equipment, such as easily erectable screens, portable projectors, simple chairs, sometimes accompanied also by a street kitchen or a drinks trolley. In connection with the attractor film, this setting can encourage people to gather in the most diverse – sometimes also very poor and difficult to live-in surroundings[1] – whereby the collective body formed in this way somehow always alters the standard cinema setting. Hence the situation created by Tiravanija is aimed at creating a connectivity among neighbours as well as strangers, and at the same time it stages a difference by bringing a Thai café and Hollywood classics together, which gave it a rather exotic touch in the Glasgow neighbourhood.

In addition, the four screens high above the intersection recall drive-in cinemas and the public survey that was realized in order to determine which films should be shown on the screen recalls production strategies of the Hollywood film industry and of the multiplex cinema, which since the 1980s have sought to integrate 'all of us' and to offend or exclude nobody.[2] Last but not least, there is a connection to 'Thai' traditions that is kept vivid not only by the setting up of a Thai café, but also by information circulated by the artist himself. In a short e-mail exchange, Tiravanija mentioned that one of the inspirational sources of this work are outdoor cinemas in Thailand, which are set up as part of temple festivals, or nearby Chinese shrines where the film is offered to the gods or goddesses (of the shrines) to thank them for the fulfilment of a wish.[3] With this mix of associative references, the cinema installation presents itself as a cross between bottom-up activism, commercial and religious operations and local and global procedures.

At the same time, *Community cinema for a quiet intersection* not only relates explicitly and implicitly to other contemporary cinema phenomena on a local as well as global scale but also distances itself actively from certain traditions – most notably from those rooted in the classical modernist art world. The subtitle of the installation is 'Against Claes Oldenburg'. Accordingly, part of the information that Tiravanija himself circulates about this urban intervention is a drawing (Figure 3) in which the American artist Claes Oldenburg drafts a protest installation against the Vietnam War.[4] In sketching a big cube occupying the intersection of Canal Street and Broadway in New York City (1965), a *Block of Concrete with the Names of War Heroes*, Oldenburg staged his intervention as a kind of provocative obstacle for city dwellers. In doing so, the artist drew on the convention of 'irritating' and 'awakening' the public and of stimulating viewers to reflect on existing attitudes.

14

Figure 3: *Proposed monument for the intersection of Canal Street and Broadway, N. Y. C. – block of concrete with the names of war heroes,* Claes Oldenburg, 1965 © Claes Oldenburg, 1965, courtesy digital image: New York, The Museum of Modern Art (MoMA)/Scala Florence.

By quoting Oldenburg explicitly, but by deploying at the same time a much less hierarchical relationship between artist and public, Tiravanija's installation distances itself from this convention and in this way highlights the innovative and anti-modernist character of his alteration. *Community cinema for a quiet intersection* not only stages the fact that it is meant to be used in order to constitute a community, but the installation is even presented as responding to choices made by the public. As already mentioned, the films shown on the four screens were determined by a survey conducted in the neighbourhood – similar to those made by sales departments of production companies, by media or the public sector. However, through the brusque, montage-like arrangement of the four screens directly above the traffic intersection and the achieved interruption of everyday traffic flow that this creates, the installation presents at the same time an unusual and uncomfortable solution – one that challenges our ability to make sense inside urban environments that, because of the above-mentioned tendencies towards segregation, are often too poorly adapted to create a shared public sphere.

Tiravanija's temporary urban intervention thus shows a strong contrariness, it offers involvement and at the same time reflective dissociation, which makes it difficult to inhabit it and to create the very connectivity that it seems to be designed for. Correspondingly, photographs of the screening show the setting being rather loosely populated by visitors mostly individually absorbed in the performance on the screen. This contrariness, however, is also able to stimulate an (ad hoc or retrospective) observation and reflection of the function that the cinema has in creating a public sphere, a function that, as I will show in the following chapters, persists despite the dissemination of new media such as TV and the Internet. To put it another way, there seems to be a potential for creating a public sphere inherent in the cinema setting that is responsible for its persistence in the age of video, TV, Internet and digital media since this somehow counteracts the further 'privatization' and 'fragmentation' of the political that goes along with these new media – and Tiravija's community cinema invites us to examine this.

As Georg Simmel (1997) has pointed out, there is a power of cinema in respect to socialization that is related to the particular and strongly standardized arrangement of space, light and bodies that characterizes the cinema setting. What we usually understand by 'cinema' is either a space marked off by four walls or an outdoor situation that uses barriers to somehow simulate this. On one of these walls we find an enormous screen that can be covered by curtains. On the opposite side – even if in most cases behind some further covering, and so invisible to the viewer – we find the film projection machinery and the projectionist. In between there are a great many numbered seats, in orderly, narrow rows, all facing one direction: towards the screen. Already the size of the space and the physical closeness between the people in the seats can create an exciting effect, an impulsiveness and a sweeping-away of the public, which enhances the feeling of being part of a collective. In addition, the darkness of the cinema space creates an uncertainty of the spatial frame, which further amplifies these effects. In the cinema we are huddled together with those next to us in a pronounced bodily way, and at the same time the boundaries of the space as a whole disappear and allow fantasy to expand it towards infinite dimensions.

In *Community cinema for a quiet intersection* this familiar setting is quoted and at the same time rearranged. We have four screens instead of one and they are placed in the middle rather than at the side. Consequently, the space around the four screens is in no way confined and can, theoretically, be endlessly expanded as the audience grows. There are no fixed seats but people can stay or sit wherever they choose and are challenged to watch the films, but also to make sense of the unusual situation they find themselves in. This way the situation turns into a 'cinema to think with'. At the same time there is still darkness, a gathering of people from the neighbourhood mixing with strangers related to a screen, and a physical excitement responding to the presence of others and the exposition of the film.

As will become clearer in connection with further examples we will encounter in this book, there is a standardization of the cinema setting that is so well anchored in habit and collective memory that it remains somehow present even if it is as drastically rearranged as in this example. A further effect of this standardization is that cinema generates a familiar feeling even if one enters a place one has never visited before – which, however, not only has to do with the consistently similar organization of space but also with the information available about films being shown. In cinemas in bigger cities in quite different countries there is usually some place where one can see a recent film one has heard or read about even if there are major differences between various cinema worlds in terms of regional, global or genre attribution (for instance: Bollywood, Hollywood or European art house cinema). Cinemas thus also function as temporary, familiar shelters even in places one is living in as a stranger on a business trip, as a tourist or as a migrant. And it is this strange familiarity of cinema that Tiravanija evokes and brusquely combines with the anonymity of an urban intersection.

Interventions in contentious territories

Tiravanija's installation combines two situations that usually do not belong together: the cinema and a traffic intersection, and in this way he alienates them and turns the situations he creates into a riddle. Cinema is transformed into a work of art, however, into one that strongly interlinks with the various elements and agents that already exist in the place it has been created for: the intersection and a local flow of traffic in a Glasgow neighbourhood, an international art discourse, a canon of classical movies, management strategies concerning the dissemination of movies or people's personal choices concerning film.

Every attempt at setting up a cinema intervenes in a similar way into what is already present in a situation. But a still dominant idea of space being created by architects and urban planners and only afterwards populated by people conceals this. The riddle-effect that goes together with this art installation points to the fact that cinema is always already an intervention into a space that in itself is shaped, perceived and loaded with feelings by various agents. Tiravanija's installation thus is able to serve as a starting point for presenting and clarifying key concepts used in the present study such as 'social space', 'contentious terrain' and 'public sphere'.

Why is the spatial dimension singled out in this way as one being particularly important to the investigation carried out in this book? First of all, because cinema is, as we have seen, primarily a spatial connection emerging between a simple architectural box, a multitude of bodies brought physically close to each other, darkness and a film shown on an enormous screen – whereby the darkness allows fantasy to expand space almost infinitely. Roland Barthes, for instance, writes that when he says 'cinema', he imagines 'hall' and not 'film' and further defines this setting as being a dark, anonymous cube, where a celebration of affects, called 'film', is capable of taking place (Barthes 1975).

The importance of space, furthermore, comes up in connection with cinema activism in particular. In 2004, during the research process for a previous book (Schober 2009b), I frequented an urban space in Belgrade, the Cinema Rex, which had an important function in public and urban life in the 1990s.[5] It served as a haven but also as a connecting and motivating factor for various oppositional movements against the Milošević regime. Although the architecture resembles an old, perhaps art deco cinema hall, the Cinema Rex was never really a cinema. It was built as a Jewish cultural centre in the early twentieth century, and later became a location for several activities of the Communist Party and its sub-organizations. Only in the 1980s was it 'dressed up' as a cinema in the course of a film shoot, and after this it was adapted as a cultural centre by various cultural and political groups. For example, Low-Fi Video activists, whose procedures I will present later on in more detail, constituted themselves in this space and drew their first audience from people who were already connected to the Cinema Rex in one way or another. In turn, the enthusiasm that these activists created with their video screenings further connected other people to this urban nodal point.

Just as Cinema Rex stands out as being an important spatial haven for various kinds of cultural and political activism in Belgrade during a particular period, a space, or actually two connected spaces, with a similar function also emerged in Vienna in the 1990s. They were cinemas in a more straightforward way – even if they had an adjoining bar or restaurant and a very open policy regarding the events staged in them: the Schikaneder cinema and the Topkino, both located in a central district in Vienna and run by the same team. As the cinema operator Johannes Wegenstein stated in an interview, first the Schikaneder and then, in 2003, the Topkino acted as a nodal point for cinema activism carried out by migrant communities, queer groups as well as young film-makers and artists (I JW) – which I will analyse later on in chapter four of this book. The various groups temporarily squatting there also made their own clienteles familiar with these spaces so that they became a regular hang-out for quite a mixed intercultural scene, which encouraged further activities – in other districts and cities as well.

The bonding some visitors experienced with these spaces was sometimes very strong and long standing. So, for instance, after a talk I gave at a conference in Yerevan, Armenia, about the history of cinema activism, in (among other places) Austria, somebody in the audience piped up furiously. He was agitated and asked me why I had left out the Schikaneder Kino and 'discriminated' against it this way. After I explained that the focus of my paper was on cinema activism in connection with the student movement in the 1960s, he calmed down a bit and explained that during an artist stay in Vienna he used to go to this place almost every evening and participated in various film and video events there and that he had somehow felt threatened and excluded when I had failed to mention this space. From this experience I learned – and later this awareness was confirmed by other events – that the Schikaneder and the Topkino acted – and are still acting – as an important haven for foreign visitors to Vienna, in particular for artists and cinema enthusiasts from the eastern regions.

These examples show two interrelated things: firstly, that cities seem to generate spaces that such modes of involvement can spread from. City life seems to be somehow in need of such 'public' urban havens. Secondly, they demonstrate that activist groups constitute themselves through an occupation of space as well as through ways of showing (or making) films or videos and – sometimes, for example, in the case of 'Low-Fi Video' in Belgrade around 2000 or the 'First Turkish Women's Film Festival' in the Topkino in Vienna in 2007 – by naming themselves as collective beings in connection to these places. Hence, these collective bodies did not exist beforehand but gain visibility and presence only through this kind of anchoring in the city, that is, by re-using existing cinema spaces and by creating new viewing situations from where they could then attract an audience and so expand their radius of action. In addition, through this occupation of space and creation of events, these groups are also staging a difference vis-à-vis other viewing options and so become involved in a struggle over the qualities of our shared world.

Yet in order to understand this spatial dimension more fully, we have to ask not only what happens in and around the cinema setting but also how the space that cinema intervenes in can be conceptualized. The examples mentioned so far already show that space is not just constructed out of buildings, streets and other traffic routes, parks, walls, squares and trees and only then inhabited by people, but it is also always constructed by relations among people and replenished by various and invisible charges: enthusiasm, fascinations, wishes, imaginations, memories, fears, disavowals as well as various projects and projections.

Usually, these relations, projections, projects and feelings are not visible and, because of that, go unnoticed. Italo Calvino however narrates the story about a city named 'Ersilia', where its inhabitants translate these things into the visible: 'In Ersilia, to establish the relationships that sustain the city's life, the inhabitants stretch strings from the corners of the houses, white and black or grey or black-and-white according to whether they mark a relationship of blood, of trade, authority, agency. When the strings become so numerous that you can no longer pass among them, the inhabitants leave. […] Thus, when travelling in the territory of Ersilia you come upon […] spider-webs of intricate relationships seeking a form' (Calvino 1978: 76).

Henri Lefèbvre tries to grasp such space-constructing relations and emotional and often conflicting loadings of space with his notion of 'social space'. He coined this notion in order to oppose what he calls a 'double illusion' (Lefèbvre 1999: 27) of transparency and opacity. The first deals with space as initially empty, transparent and manageable, that is, as an entity that offers itself for creation like a white 'virginal' sheet of paper. This vision is attractive because it reduces the multifaceted and often conflicted dimensions of space we have to deal with daily and because, after having entered in it once, we can succumb to a feeling of mastery. The second and complementary illusion that Lefèbvre wants to counter sees space solely as filled with visible objects, and rife with substance, naturalness and density. Here space becomes inflexible, rigid and unified. Both attitudes, however, conceal the fact that space is always already populated by often conflicting feelings, imaginations, projections and projects, and is produced not only by architects and urban planning but also by relations of exchange and struggle among those who inhabit it.

Besides, space is always already claimed by various agents: diverse groups – such as city planning, security services, big cinema chains, as well as school children, consumers or urban cultural activists – will perceive one and the same space differently, will use it in an always different way and will create diverse representations of it. In relation to this struggle over space, we always deal with 'lived, perceived and represented space', a triad, that Lefèbvre made the central constituent of his concept of space (Lefèbvre 1999: 40).

In doing so he particularly insists on the fact that every perception, every use and every representation involved in this collective creation of space will feature a 'blind spot', that is, bias, distortion, misunderstanding. These blind spots are 'not merely dark and uncertain, poorly explored: they are blind in the sense that there is a blind spot on the retina, the centre – and negation – of vision. A paradox. The eye doesn't see; it needs a mirror. The centre of vision doesn't see and doesn't know it is blind. Do these paradoxes extend to thought, to awareness, to knowledge?' (Lefèbvre 2003: 29).

The 'blind spot' concept thus tries to grasp that all the various attempts to use, perceive and represent the space we are living in are disjoined by a gap – a gap that is not avoidable but is something constitutive for our dealing with the world. There is no place from which this intertwining and this struggle of perceptions, representations and ways of life can be represented in the 'right' way. Even a scientific account such as the one I am trying to give in this book can only present an approximate assessment of the distribution of power involved in such processes of space creation.

However, I do not want simply to adopt Lefèbvre's approach for the investigation in this book; because even if Lefèbvre conceptualizes space in this plurality, his theory is also characterized by quite a rigid Marxist evolution theory in which in the end spatial processes are again reduced to a linear and teleological process determined by one singular level: that of production.[6] Furthermore, he distinguishes between 'producers' and 'users' of space, with the former being seen as imposing orders and as manipulating the latter, who have only the role of being passively manipulated and becoming 'thoroughly inserted' in what was defined for them (Lefèbvre 1999: 43f.).

In this way Lefèbvre again eliminates the openness and plurality in which space is otherwise conceptualized by him and leaves out the questions of why users accept certain representations of space, and if they always do so or if they are not, at some points, contesting the reigning allocations of spaces, too. This is why in the following pages I will adopt his concept, which sees space as always already lived, perceived and represented by various agents and filled not only with buildings, streets and inhabitants but also with invisible charges of feelings, projections and projects, by combining it with investigations focusing on struggles about political power, meaning and sense. Particular attention is dedicated to conceiving such a struggle as constitutively open – which also means that its result often comes as a surprise.[7]

In this opening chapter I do not want to outline a theory of space in a capillary way that then can be adopted in an unchanged way for empirical investigation. Rather, I seek to propose initial reflections on some key notions. As a starting point, this investigation maintains that space needs to be conceptualized as the place for real, imaginary and symbolic struggles. This means that even if space is part of the strategies of various institutionalized and bureaucratic agents, such as city councils or big production companies like Warner Brothers, it can always be claimed and adopted by other agents that also constitute themselves as acting entities through such an occupation of space.

Seen this way, the territories in which cinema interventions take place appear to be radically plurivalent. They are occupied, perceived and lived in by various agents at the same time – which, however, enter this struggle with different qualifications and with an inequality of assertive power; they are claimed, contested and crossed by practices of articulation; they are characterized by insurmountable antagonisms, and they never fully fit in with the various definitions they are subjugated to.

Strategies, tactics and the limit of our knowledge of spaces

The above-described power that cinema has in respect to socialization has led a variety of social forces to use it to expand their sphere of action: since its beginning, cinema has been part of educational and promotional discourses of cities, nations, political parties, transnational organizations, corporations and even religious institutions. At the same time, the gatherings of consumers and citizens in and around cinema spaces (or other localities where films are projected) also brought communities into being, and even led to the formation of particular cinema-related political movements.

There were the working-class cinema movements in the 1920s, the Expanded Cinema and cinema clubs or community cinemas in pluralist democratic countries and the different shades of amateur-film movements in socialist countries in the 1960s. Since the late 1980s and 1990s, there was cinema activism created by immigration groups such as the Cinema Beur in France or the Turkish or Kurdish cinema activism in Austria and Germany, as well as cinema events in connection with political questions such as 'women', 'gender' or 'queer'. In post-socialist Eastern Europe, cinema activism then appeared rather in connection to new media, such as video, or to various affirmations of 'ethnic' difference.[8]

The conceptualization of such interventions sometimes goes in a complementary direction to the one I have interrogated before. As outlined above, Lefèbvre starts from the assumption that there are dominant producers of space who manipulate the consumers – something I have criticized by maintaining that even if space is incorporated into strategies of powerful and often institutionalized agents, there is always the possibility that it might be reclaimed and used by other actors – which makes space an essentially contested terrain.

In recent decades, however, one has also seen a complementary tendency in the form of a celebration of consumer and citizen activism, especially in the form that uses media such as film, video or TV.[9] In the case of the arguments discussed in this book, such an attitude would lead to a focus on the actions emerging in spaces such as Cinema Rex in Belgrade or in the Schikaneder cinema in Vienna, celebrating them and opposing them to 'dominant' or 'mainstream' cinema culture by classifying them as 'subversive'. Any correspondence that, despite all differences, would emerge between this kind of cinema activism and broader cinema cultures would be disregarded.

This strand of argumentation usually adopts a distinction coined by Michel de Certeau, who in response to the writings of Michel Foucault and in continuation of those of Carl von Clausewitz tried to differentiate the strategic practices of big companies or bureaucratic apparatuses from the 'tactics' of consumers. According to de Certeau, 'strategies' endow their agents with will and power by demarcating a domain from their surroundings and by developing procedures in order to affect these surroundings and to expand their radius of action. He used the contrasting notion of 'tactics' for all those practices operating, as he calls it, in the lee of strategies and through which consumers gradually and without securing an overview exploit favourable moments blow by blow and try to realize their own interests and wishes by subterfuge (de Certeau 2002: 35f.). Following this argumentation, initiatives employing cinema or other media compounds are called 'strategic' when they come from institutionalized agents such as multinational companies and state or municipal entities, and they are called 'tactics' when referring to claims and deeds of consumers and citizens.

In approaching interventions into city spaces it is certainly important to take account of the fact that various groups already dispose of a different power of assertion as well as different instruments and supporting areas for their participation in struggles over hegemony. Nevertheless, this struggle is always already also one about becoming dominant or remaining marginal – which means that the result of this struggle cannot be decided ex ante, as Michel de Certeau suggests, but is strongly characterized by the unforeseeable and by surprise. This further implies that the two types of acting cannot be attributed to different agents in such a schematic and univocal way as de Certeau suggests. 'Strategies' and 'tactics' never appear in a 'pure' way but are always already mutually contaminated, because consumer practices are also directed towards a demarcation of an 'own' area and a penetration of the surroundings, and the entrepreneurs and state institutions do not always operate from a guaranteed outlook, but also take part in an open contest, in which they too have to exploit favourable moments and search for alliances.

Precisely because of the fracturing of handed-down traditions and conventions that are so symptomatic, as I have shown elsewhere, of our modern being in the world, however, processes of an emphatic re-invention of new traditions are emerging (Schober 2009a and Schober 2009b). Very often, schematic and dichotomous assignments such as those between 'strategies' and 'tactics' are made and are connected to fantasies of 'purity': for instance, of the self and the other, of 'we' and 'them' or of 'our' and 'their' communities. But in spite of such claims, the intentions and the motivations nourishing urban interventions cannot control the effects triggered by them, nor the plurality of utterances involved in them – which also means that the cinema or certain ways of inhabiting it cannot per se be classified as 'counter-cultural space' or as 'other space' (or 'heterotopia') and be opposed in a binary way to 'mainstream' or 'dominant' forms of urban dwelling.[10]

The various forms of employing the cinema setting, both from official, institutionalized agents and from non-institutionalized bottom-up activism, can thus be understood as, in fact, calculated but nevertheless non-calculable appropriation, because – even when they are drafted and realized to be guided by intention – they will interact and collude with all other charges, perceptions and projects present in urban space in a usually unforeseeable way. Thus, they call into question the apparent coherence, totality, manageability and certainty of spatial systems in general. As Salman Rushdie described it from the viewpoint of one of the characters in his novel *The Satanic Verses*: 'The city in its corruption refused to submit to the dominion of the cartographers, changing shape at will and without warning, making it impossible for Gibreel to approach his quest in the systematic manner he would have preferred' (Rushdie 2008: 327).

1.2. Difference and the unfamiliar

In February 2004 I had the opportunity to take part in the dress rehearsal for the 200-year celebration of the State Union of Serbia and Montenegro in the Sava centre in Belgrade – a celebration that had to be invented from scratch since the state union was (re-)established only in 2003, and other parts of the 'old, communist Yugoslavia' had long before split off in 1991/1992. Nevertheless, one of the entrance slides made it immediately clear, that the state celebrated there was anything but new: '200 years ago', the text on a scroll-like background reads, 'the modern Serbian state came into being'. This announcement was accompanied by dramatic music, colourful lighting and flag-like compositions. One of the most striking things in this celebration, however, was the complete lack of clearly identifiable nationalist symbols. On the contrary, abstract compositions recalling rod patterns and snow and very empty symbols of hope such as light cloud-compositions in various forms dominated the event. There was a montage of elements that seemed to have no connection to each other whatsoever: vague and 'empty' symbols and a pronounced modernist aesthetic, dramatic music and lighting and the announcement of a century-long history. Only at the beginning did a chandelier appear as a reference that what was happening had to be seen in the tradition of powerful state representation. Yet the whole montage conveyed the impression of participating in the invention of a story and the construction of a celebration that nobody really believed in. It was necessary to invent such a new story because former states and the stories connected to them had collapsed, but also because none of the other nationalist, folklorist or Yugo-nostalgic stories circulating at the time was presentable enough for such a major ceremonial event.

A local acquaintance who took me along to watch this rehearsal shared my impression. She mentioned that two years previously people were still celebrating the main high days of socialist Yugoslavia, that is 29 November, the anniversary of the Socialist Federal Republic of Yugoslavia as established in 1945, as well as May Day. On our way back from this event we passed by the construction site of a church, which triggered some caustic remarks from her, but for me helped to interweave the local superimposition of symbolic dwelling sites, and the stories connected to them, even more tightly.

These events are testimonies of the dismantlement of existing worlds and of the necessity to re-invent or, better, to regain sense – a dismantling and a necessity that in general define our contemporary condition, but that in this part of the world, in the course of the twentieth and early twenty-first century, appear in a particularly sharp way. (Geertz 2000: 229) Since the First World War, monarchy, parliamentary democracy, National Socialist occupation, the communist one-party system and again parliamentary procedures in a struggle between a multiparty system and 'democratura' have followed one another here in a long sequence, and each phase has led to the need to re-construct sense – a reconstruction for which various agents with different goals have competed with one another.

But also in countries such as Austria and Germany there has been a dense succession of erecting and breaking down borders and of re-arranging the arenas in which identity-conflicts have been fought. There was the First and Second World War, the NS regime, the erection of the Iron Curtain as well as the new demarcations emerging in connection with the construction of the European Union and after 1989 with the re-unification of Germany and the integration of new EU member states. In recent decades, in addition to growing exchange, interdependence and conflicts between agents in various territories, usually described as 'globalization', migration processes across the newly created borders and from the newly defined 'outside' into the European Union have led to further connections as well as to the augmentation of differentiation. It is not so much what is in common and shared, but rather that what is missing as well as the faults and fissures or the cross-indexing that today seem to constitute the landscape of collective belonging. 'Cultures', 'ethnic groups' or 'political agents' are, as Clifford Geertz put it, not 'lumps of sameness marked out by the limits of consensus' (2000: 250) but 'modes of involvement in a collective life' (2000: 254) that take place on various scales and in different realms at the same time. Regionalism and globalization, pride and hatred, cultural events and ethnic cleansing exist side by side, able to pass quickly from one to the other.

At the same time, our common world is entrusted to the fragments dispersed inside this world in a new way. Ordering principles such as God, history or science have been called into question in various ways. Part of this is that meaning and sense appear mobile and particularly ambivalent: on the one hand they are regarded as present, visible and graspable within the realm of mundane appearances, but on the other hand they are seen as missing or at least difficult to reach and as hidden behind words and things.[11]

In this environment the cinema operates as an important place for re-negotiating sense. It belongs to the street and to our public life, but acts simultaneously as a shelter, where the watching of films is able to confront our private, habitual world as spectators (Merleau-Ponty 1964b). Besides, in cinema, contrary to other cultural forms, a (new) sense of the world can be experienced through a variety of environments and their surfaces, people, gestures, gazes and facial expressions and things – sometimes distant, sometimes well known, but alienated through camera, zoom and film, and presented via montage in a temporary form.[12] As spectators, we enter into various viewpoints, encounter surprising cuts where something other can break in or shots with the capacity to evoke and to affirm reality. Yet in doing so we are also somewhere else: in conversation with the various 'selves' and 'others' that suddenly come up in the viewing process.

Hence cinema enables a particular kind of encounter with the other. Thereby what is unfamiliar, new and strange often is perceived as belonging either to 'we' or 'them' communities and is in this way kept in check. In this sense, cinema can become involved in the modern struggle against ambivalence or in a postmodern celebration of various but nevertheless neatly divided and assignable 'cultures' (Bauman 1991: 58). It becomes part of a culture that tries to avoid and 'neutralize' everything that is strange and that is directed towards an enhanced partition of various communities based on identification, enforced security efforts and the surveillance of self and others.

At the same time, however, what we encounter in cinema is also capable of introducing cracks into our private and public world. There is always also the possibility that we might encounter 'glancing moments' in which something unfamiliar can come in that confronts our divisions and assumptions. Hence, perceiving can also mean being provoked to respond to the presence of the other, of something or somebody strange or foreign that suddenly stands out from the smooth viewing process (Mersch 2002: 28f.). This can be specific films or details in films that confront the viewer with unexpected and somehow revealing narrations about their environment or themselves,[13] but it can also be a certain style or other not so easily nameable features of film-experience that can be described as 'forces' or as 'events redirecting life'.[14]

In cinema such a re-exposition to the sense is usually a collective one; not in the way that we are all captured by the same details or that there is immediately any communication about what a film shows happening, but rather in the sense of a multifariousness of a linking-up of affects, bodily reactions and processes of judging. Hans Hurch, the Austrian film critic and later director of the Viennale film festival, for instance, described this potentiality of the cinema setting in an interview as follows: 'When are you otherwise in a space with a lot of people, at the university, in church, where the light is turned out and there is no talking. [...] Especially because of that, cinema is a collective space, because there is no communication, because communication is shit, is horrible, is a capitalist invention. The cinema is communion, that is, not in a reactionary way; it is a space that creates a community, where people are equal. But there is no exchange in cinema and that's the beautiful thing' (I HH).

In this way, however, he reduces the multiplicity of viewing events and their linking-up processes to a phantasm of the *corpus mysticus* (Balibar 2006: 85), that is, he is re-inscribing cinema experience into a Catholic tradition. But simultaneously, he also describes being in the cinema as an 'equalizing'[15] experience, because in the cinema setting, darkness reduces the visible hierarchies that otherwise reign in social space, transforming the various visitors into not further differentiated bodies that are posited in the same relation as myself vis-à-vis the glowing screen. With that he touches on an important function of cinema space – the obfuscation of social hierarchies – but he also reduces the interplay of affective investments to a mute co-presence.

Despite such views, the linking-up of affects, judgements and bodily reactions happening in cinema spaces is not so much characterized by 'something' held in common, but rather by an involvement driven strongly by what in everyday life appears to be lacking. This also means that every inhabiting of the cinema setting occurs in relation to an ever specific environment and is nourished by the compulsions, forms of training, shortcomings and insufficiencies that determine everyday life.[16]

Body experience and the creation of an (informal) public sphere

In the cinema – like in a modern factory – the body of the viewer is 'pinned down' in a specific position: it is placed in a numbered seat, one amid several rows of uniformly designed positions, all facing the same direction, towards the screen. Usually in the classical cinema set-up it is not possible to move the seat, nor is it easy to turn around and watch at the projector or projectionist. In most cases there is only one entrance and one exit, with these doors often kept separate to better control the flow of the masses of people passing through this space. The numbered seats provide an atomized space for every individual, and at the same time the auditorium assembles them into a particular form of collectivity. By these means the cinema subjects the bodies of the viewers to a certain kind of ordering force that operates through territorial and functional separation – it calls the body of the viewer to rely on one sense in particular: that of vision. The cinema is thus a space that provides a separation, but acts also a kind of shelter from the entanglement of the streets. In this way the cinema setting is the expression as well as the agent of what Zygmunt Bauman has called the typically modern 'task of order' (Bauman 1991: 4f.).

At the same time, however, the showing of films counteracts the various modern efforts to create order and to eliminate ambivalence, because it holds the potentiality that something or somebody strange and unfamiliar is glancing back from the screen at the viewer, touches him or her and turns their world in a contested, problematized ground.[17] In this sense the cinema is part of modern consumer culture which also fails to remain firmly within orderly circulation systems. It is able to embody an excess that can challenge the status quo.

Nevertheless, in cinema an important dimension that characterizes our being in respect to others in a variety of modern institutions and public arenas is missing: there is no 'look at me', no solemn exposition of myself to others such as during official celebrations like the one in the Sava Centre in Belgrade described above. On the contrary, the cinema's character of a shelter (in contrast to that of a factory) derives from the fact that I am able to disappear, to draw back from being directly addressed, but I am nevertheless together with others in a shared cover of darkness where I am capable of encountering 'the other' on film, in a fragmented way, framed by darkness, so that the relationship becomes one of observation, comparison, identification – whereby events of perception are always able to redirect perception.

In spite of this absorption of the viewer into the dark space, and in spite of the cinema being a space that privileges the visual, the re-negotiation of sense that takes place in cinema has various bodily dimensions. As viewers we are with others, but at the same time alone; we sink relaxed into our chairs, and our body opens itself up to the images and can be touched – by colour, faces, expressions, occurrences or by the whole scene. Bodily points of contact between viewers and film emerge, with cinema communicating 'less as a whole with consciousness than in a fragmentary manner with the corporeal material layers' (Siegfried Kracauer, quoted in Hansen 1993: 462). These points of contact have the capacity to disorientate the world as we know it, break it up into stories and offer components to be rearranged anew.

At the same time, the cinema setting re-assembles bodies not only between the auditorium and the screen but also inside the auditorium itself: it creates a bodily proximity between a multitude of bodies. The darkness of the cinema space that enfolds the viewers is thereby saturated with a certain kind of casual eroticism. Roland Barthes refers to this dimension too when he says that precisely because as a viewer in a cinema I am not visibly exposed to others and enclosed in my seat, 'I can light up in all my desire' (m. t. Barthes 1975: 105). Inside the cinema setting I can thus be fascinated twice: by the images and by the ambience, by the touch of colours and faces and by the soft plush chairs, by the body next to me and by the conversations over a beer or a coffee before the show. So the imaginary dimension is able to persist, even when one inhabits the place guided by a kind of 'amorous distance' that can be seen as essence of a cinéphile enjoyment of the cinema-setting (Barthes 1975: 108).

As I have already pointed out, the cinema has the potential to provoke its viewers into responding to the other, to something or somebody interrupting the smooth viewing process. In doing so, it re-exposes the viewer to the sense, that is, it challenges well-known certainties and allocations, but can also redirect our judgements and even our actions. That is why the viewing experience in the cinema setting is politicized and is in itself already involved in the collective constitution of a multivocal political, public sphere.[18]

The public dimension of cinema experience thus lies in the fact that such events of perception can call judgements and viewpoints into question and trigger various kinds of deeds and this way outgrow the cinema spaces and expand into everyday life. Usually, the shared connectivity characterizing the cinema setting mentioned above is sharply interrupted with the end of the film, when we step back onto the street. Then an exchange and discussion of what was experienced occur, various viewpoints are posed and sometimes even more or less spectacular actions or the making of further films are stimulated. In all these various ways cinema and film are involved in the construction of a public sphere where a civil interaction between strangers as well as an expression of diversity take place – they are involved, together with spectators and critics in constituting such a sphere (Hansen 1991: 90f.). In stating this I see the political and public sphere not as an already pre-given entity that we can just step into, but as one that is always constituted anew through our mutual provocations, perceptions and deeds that stage judgements and desires and challenge the status quo (Rancière 1999).[19]

In connection with this involvement of the cinema setting in constituting a public sphere, however, we also encounter one of the biggest differences between cinema cultures in pluralist democratic societies such as Austria and Germany and in state-socialist societies such as Titoist Yugoslavia – a difference I will explain in more detail in the course of this book, also in relation to what this means for the political culture emerging since 1989. Democratic political systems are characterized by the presence of different, competing actions, perceptions or representations that constitute a public sphere. In state-socialist political systems, however, it is exactly such a struggle and such a competition that is to a large extent restricted. There is a denial that difference is constitutive for society – the only accepted division is the one between the 'people-as-one' (which, at the same time, is represented in the party and the egocrat, here Josip Broz Tito) and its enemies (the old society, which is simultaneously the bourgeois, capitalist, imperialist world).[20] In this way, as soon as they became audible in public, non-conformist voices were slandered as 'enemies of the people and of the state' and forced underground.

Nevertheless – as cinema movements such as the 'novi film' movement (also called Crni Talas) demonstrate – in one-party systems, too, actions around urban spaces could initiate something like a 'movement' that involves others, creates discourse, triggers discussions in newspapers, magazines and public places and challenges the ruling authorities. So any strict distinction between democratic and totalitarian societies with regard to the possibilities of the emergence of a political public sphere also needs to be questioned (Garcelon 1997); and it can be shown that even in state-socialist societies like Yugoslavia, non-conformist movements appear to have formed something that can be called the 'informal public sphere'.[21] Yet the two political systems shaped cinema activism differently and also keep influencing the public realm created after 1989 – something that will be subjected to further investigation in the chapters ahead.

The political and the social

With regard to the involvement of the cinema setting in creating a public sphere, we sharply encounter the political dimension of our being with others – a dimension that cannot be equated with its social one. Hence, in respect to the multifaceted space that we create with others, the political and the social are not congruent. What we encounter in cinema can trigger a re-negotiation of sense and, consequently, a staging of judgements, perceptions, representations and initiatives that call the reigning structures of our living together into question, contest usual allocations or propose new ones (Laclau 1990: 68f.). The challenging and the provocation of existing structures constitute the political dimension of our deeds, perceptions and representations. Hence the space we create with others is transformed into a public, political sphere – although in state-socialist systems such as Yugoslavia such a politicization remains closely monitored and is legitimate only to the extent that the central uniting principles, the 'people as one' and the egocrat Tito are not called into question.

In contrast to this stands another realm as an intermediate one between public and private: the social, where exchange, mingling and re-assembling between a multitude of actors occur (Wolfe 1997). The notion of the 'social' is often employed to describe the individual or certain places as taking part in a system of common life, as 'associated'. Through this term individuals are registered, described and allocated, and certain places are assigned to particular individuals or groups of individuals (Williams 1988: 294f.). Especially in the nineteenth and in the first half of the twentieth century, a notion of the 'social' became dominant that was at first connected to an assurance and a sustainment of allocations. The community was understood as an extended family in which everybody occupied a certain place that had to be secured.[22]

In modern societies, various public and private agents enter deeply into the public as well as private realms, and subject a whole range of areas, such as production, consumption and commerce, but also health, family, sexuality or the body, to new regulations. In this way public and private life became politicized, that is, opened up to a competing and mutually challenging discourse by the various attempts to manage them (Crossley 2007). At the same time these attempts have often been presented and discussed under the label 'social' – so that the emphasis was on securing dimensions of such interventions that affirm reigning allocation and counter widespread threats such as unemployment, homelessness and descent on the social scale in general and the fears connected to them. These differences between the political and the various meanings of 'the social' should be kept in mind despite all the interfaces that exist between them – in particular because, as a result of the growth of a capitalist commodity-exchange economy, 'the social' has been so heavily emphasized and to a large extent tends to replace 'the political'.[23]

A second reason for highlighting this difference is that, unlike acts of politicization, which even in connection with film and cinema were seen as threatening in the state-socialist system of former Yugoslavia, the notion of 'the social' was strongly embraced: competence for monitoring the self-managing processes of 'the people' could be affirmed through the self-description as 'social', and individual political challenges could be kept in check by labelling them as potentially 'asocial'.

The notion of the political outlined above also implies that the public sphere is not a pre-ordained entity. 'Public sphere' thus does not mean the street or buildings that are open to 'everybody' but the practices of inhabiting them and of questioning and challenging existing orders. Hence, the public sphere constitutes a realm that interferes with social space by politicizing some of its elements. In the following chapters I will point out how the public realm emerging in and around cinema in Austria, the FRG and Yugoslavia since the 1960s can be further characterized. The investigation will also seek to find an answer to the question as to how the media have altered the experience of being in common by understanding communality no longer in terms of rational exchange – as it is presupposed in Jürgen Habermas' notion of the public sphere (Habermas 1990: 161f.) – but also as a result of significant encounters.

The public is thus the realm in which we get involved with each other and in which we differentiate ourselves from others. It is the sphere in which we demonstrate and show something to others and where what we show is perceived by others – and is thereby contested and/or carried on further. It is a space of appearance to which potentially everybody can count himself or herself as belonging (Rancière 1999: 27) and can start an initiative that challenges reigning conditions of our common world. Seen this way, the scientific division of the public sphere into 'partial public spheres'[24] that can be investigated separately from each other appears to be misleading because it tends to conceal this interconnecting realm to which everybody is able to count him- or herself as belonging on his or her own initiative.

Because of its potential to challenge our judgements as viewers, cinema is involved in a particular way in activities that constitute a public and political realm. In recent decades, this has been accompanied by some follow-up phenomena: the cinema setting has outgrown the concrete cinema space and is frequently used as a reference in other arts, such as literature or the visual arts, in order to operate in a political, public way. In 1997, in Belgrade, for instance, a poster in the tradition of big film posters appeared (Figure 4). It showed the half-length portrait of a woman with a glass eye facing an older, bearded man, who we only see from behind. The poster advertised a 'film' called 'Murder' by a 'director' identified as 'Raša Todosijević'. This poster is 'political' in the sense that it holds the power to challenge various well-known and widespread certitudes: for instance, that murder is mostly a subject of various kinds of fiction and not of common life; but also that cinema is an escape from reality and not a way of redirecting our senses towards it.

Alternating glances: city-squats in pluralist democratic, socialist and post-socialist countries

I have chosen to use a comparative viewpoint to investigate urban interventions, films and the retrospective narrations of cinema activists (film-makers, cinema programmers, critics, enthusiasts, etc.) in Germany, Austria and former Yugoslavia as well as its successor states. In doing so, I will focus in particular on the cinema as a space and on cinema activism as a spatial practice that intervenes in contested territories and is involved in the constitution of an (informal) public sphere.

Such a view has to take into account the long tradition of a viewing relationship between 'western' or 'central' and 'south-eastern' European cultures that is often described as one between centre and periphery or 'Mitteleuropa' and the 'Balkans' and is full of mutual attributes and projections (Bjelić and Savić 2005). This tradition usually also implies the application of different measures in describing one culture as being the influence on the other, which is generally expressed in a different evaluation of the importance of 'influenced' and 'influencing' cultures (Belting 2008: 12f.).

Scientific knowledge cannot, as already mentioned, reduce the various struggles and gazing relationships which occur in social space and among different territories in an 'objective' way – since it is always already involved and represents in itself a kind of intervention in a space filled with various opinions, projects, projections and feelings. However, it can try

Figure 4: *Murder,* Raša Todosijević, 1997 © Raša Todosijević.

to give a comprehensive assessment of the various agents involved in certain territories, the political conflicts and the relations that emerge between them and the changing distribution, and shape of power that results from this. Gazing relationships, projections and various emotional loadings of space are part of what needs to be dealt with in such an assessment too.

In order to arrive at this, I will present a view that considers cinema cultures in pluralist democratic as well as in socialist (and post-socialist) societies as well as their interdependent relationships. In this way, similarities and differences can be highlighted in a more pronounced way than would be possible if focusing on cinema culture in only one type of society and describing 'influences' entering into it or coming from it. In particular, the public, political dimension of cinema as well as the specificity of political culture emerging in democratic, state-socialist and post-socialist societies becomes more clearly understandable.

Cinema activism and cinema movements investigated in this book are suited to such a comparative view because they emerged more or less simultaneously in various countries on both sides of the East-West divide and mutually influenced each other. All of them occurred in (bigger or smaller) cities (Belgrade, Novi Sad, Kranj, Vienna, Cologne, Munich or Hamburg). But this does not mean that all activists came from these cities or from the city at all.

On the contrary, for people who moved from smaller towns or from the countryside to big cities to study or work, going to the cinema was often a way to appropriate their new surroundings and learn to handle urban life. Sometimes, for instance, in the case of Naško Križnar, who founded the OHO cinema club in Kranj, life in two nearby cities was combined: life in Ljubljana, where he studied architecture and where he could visit the Kinoteka, and life in Kranj, where he could use local networks in order to get backing for starting the kino club (I NK). At other times cinema was a way of dealing with a move from one city to another, a way of accommodating oneself in the new surroundings. One function of the cinema thus was to provide a local reference point for (mostly young) people who left the countryside and smaller towns in the periphery and moved to the capitals or at least to bigger cities in the 1960s.

Another equivalence between cinema activism emerging around 1968 in both type of societies was that all groups situated themselves by putting particular emphasis on the ways of representation and of inhabiting the cinema setting in order to question what they see as the respective dominant viewing conditions. They repeatedly invent new rituals of cinema-going and transform the spaces they occupy into places for discussion, confrontation and self-assertion.

All these groups differentiate their own cinema space from what they see as mainstream cinema worlds. In 'their' cinema they all find everything that everyday city life denies them. Hence there is always a particular inhabiting of one's 'own' cinema space that involves utopian sensibilities (Dyer 1993). This is, as we will see, arrived at in relation to an always specific urban environment and nourished by the compulsions, insufficiencies and tensions that determine everyday life in the experience of film-makers and cinema activists. As the anthropologist Mattijs van de Port puts it, in film as well as 'in nightmares, dreams, daydreams, in the arts and other expressive genres, people abandon the everyday in order to create room for the imagination' (van de Port 1998: 134).

At the same time, all these movements and groups also indicate a historic break in the overall history of cinema movements. Unlike older grassroots cinema movements, such as the working-class cinema clubs or the newsreel movement of the 1920s, the cinema movements of the 1960s were no longer bound to relatively stable class formations and party organizations (Dörner 2001: 107) – even if these do not become unimportant with this development. A shared desire and a particular experience of something lacking in everyday life was translated into a particular aesthetic style of producing film and of inhabiting the cinema setting, in a shared taste in literature, theory and music (for example, jazz in the case of novi-film tendencies in former Yugoslavia) and in similarities in ways of dressing or moving through space. These movements are situated at the transition between movements that emerged in the inter-war years – which by fighting ambivalence suppressed a variety of differences and privileged certain ones that were universalized – whether as 'the worker' or the 'national' everyman – and those that emerged after 1968, which often programmatically rediscovered and exhibited a broader variety of cultural difference. Besides, all these movements have strongly influenced further developments throughout Europe.

The advantage of such a comparative view is that it brings the public-political dimension of cinema practice to the fore in a more pronounced way. It highlights the fact that around 1968 the public potential of the cinema space became even more visible and influential for the broader political culture emerging then in both types of societies. Besides, it also makes graspable that it is exactly the political potential of cinema that leads to the main differences between the public realm emerging in pluralist democratic and state-socialist one-party territories. The German and Austrian communal cinemas as well as some of the politically engaged cinema clubs or the Expanded Cinema that emerged around 1968 transformed the cinema setting into a site from which they tried to deconstruct dominant ideologies and to inhabit space in order to build a decidedly 'different' society. In doing so, they sometimes banked on provocation, on seduction, on attacking the public and on 'art-war campaigns' (Schober 2009b: 148f. and 253f.). In contrast to this, the Yugoslav novi-film scene (or Crni Talas) which started to emerge in the early 1960s operated with rather restrained actions that seem at first almost inconspicuous, for example, by concentrating on the *mise-en-scène* of love, alienation, sexuality and loneliness and by relating the activity of film-making to the consumption of jazz music. Nevertheless, in the state-socialist society of Yugoslavia, their cinema activities unleashed a strong politically explosive force, led to censorship and imprisonment and drove a lot of the film-makers to an inner or de facto emigration (to France, Germany, the United Kingdom or the United States).[25]

The different, democratic and state-socialist forms shaped the cinema movements, as we will see, in a quite distinct way. But they also influenced the construction of the public sphere after Titoism in the various ex-Yugoslav-successor states as well as in Austria and Germany after 1989. In all countries, cinema activism in the 1990s went along with a fervid rediscovery and figuration of difference – as aesthetic, sexual or ethnic difference. The tradition of a conflictual public sphere in pluralist democratic societies could be continued and used for various and competing assertions of public presence now emerging around cinema spaces. In addition, the existing linkages between the newly re-valuated cultural arenas of the public sphere in the 1960s and early 1970s and the stage of politics in a more narrow sense, that is, parliament and parties, could be drawn on in order to deal with conflicts and tensions that accompanied the various attempts to exhibit difference. Since Tito's death in 1980 difference was asserted in various ways also in (former) Yugoslavia's cultural arenas and was expressed through a variety of practices such as writing, filming, making music, etc. However, as much as difference was repressed and monitored during Titoism, it was emphasized and politicized all the more afterwards. Furthermore, the tradition of an informal public sphere in one-party systems provided only a very weak mediating sphere vis-à-vis the newly emerging stages of politics in a more narrow sense.

This kind of informal public sphere was sometimes called 'the public sphere in the kitchen' – an expression that attempts to grasp the fact that political judgements were often more openly and fervidly expressed in private spheres of the home or in semi-private spheres such as the cinema than in the official public realm, which in state socialism was dominated by the party and where every divergence from its official view was closely controlled and often punished. After 1989 this heritage of an informal public sphere tended to be romanticized, especially by theoreticians from Western European countries[26] – yet this sphere was too closed off from the newly emerging arenas of politics for it to be used to deal with the rising tensions and conflicts accompanying the rediscovery of ethnic difference, for example. Nevertheless, also in post-socialist environments there is not only rupture but also the re-creation of tradition: in ex-Yugoslavia in the 1990s, too, the cinema continued as we will see to be used for the regaining of sense as well as mastery in a world that even in terms of states had fallen apart.

1.3. The subject in process: rituals, revolt and storytelling

In this book I am tracing the processes by which cinema spectators in various ways are turning into cinema-makers, film-makers and temporary urban squatters. I am thus addressing the phenomenon that in the decades following '1968' people increasingly do not feel represented by the authorities and images claiming to represent them and are led to enter the political stage themselves – often through gestures that in themselves seem to be more 'cultural' or 'artistic' than political in the strict sense of the word. By showing or making film, video, performance and/or multimedia spectacles, they articulate a difference in the public sphere that is linked to a constitution of themselves as political subjects and as individual actors.

In order to grasp this, the subject itself has to be understood as a 'subject in process', that is, as someone in a constant state of becoming and in the need for completion, pervaded by various acts which attempt to create meaning and sense and that again and again reconstitute us. We are thus born into an ever specific plurality of sense created by others, exposed to others in our attempts to create sense and meaning and we are, at least for certain moments, subjects of this sense – understood as an ever specific position of articulation. As 'subjects in process' we are, however, also driven by unconscious elements and fantasies that exceed and undermine any ideal vision we create vis-à-vis ourselves.

From a (Lacanian) psychoanalytical point of view, the subject is a divided unity: there is a lack of being in the heart of the subject that keeps our desire in motion. In the development of the subject, sexual difference and the unconscious play a constitutive role – they are operative on another level than other kinds of (ethnic, for example) differences (Copjec 1994: 207). But the main aspect that the notion of 'subject in process' (Laclau and Zac 1994; Kristeva 1998) highlights is that we constitute ourselves in exchange and confrontation with others – a process that is never completed, but which is a necessary one in the sense that we are not able to escape it.

The cinema is involved in the transient re-constitution of the subject in various ways. As I have already shown, in cinema we are able to experience significant encounters that stand out from the smooth viewing process and redirect our exchange with the world and others. Hence, going to the cinema also means that we experience 'passages' through images, whereby sometimes we leave more deeply affected than other times. In order to show such a passage, to make it evident and to communicate it to ourselves and to others, we start to pose differently, to buy certain clothes or accessories or to try out a slightly different way of walking or of playing with small gestures. We start to use certain new phrases, change our judgements and set unusual and sometimes also politically relevant initiatives. And with the aid of such adoptions of objects, gestures and expressions we are linking ourselves to some of our fellow citizens and we are distinguishing ourselves from others (Schober 2004: 122; Schober 2012).

Certain details, scenes or even entire films can thus extend into the everyday manifestation of ourselves, into our gazing, perceiving and talking. In this way we are somehow 'reborn' in cinema spaces – here we can find the 'zero point […] the good origin' as Serge Daney (2000: 22) calls it. He thus relates the cinema to an always possible new beginning.[27] This however, is also a political capacity. There is a potential of interrupting the regular flow of things and of starting something new by the encounters we experience in the cinema setting as well by setting up film and cinema initiatives ourselves. At the same time, such a new beginning is never sovereign, since whether or not such initiatives are carried further depends on others. Nevertheless, in cinema a starting anew through films, perceptions, artistic action, discussion or the creation of new and 'different' cinema settings is always linked to our experience of sense. This has to do not only with the images and their montage but also with cinema as a space. Since in the black box of the cinema setting one can, so to speak, open oneself to a 'rebirth' through images.

Figure 5: *Cinema nomads*, Volxkino, open air cinema,
Vienna, 1996 © St. Balbach Art Production.

At the same time not only the involvement triggered by the image but also the ritual dimension of cinema-going participates in the constitution of ourselves as a subject in process. This ritual dimension derives from the fact that we generally do inhabit a quite defined model of going to the cinema in our own, slightly different way: some of us like to go alone, some with others, some like to sit near the screen, some far away, some like to eat, some hate the noise of eating, some like to talk or to kiss, others prefer the silence, etc. We thus do not go to the cinema in the first place in order to do something to the world or in order to involve ourselves in communication, but we go there in order to perform movements within certain stereotyped parameters. We perform them because we find pleasure in performing such ritual gestures, that is, in projecting our own, specific and unique existence out of ourselves, recognizing ourselves in our own style of carrying out this public ritual.[28]

As the examples I will present in the next chapters show, the invention of new cinema rituals is often linked to revolt, that is, to a more or less consciously expressed rejection of other forms of cinema-going – a rejection that can be acted out more fervidly or more playfully and that can dominate the new rituals invented to various degrees, but has the effect of affirming the 'innovativeness' and 'individuality' of the acting subject.

In this way also new collective subjects emerge as a result of inhabiting the cinema setting – although it is important to see that such subjects are not constituted beforehand and then 'expressed' through an ever different way of re-assembling the cinema situation, but that on the contrary the process of acting and squatting is constitutive for the emergence of new collective actors in the public sphere. Besides, this again highlights that it is through our deeds and gestures that we differentiate ourselves from some of our fellow citizens and link ourselves to others.

But why has the pleasure of recognizing oneself in the world been acted out so frequently in the ritual of cinema-going throughout the twentieth century and still today? In order to answer this question, let us come back to the city and everyday life, and to the relationship that the cinema maintains with it.

Modern but also postmodern life is characterized by an intensified encroachment on our bodies: in the workplace, in the traffic on the streets and in new means of transport such as trains, streetcars, buses, cars and airplanes; in the news, transmitted via media such as radio, film, television, computer, via new hygiene-products and modified food. All these implements together form a kind of training for our bodies, a training that produces a specific bodily experience of insufficiency, as well 'ideal bodies' of our imagination and desired and feared demonstrative bodies of teachers, instructors and other role models (Schober 2001: 38). Cinema, as argued above, is one of the places inside the city where we can observe the other. Here we are able to experience significant encounters and can compare ourselves to as well as identify or dis-identify with various, idealized or feared others. The cinema thus seems to be a space that is in a particular way suited to confronting the tensions and insufficiencies of daily life through self-mirroring, imagination and fantasy.

In the following, I will present a narration that brings together various stories and perspectives about the web of judgements and initiatives involving cinema and film in several milieus.[29] I came across some of these stories in other people's books and in the form of published interviews with film-makers and cinema activists. Most of them, however, have been produced through my own interviews while doing research for this book. Hence in the following I will refer to a corpus of about 45 interviews I have conducted over the past decade with different generations of film-makers and cinema activists in Germany, Austria, Italy and former Yugoslavia and its successor states. I am not using these quotations primarily as markers of authenticity, but rather as traces of a plurality that exists in relation to the reflection about the issues brought up in this book.

Hence, more so than in any of my other works, in which I have sometimes also used interviews, this book originates in various encounters with others: in listening to their stories, following up on analyses initiated by them and tracking down what was staged in them. In stating this I do not want to hide behind these interview partners or to impute my views to them. But since the research process for this book was so strongly characterized by an experience of a plurality of stories and points of view, I wanted this plurality also to be present in this final text. The public sphere in its multiplicity should not only be the subject of this book, but it also should be represented in it to some extent – even when it is obvious that it is me as the author who conducted the interviews, who has chosen the quoted passages and is responsible for the theses presented here.

This plurality of the public sphere is not a harmonious one that is free of conflict, the inequality of power and dispute. On the contrary, just as the public sphere is genuinely a conflicted one where various viewpoints and initiatives not only find a response and are taken up but are also challenged and sometimes severely contested, so too does the plurality of stories narrated in respect to cinema activism also involve struggle and conflict. Even though I found many interview partners who responded in a very positive way to the initiative started by this research project, there were also some who refused to be interviewed. Not all of them justified this move – sometimes, however, film-makers and cinema activists or their agents gave me the impression that they wanted their story to be told in a particular way and did not trust me to write what they wanted to read. Cinema as a star system was also relevant in this because sometimes (agents of) potential interview partners were only interested as long as they had the impression that I was a journalist who would make publicity for the director's latest movie and lost interest on discovering that I was involved in what they concluded was a rather academic undertaking.

But the opposite also happened: some former activists, who came across this research project through public events in which I participated during its realization or through rumours, got in touch with me on their own initiative because they felt that they too had to be part of it. Sometimes it was not the former activists themselves who approached me but colleagues or friends who thought a story might be relevant to the narration they knew I was working on.

Conflicts sometimes emerged after the interview. Some interview partners subsequently wanted to correct what they had said and some tried to influence or even to control strongly the theses I drew from my research.[30] Such conflicts have to do with the fact that the desire to hear a story told by others about one's actions and the sense of identity that is conveyed in this way can clash considerably with one's own self-image.

As already briefly mentioned, in respect to the disposition of having one's story told, the tradition of gazing relationships that have emerged between 'south-eastern' and 'central' Europe was also influential. So, for instance, most film-makers and cinema activists in former Yugoslavia responded positively to my request to interview them – some, however, only after various, persistent attempts and after they had understood that my interest was serious. During the interview, however, most answered my questions generously and, since they were mostly male, the interest of a middle-aged women researcher from Austria also aroused a certain curiosity. In contrast, several of the film-makers and cinema activists in Austria and Germany, especially the well-established ones, refused to be interviewed or, if they agreed, gave only sparse answers. Here, too, gender was influential, since this happened more often when the interviewee was male.

Obviously, this plurality of stories I had gathered and the occurrences I experienced while listening to them and describing them posed the challenge of how to incorporate them into the final text. It would have been possible to render all the interviews anonymous, which would have had the advantage of avoiding the question of why I had spoken to some and not others and to a certain extent obviating the cinema world's star system. At the same time, however, important information would have been lost to the reader and it would no longer be possible to attribute the various viewpoints and deeds to certain actors.

Besides, I in no way claim to be exhaustive in respect to the range of my interviewees. My interest was focused on encountering people with various backgrounds and representing different ways of getting involved in cinema and film. Because of all this I decided to mention the names of my interview partners, not of all of them of course, but only of those to which I refer in this final text, and to include brief quotations from them.

Finally, the issue of storytelling and how it is linked to us as subjects also leads to a further question that will be taken up in several of the following chapters: there are usually official, legitimate stories that feature prominently in the public sphere and there is what lies beyond these legitimate expressions. The latter, too, is sometimes expressed by often rather unconventional representations (films, but also literature and fairy tales) that challenge that which is seen as legitimate and at some point enter into conflict with it. Especially in state-socialist societies where official propaganda occupied the public sphere and was to a large extent cut off from people's experience of their own situations, what was officially regarded as unspeakable just slumbered below the surface and began to flourish and to be re-created and sometimes even celebrated as soon as the official public world faced a crisis (van de Port 1998: 101). Initiatives employing cinema as a space and film as a medium are usually involved in the creation of stories that challenge and sometimes even undermine the reigning world. Hence, in several of the following chapters I will trace these worlds in stories represented in the cinema settings and show how they are linked to other stories that fall apart, are sometimes contested and reassembled into new ones. In this way it will become manifest that cinema initiatives are at times explicitly staged as a political protest and revolt, but that at other times they can be rather political in an involuntary way. By depicting seemingly apolitical themes such as love, sexuality or loneliness or our views and projections it is also possible to address a conflict about our common world.

Notes

1   As for instance the temporary open-air cinemas set up by Slum-TV in Mathare, Nairobi/ Kenya and the DVD-cinemas emerging there show (interview with Biki Kangwana, adviser Slum-TV and Ghetto Filmclub, 30 April 2009); see also http://slum-tv.org/ (22 February 2010).

2   Blockbuster films, like *Titanic* (1997), were no longer designed to address a segment of the pubic but the 'whole' public in order to make up for the enormous production costs. This had effects on the stories chosen as well as the aesthetic language of the films. With this, films were expected to also be convertible into a series of other products – from CDs and computer games to plush figures or T-shirts (Corrigan 1991: 20ff.). In parallel cinema producers like Warner Brothers started in the 1980s to market films themselves through multiplex-cinemas, temporary adjusted PR campaigns and simultaneous film-openings in as many markets as possible. In the 1990s the multiplex cinema became the dominant cinema form. Since then the Motion Picture Association of America only counts screens and no longer cinemas (Paul 1994).

3   E-mail conversation with Rirkrit Tiravanija, 22 April 2009.

4   This drawing was also brought up in the already mentioned e-mail conversation in April 2009 with Rirkrit Tiravanija.

5   In order to investigate the anti-Milošević movement, I went through the archive boxes of Cinema Rex, which contained a wide range of material of these various opposition groups. In the course of this I came across material of several kinds of film and video activism – among it was a book about the Belgrade kino club written by one of its veterans. Since I had been interested in cinema movements for quite a while, and saw a connection with the aesthetic political activism of the 1990s, I started conducting interviews with some of the cinema-makers of the 1960s as well as with younger cinema and video activists. The main reason for continuing these interviews, however, was that in the course of conducting them I found out that some of my interview partners from the cultural and political scene of the 1990s spoke more openly about their views of the past and present when they were asked to remember their actions in connection with their cinema memories. When I talked to them directly about their activities in the recent past, they were sometimes reluctant to enter into conversation, considering their views of no or little importance, or they were suspicious of my motives for conducting the interviews; but as soon as I brought the conversation to films they had seen (or made), they often warmed up and spoke more openly. They not only talked about films themselves, but usually also located their viewing experiences in the city and highlighted the importance of certain urban anchoring sites such as the Cinema Rex or also the CZKD (Centre for Cultural Decontamination).

6   He distinguishes between various stages of evolution with every stage being dominated by a fixed ensemble of meanings: 'absolute space' is followed by 'abstract space' and this is followed by 'differential space' (Levèbvre 1999: 229ff.). A critique of this legacy in his work can also be found in Keith and Pile (1993: 25).

7   Such approaches have emerged in recent decades, for instance, in the adoption of the writings of Antonio Gramsci and around the notion of 'hegemony' in works by Ernesto Laclau and

Chantal Mouffe (1985), Stuart Hall (Hall and du Gay 1996) and Doreen Massey (2005) or in the continuation of theories by Hannah Arendt and Michel Foucault in the work by Jacques Rancière (1999).

8   On the history of cinema movements, see, for instance, Gauthier 1999; Bloom 2006; Schober 2007.

9   This can often be observed in relation to investigations of fan communities. See, for instance, the in many aspects excellent study by Jenkins 1992.

10 Michel Foucault used the term 'heterotopia' or 'other space' for the cinema – and in this way related the cinema closely to spaces such as the theatre, the luna park or the hotel room, which for him too are 'heterotopias'. There is, however, an inconsistency in what he understands as 'other space' or 'heterotopia'. Foucault used the concept in two texts: a short article called 'Des Espaces Autres', written in 1967 and re-published in 1984, and in 'Les Mots et Les Choses', published in 1966, in a passage linked to the Chinese encyclopaedia of Borges. Foucault did not expand the notion of 'heterotopia' in any further work nor did he make it the object of a monograph. This contrasts sharply with the broad dissemination and reception of the notion in cultural studies literature since the 1980s. As a result, a contradiction between these two negotiations of the concept in Michel Foucault's work is often overlooked. In 'Of Other Spaces' (Foucault 1986), he identifies 'heterotopia' with certain nameable spaces such as the cinema or the theatre, without, however, asking if the 'other' of space can be named, identified and described as such or if it is not rather that what exists beyond the order of language and representation. In 'The Order of Things' (1989: xviff), he uses Borges' Chinese encyclopaedia, in which things of different orders such as animals and mythical creatures are assembled side by side in order to question the coherency and totality of spatial and linguistic systems as such. This enunciation of mythical and real things is a 'heterotopia' in the sense of a discursive demonstration of the limits of Western systems of knowledge. On a discussion and critique of the reception of this concept, see Genocchio 1995.

11 On this ambivalence owed to the repeated fracturing of stories that goes together with modernity, which led to the need to find other stories in order to give meaning to the world, see Nancy 1986.

12 As an important institution for a new way of negotiating sense that draws strongly on our capacity to decipher the world as well as the actions of others, the cinema enters into a strange complicity and equivalence with twentieth-century philosophy, which also dwells persistently in a quite similar way on the sense (Merleau-Ponty 1964b; Merleau-Ponty 1964a).

13 I investigated such a cinema event related to the unexpected confrontation (which happened in 1958/59) with a documentary about the Nuremberg Trial in Schober 2004.

14 This is in turn taken up again by cinema-makers, for example, the GLBT Film Festival in Turin, Italy, 2010 had a programme venue *I film che cambiano la vita* (Films that Change Life).

15 Marguerite Duras also describes the cinema as 'equalizing' and 'democratic'. Suzanne, the young protagonist of her novel *Un barrage contre le Pacifique*, speaks about the 'artificial and democratic night, the enormous, all-equalising night of cinema'. The big merit of cinema, she further explains, is that it attracts young women and men and lets them escape their families (Duras 1963: 188 and 199).

16 Roberto Esposito uses a conceptualization of community as a lack in order to challenge Arendtian notions of a communal character of aesthetic judgment (Esposito 2006: 66 and 76). However, the two conceptualizations are not completely opposed, since what is lacking can be projected onto elements of the sensible world (onto aesthetic languages, certain film styles, a particular way of going to the cinema), which can then be shared as indicators of belonging.

17 Even if Zygmunt Bauman dwells in detail on the double move of modernity in creating order and involuntary increase of ambivalence, his account of media sites such as the cinema remains in itself univocally pessimistic when he writes: 'The frame of a cinema or TV screen staves off the danger of spillage even more effectively than tourist hotels and fenced-off camping sites; the one-sidedness of communication firmly locks the unfamiliars on the screen as, essentially, incommunicado' (Bauman 1991: 58). In relation to film and cinema he does not present their antidromic potentiality of providing also an encounter with the strange and unfamiliar that can call usual allocations into question. In this respect, he uses a binary opposition of modern consumer culture and political solidarity and thus gets himself caught in modern attempts to eliminate ambivalence.

18 This notion of the 'political' follows a definition given by Ernesto Laclau (1990: 68f.), who uses the term for every provocation and intervention that challenge reigning allocations, call principles of society into question or proposes a different order of things. In contrast, the term 'politics' denotes a separate social complex, which has to deal with this precarious logic of the political.

19 However, I do not follow a binary division of what Rancière calls 'politics' and 'police'.

20 In the following, I refer to the notions of 'democratic' and 'totalitarian political systems' as coined by Claude Lefort (1986: 297f.). As outlined in the course of this book, however, I also aim at a questioning and modification of these concepts through reference to recent research.

21 The notion of 'informal public sphere' in order to designate the politically relevant diversity of state-independent activities and interactions in totalitarian societies was formulated by Oleg Yanitskii (1993).

22 Connected to this, the idea of the social as a separate sphere emerged that could be used to explain other phenomena. Bruno Latour (2007: 9f.) opposes this conception of the social and proposes understanding it as circulation and reassembling.

23 Hannah Arendt (1958: 46f.) strongly contrasts 'the social' and 'the political'; she sees the emergence of 'the social' in the public sphere as negative, since for her the social is mainly related to a securing of the place one occupies in a community; political action, on the contrary, is also in her view able to question such allocations of the individual.

24 The notion of 'partial public sphere' (*Teilöffentlichkeit*) in relation to cinema cultures was made central, for instance, by Mueller and Segeberg (2008).

25 The novi-film-makers emerged out of the amateur film scene in the early 1960s and soon became a hotly discussed issue in Yugoslav cultural politics. The movement was formed by way of the activities of prominent film directors (as well as film writers, journalists, directors of photography and film editors) such as Dušan Makavejev, Živojin Pavlović, Kokan

Rakonjac, Branko Vučićević, Marko Babac and Želimir Žilnik (Goulding 2002: especially 59 and 66; Babac 2001).

26 This, for example, became evident during the conference 'The Public Sphere: Between Contestation and Reconciliation' organized by the National Association of Art Critics in Yerevan, Armenia in 2005, where contrary to some colleagues from Western Europe most of the Armenian participants strongly criticized a positive, optimistic notion of the 'public sphere in the kitchen'. This debate is in part depicted in Miles 2009.

27 In this quotation Daney implicitly contrasts the 'good origin' we can encounter in the cinema with another one, which presumably is not as good: our birth. This can be confronted with a view by Hannah Arendt (1958: 177f.) who sees every action and initiative as a new beginning that is rooted in human natality, that is, in the fact that every birth already represents a new beginning. This human capacity of being able to start anew constitutes the core of her conception of the public sphere and of freedom.

28 Vilém Flusser (1994: 162f.) points out that our desire organizes itself as a series of meaning-granting practices, some of them rituals, in which we give ourselves meaning as subjects. In this way, through rituals, that is, through actions we carry out inside fixed parameters for the sake of the pleasure we find in them (and not in order to do something to the world or to communicate), we produce meaning as an always already shared sense. Thereby, an already transformed religious experience unfolds itself inside what he calls 'our artistic life'.

29 The subject also gets recognition from the stories that are told about its actions. Since our deeds constituting a public sphere are volatile, it is only through storytelling and other artistic practice that they can be actualized and provided with durability (Arendt 1958: 186; Cavarero 2000).

30 Generation was an important factor in this respect since such conflicts sometimes happened with interview partners from the 1968 generation, mostly in the 'Western' context. But also gender was influential, since quite often women from this generation tried to control how their deeds were represented.

Chapter 2

Movements and places: modern order and the cinema-squats of the 1960s

The cinema's spatial setting is, as pointed out in the previous chapter, characterized by a strong ambivalence: it possesses a particular socializing force, yet it allows at the same time for a coexistence of diverse identifications; it is included in modern strategic attempts to create order and acts as a place where encounters with the unfamiliar and the strange can occur. For several institutions of modern society, it was exactly this ambivalence associated with the cinema that was problematic in a particular way. In this chapter I will show that the rediscovery of difference that we encounter with the cinema movements in both pluralist democratic and one-party socialist societies around 1968 needs to be understood as a reaction to modern tendencies to eliminate ambivalence and suppress or control certain kinds of differences. The latter are the foil against which urban cinema squatters in both multiparty as well as one-party societies acted.

The fact that there has been a pronounced rediscovery of difference accompanying cinema activism since the 1960s, however, does not mean that ambivalence is re-evaluated and accepted in the same way. As war and ethnic cleansing some decades later in former Yugoslavia show, the rediscovery of difference can go along with clear definitions of 'us' and 'them' groups and fantasies of purity connected to this. Nevertheless, in order to be able to grasp the changes that occurred along with cinema movements since the 1960s, the modern tendency to fight ambivalence and to monitor difference needs to be presented in more detail.

This chapter begins with an account of how the cinema is involved in the various attempts to create order in modern nation states. In this respect, it also focuses attention on the very influential cinema politics of the German Reich, which represented these attempts in a heightened form. It then shows how cinema-activist groups in the 1960s started to call themselves into being through events organized around film and also an aesthetic staging of themselves in the city – a collective experience which led to the assertion of a 'different' way of inhabiting a city and which set them in conflict with other forms of cinema culture present in their environment. At the same time the emotional intensity that emerged around some of these cinema-squats encouraged other people to join in – temporarily or more permanently – or to create follow-up groups – so that cinema transformed itself into a kind of 'movement'. All these collective bodies emerging in the 1960s came together in reaction to and in the process of dealing with official interventions into social space – although, at first glance this seems to be less evident in the case of the movements in the FRG and in Austria. Despite this, however, the multiparty and one-party political contexts shaped the cinema movements quite differently.

Particular attention is given to the fact that, in both types of society, an encounter with strange and foreign movies caused viewers to become activists and cinema-makers themselves. As a result, films, urban interventions and particular alterations of the cinema setting contributed to the re-creation of a conflictual public sphere in the FRG and Austria and an informal public sphere in former Yugoslavia. The aesthetic productions of these movements did not remain inside the typical East-West, Cold War frame of reference, but displaced it by instead highlighting the discrepancies between the 'First World' and the 'Third World'. At the same time these movements also acted as a kind of avant-garde for a privatization of ambivalence and further individualization.

2.1. Cinema and the modern attempt to eliminate ambivalence

The modern state was a designing power engaged in 'social engineering' and in this way has promoted assimilation and linguistic, cultural and ideological unification rather than cross-cultural exchanges and a heterogeneity of cultural forms. 'Modern mastery' thereby operates, as Zygmunt Bauman points out, through 'the power to divide, classify and allocate' (Bauman 1991: 4f.). The various modern efforts to create order were supported by an assessment that had been spreading since the Enlightenment: the more we are able to push cultural particularisms back, the more modern we are. People should be made to step out of their limited state of dialects, clans and religions and be guided towards the universal (Wieviorka 2001: 19).

With this, differences were repelled and even regarded as threats, in particular in totalitarian political systems that tended to universalize a single difference (a nation, the proletariat) and to monitor and control the emergence of others. Nevertheless, modern institutions obviously did not succeed in these attempts. Every effort to create order produced ambivalence: phenomena of contingency, polysemy and non-univocal allocation. Simultaneously, and again in antinomy to universalism, capitalist consumer culture is based on continuous differentiation. In this way ambiguity, contingency, the unfamiliar that resists classification and non-univocal definitions function as the 'other' or the 'demon' of Modernity (Bauman 1991: 8). They were targets for new attempts to create order, which, however, in turn produced further ambiguities.

In the way cinema spaces place the bodies of the viewers in that space, separate them from the entanglements of the everyday, privilege their sense of vision and try to channel the perception of the public, they correspond to modern practices of creating order. The cinema setting thus appears in a particular way to be suited to take part in such essentially modern activities such as the *mise-en-scène* of the nation state, the promotion of productivity and of social reform. From the beginning, the cinema was implemented in educational and promotional discourses of cities, nations, political parties, transnational organizations, corporations and even religious institutions.

In order to make the merging of the cinema setting and strategies of modern institutions even more efficient, film screenings were framed with various (national, corporate, political party, religious) symbols and were incorporated into newly invented rituals intended to influence the perception of the viewers further (such as announcements, explanations and speeches, music, the distribution of leaflets and samples and sometimes even the singing of the national anthem). Simultaneously, however, the exposition of films strongly counteracts these efforts since it is able to cause significant encounters with the strange and unfamiliar, which throws concepts of national purity into disarray and triggers the persistent involvement of the viewers in unexpected stories and images as well as new ways of self-presentation and of inhabiting the city. There is thus a 'threat' connected to the exposition of film in cinema – which led to the persistent invention of measures to control what is happening in this particular urban space.

The pronounced involvement of the cinema in official strategies first took place in the urban centres of the modern state, where the cinema established itself as one of the most important visual entertainment and commercial resorts. But soon, and particularly with the various kinds of fascist and communist regimes emerging in the inter-war period, it started to spread to the countryside. National Socialist (NS) politics and Stalinism are the most extreme cases of a belief in global 'social engineering' (and not – as is often believed – the 'barbaric counterpart' of a development essentially viewed as directed towards progress and enlightenment) (Bauman 1991: 29) – something that appears to be closely entangled with cinema politics.

Transition spaces between NS politics and post-war re-education efforts

In Austria and Germany the Second World War and the NS regime had an especially strong and long-lasting impact on the transporting of the cinema setting into a variety of new urban as well as rural situations and in creating a whole range of new institutional intersections that specialized in the public dissemination of film and cinema. Regional *Gau-, Kreis-* and *Ortsgruppenfilmstellen* were set up in order to show some particularly 'important' films in a spectacular way and to include a large part of the population in these events through *Filmfeierstunden* (film-celebrating hours). Besides established cinemas, areas in taverns, schools and (courtesy transportable equipment) open-air arenas were used for projection.[1] A monitoring system as well as carefully planned rituals and an array of symbols were mobilized to maximize the control of what happens in these spaces. From 1934 onward it was almost impossible to see 'non-authorized' films in any cinemas within territories under NS control.[2] The films were framed by addresses delivered by the Hitler Youth, the reading of political texts or poetry or collectively shouted slogans. Swastika banners draped the outsides of cinemas and framed the screen along with evergreen branches or statues of eagles. Through such a setting the party tried to eliminate the multiple and ambivalent identifications the cinema setting might have triggered and to direct the reception unequivocally towards one that celebrated the event of the community in NS terms as a *Volksgemeinschaft*. In interaction with radio programmes or newspaper articles, these screenings were intended to get the audience to dwell exclusively on either the 'Germanness' or 'foreignness' of the characters shown.

However, even the fascist one-party state could not control the reception of films and the events in cinema spaces completely. Even after 1933, American films were to some extent still shown, if they had been produced without Jewish actors, directors or scriptwriters, and magazines continued to report on popular US stars like Clark Gable (Zimmermann 2007: 205). But also in relation to films produced in NS Germany, plural identifications and fascination, mainly with certain stars, remained prevalent (Hake 2002). One of the people I interviewed with respect to their cinema memories, Herta Konstantin (born in 1926), a former clerk and functionary of the Bund Deutscher Mädchen [BDM, Association of German Girls], remembers having been a fan of 'Willy Birgel in particular in [the NS film, A. S.] *Reitet für Deutschland* (1940–1941)' as well as of 'Kristina Söderbaum and, certainly, Marika Rökk' (I HK).

Particularly towards the end of the regime, the cinema seemed to have been functioning for her as a kind of 'transition space'. Herta Konstantin recounts having frequented one of the cinemas in Vienna fourteen times in February 1945 alone – that is, every other day – of course, also because 'it was warm there'. She remembers that '[t]here were films like *Jud Süß*, certainly *Tendenz*, Marika Rökk films, revue films' (I HK). Also, during the time immediately following the end of the war, she and her parents continued to go to the cinema. Her parents also watched 'rather German films'. But she herself went also to see US films and used them as a source of inspiration for new fashionable clothes: 'In general, the Viennese films with Hans Moser and Paul Hörbiger were almost all from the 1920s and, because of that, one was not able to get fashion inspiration from them. Actually only the American films were stylish' (I HK). With such appropriations, however, fashion styles from US films left the cinema spaces and emerged in everyday city life, where they, in turn, could be viewed by others as indicators of a new diversification of identification and of change.

Whereas several other spaces disappeared or changed their role with the end of the NS regime, the cinemas, if they had not been physically destroyed, often remained in place, even though now other films were shown there and the framing had changed. And due to the strongly standardized spatial setting, newly built cinemas, too, could give a feeling of familiarity. Because of all this, cinema spaces were able to act as transition spaces by providing a spatial frame in which new possibilities of accommodating a sense of temporary belonging and of developing aesthetic style could be advanced and different 'selves' could exist side by side without an immediate urge towards a univocal self-assignment.

In order to redirect public life after Nazism and to signify a change, a solemn *mise-en-scène* made out of banners, evergreen branches, eagles, political speeches and collectively shouted slogans such as those invented during the NS period was omitted and counteracted with a more decidedly modernist style.

However, the newly established official entities in the FRG or Austria again immediately made cinema part of their now diversified and sometimes conflictual encroachments

Figure 6: Löwen Cinema, Vienna 1947 © Votava Vienna.

into social space. Besides the commercial cinemas, several influential institutions such as trade unions and the Protestant and Catholic churches again included the cinema setting in their strategies to re-educate the public in West Germany and Austria and therefore expand their sphere of influence. For this they used established offices, trade union localities or the community spaces in parishes as well as travelling equipment in order to reach the population in various parts of the cities and countryside (Reichert 2007; Veith 1974; Kuchler 2006, Schwanebeck 1990). In addition, US offices and French, British and Russian cultural authorities also organized screenings, film programmes and lectures (Rupieper 1993: 101; Grafl 1995).

Sometimes there was collaboration – for instance, between the US and the Catholic re-education bodies (Schlemmer 1999: 297). But at the same time there was conflict (Reichert 2007: 236) as well as competition for similar target groups. And industry – especially food and consumer goods – also focused on cinemas to reach a large and rather general audience and framed screenings with fashion shows or with usherettes distributing samples in sexy and spectacular outfits.[3] Bigger cities such as Vienna, Munich, Berlin and Cologne became battlegrounds for these various efforts to use the cinema to re-educate and/or seduce the public.

Furthermore, in the early 1950s several city governments started to include film screenings and seminars in their cultural programmes – the communal film festivals in Mannheim and Oberhausen in the early 1950s, for instance, grew out of the active roles town governments assumed in subsidizing culture (Fehrenbach 1995: 214). In the course of these various strategic incorporations, feature films were again framed by newsreel and commercials as well as by posters and leaflets that visibly linked the screening to the broader strategy it was part of. Sometimes lectures and addresses were included too, or – in the case of foreign-language films – live translators, and usually, the opening images of films presented the production company and the country or organization that produced the film.[4] Together with these attempts to eliminate ambivalence again went the fact that – in the form of 'the nation', 'the worker' or the 'new democratic everyman' – the focus was on the universal, and cultural differences were consigned to the background or subordinated.

From NS occupation to cinema as a site for celebrating the Yugoslav 'people as one'

In Yugoslav cities such as Novi Sad or Belgrade the perceptual regime that emerged in connection with cinema spaces during the Second World War was closely connected to the developments in Austria and Germany – even if the one-party and multiparty context developing after the war soon shaped the activities around cinema in quite different ways. After the April War in 1941, Nazism and, as a part of it, measures to direct cinema reception univocally towards one that celebrated 'Germanness' also entered the territory of the former Kingdom of Yugoslavia: Jewish-owned cinemas were confiscated and others were asked to hand in their pre-war stock of films and to exhibit NS films as well as films from German allies or from 'neutral' countries such as Spain or Sweden (Kosanović 2004: 43). In parallel, cinema here too became more widespread as part of NS propaganda policies. The number of cinemas in Belgrade increased (to 21) and had a daily attendance of between 12,000 and 15,000 people (Savković, 1994: 59).

With the liberation of Belgrade by Tito's partisans and the Liberation Army of Yugoslavia in October 1944, the screening of films was again reorganized. At the end of 1944 a film section was installed in the department of propaganda of the Superior Headquarters of the liberation forces (the Partisan Units of Yugoslavia and the National Liberation Army), which, for lack of its own productions, mainly distributed films obtained as allied aid from Soviet, British and American forces, but also supervised the production of new films and operated the nationalized cinemas (Kosanović 2004: 43; Goulding 2002: 2). However, when the war was over, there were fewer than 500 cinemas in Yugoslavia, approximately two-thirds of the cinemas were damaged and the projection equipment had either been removed or destroyed (Goulding 2002: 1).

The Tito-led government elected in 1945 oriented itself on the Soviet model of employing film as a central means of mass education and as early as June 1946 set up a separate committee for cinematography as the highest state organ for the development of film, which quickly established separate regional committees for cinematography in each of the six republics except for Montenegro, where a special commission was formed. National film studios such as Avala film in Belgrade, Jadran film in Zagreb and Triglav film in Ljubljana as well as the first state film school for acting and film direction on Yugoslav territory were founded in 1946–1947 (Goulding 2002: 4f.).

In contrast to Austria and the FRG[5] after fascism and the Second World War, where a variety of societal forces competed in employing cinema for their strategic activities, in Yugoslavia an institutional structure was installed, dominated by the Commmunist Party and its leader, Josip Broz Tito. With this, power and society were again fused together. The party and Tito as its head were staged as representing an undivided 'people as one' (naši narodi/our people; Fischer 2013), and at the same time the propaganda they circulated was characterized by a denial that difference is constitutive for society – the only difference accepted was the distinction between the 'people as one' (represented by the party and its head, Tito) and its enemies (the old society, which was simultaneously the bourgeois/capitalist/imperialist world).[6]

Under Aleksandar Vučo, a well-known writer who was appointed the leading officer for cinematography by Tito himself, the cinema was used in this structure to redirect the population towards a single 'direction that shows the nations composing our country involved in an unparalleled aspiration to change all of the old relations and ideas and in an unparalleled struggle to achieve a richer and better future for man' (Vučo 1946: 4; quoted in Goulding 2002: 8). With this, non-conformist voices could be slandered as 'enemies of the people and of the state', in film production as in other sectors of society, and they were forced underground and their productions banned, or 'put in the bunker' as it was known in former Yugoslavia (I MB).

In keeping with this logic, film was called on to represent partisans, party members and collectives of workers engaged in socialist reconstruction as incarnations of the new, socialist society and to be visibly divided from, for instance, 'bourgeois' productions characterized by individualism and the 'star' system, by 'the dangers of formalism' or 'vulgar entertainment' (Vučo 1946: 3f.; quoted in Goulding 2002: 8). Hence, the strategies employed by the one-party system in Yugoslavia in relation to film and cinema again tried to make the viewers' perception unambiguously concentrate on, and celebrate, an undivided 'people as one'.

In 1948 the Titoist regime decided to break with the Soviet Bloc and embark on an independent way of Yugoslav socialism, and in 1950 a self-management system[7] was implemented that strengthened the initiative of individual units and collective action. As a consequence, between 1950 and the 1960s there was an 'opening' that consisted in a growth of film imports from the United States and Western Europe (France, followed by Britain and Italy) as well as in a diversification of homemade film production which now also included light comedy and satire as well as adventure films, historical-literary films and children's films (Goulding 2002: 37 and 43). As Dubravka Ugrešić recalls: 'My childhood culture consisted of Greek myths, stories of brave partisans and Hollywood films. My childhood idol was Audie Murphie, the hero of American Westerns. American films were the most effective and cheapest propaganda support for Tito's famous NO to Stalin' (Ugrešić 1998: 4). This, however, did not change attempts to control ambivalence and multiple identifications in cinema spaces, since party bureaucracy at the same time remained very concerned that the newly demanded collective action and initiative would not develop into political opposition.

In Yugoslav state-socialist society, the focusing on the universal and attempts to eliminate the ambiguity so characteristic of modernity were carried out in a particular way. Film was urged to represent the worker, the party and its leader, Tito, but at the same time there was latitude for individual and collective initiatives and experimentation, which created difference and augmented ambivalence. On an official level, however, there were no doubts. As Dušan Makavejev, then a young activist who would later become a famous film director, recalls: 'At that time, you know, everything was one. One youth organization, one film-maker organization, one popular front. […] And then the Cinémathèque opened in 1955' (I DM).

Around 1960, films shown in regular cinemas were more diverse than those exhibited immediately after the war and also included films from the United States as well as from Western Europe, and the homemade production was, in terms of genres, more diversified, too (Goulding 2002: 62ff.). Nevertheless, any form of appearance of difference that related to the Yugoslav people remained closely controlled. For instance, when Marko Babac in 1964 attempted to call a short film he had produced in the kino club *Kain i Avelj/Cain and Abel* he was explicitly asked to change this 'conflictuous' title and to rename the film *Braća/Brothers* (I MB) – something that takes up the Tito dictum of 'brotherhood and unity'. This shows that alongside the expression of political differences, any assertion of conflict between the 'brothers' was, even before the Croatian uprising (1967–1971), one of the most threatening issues in former Yugoslavia. The presence of different positions and of difference or conflict as such were only allowed as long as neither the 'people as one', the party nor the egocrat[8] Tito were called into question or challenged, and it was of course up to 'the party' and Tito themselves to decide whether or not this was the case.

The cinema created from below

In both post-NS West Germany and Austria as well as in Yugoslavia, cinema and film were used for redirecting public life and were for this purpose implemented into official strategies. This notwithstanding, the various efforts to control what was happening in cinema space in all countries were trapped in the same, already mentioned dual tendency: in the form of 'the nation', 'the worker' or the 'new everyman' – the focus was on universalizing a particular difference and subordinating, monitoring and controlling the emergence of other ones. Yet the public did not simply carry over what was available through official, institutionalized strategies – even if their deeds were informed by them – but followed what they themselves encountered in the course of the viewing process and stuck, often emphatically, to these events.

This involvement of the public is closely entangled with modern consumer culture, of which the cinema is a part. Consumer culture also operates through diversification, which, for instance, became manifest after 1945 when American re-education bodies in the FRG and Austria tried to 'preach' democracy, but, as the above quotation from Herta Konstantin shows, the American films screened were mainly seen as sources of fashion, or similarly, when the Yugoslav state, in order to popularize its 'No to Stalin's Russia', imported a wider range of movies from the United States and Western Europe the public responded mainly by travelling to Italy to buy the sort of consumer goods they had seen on the screen (Drakulić 1996a).

Related to this, cinema consumers started their own initiatives and turned into cinema-makers.[9] Their deeds were, however, not limited to a mere affirmation of consumer culture but exceeded it by politicizing the everyday and by participating in the construction of an (informal) public sphere. Groups and movements formed by inhabiting the cinema setting in a non-conventional way, by making films themselves and even by transforming cinema and film into artistic action.

Early groups emerging in the 1950s in Vienna, for instance, were more related to the tradition of working-class cinema clubs of the 1920 and 1930s – for instance, the workers' league (Abeiterbund) Brücke der Roten Armee (Bridge of the Red Army), which organized film screenings in Vienna's second district and also published a magazine advertising films and promoting certain 'red actors' (*Unser Arbeiterbund* 1954:3). In the late 1960s, however, cinema-activist groups constituted themselves as new initiatives by exhibiting a 'difference' that could no longer be subsumed under the criteria established by the working class. And, sometimes, they also explicitly challenged a 'straight' Marxist party tradition (Wieviorka 2001: 30f.).

In doing so, these groups usually highlighted the aesthetic appearance of their activities, connected it with a political message and invented new differences by staging particular filmic 'everymen' and 'everywomen', that is, the 'young, modern, independent women', the 'marginalized black or third-world person', the 'urban rebel', the *flâneur* or the 'Gypsy'. These figures and styles thus became publicly disseminated and started to contest older universal figures such as 'the worker', 'the partisan' or nationalist heroes. Quite often aesthetic productions from 'another America', shaped by jazz, beat and 'underground' culture or inspired by pre-war aesthetic subcultures, such as Dadaism or Surrealism, or from Soviet 'revolutionary cinema' triggered the creation of a cinema setting and films that exhibited a pronounced difference vis-à-vis what was viewed as 'old', 'bourgeois', 'consumer' or 'cultural ghetto' cinema.[10]

In Vienna, Munich, Cologne, Hamburg or Berlin, for example, transnational networks were established that were quite compact. They consisted of artists, film-makers and cinema activists whose activities to some extent became involved in the formation of the

Figure 7: xscreen, Cologne, 1968 © xscreen archive berlin, courtesy Wilhelm Hein.

broader student movement of 1968. One of these networks, also known as 'Expanded Cinema', was, for instance, composed of the xscreen group in Cologne and Munich (Christian Michelis, Rolf Wiest, Hans Peter Kochenrath, Birgit and Wilhelm Hein and others in Cologne, and Karlheinz Hein and others in Munich, Figure 7), the Viennese Aktionismus (especially Otto Mühl, Günter Brus and Rudolf Schwarzkogler) and the Austrian Filmmakers Cooperative (Valie Export, Kurt Kren, Hans Scheugl, Gottfried Schlemmer and Peter Weibel). Connections also existed to Peter Konlechner and Peter Kubelka, who by 1963–1964 had already founded the Austrian Film Museum, which had a strong avant-garde orientation (Peter Kubelka in Jutz and Tscherkassky 1995: 37). These Austrian and German Expanded Cinema groups were set up in contrast to leftist cinema clubs that were more explicitly rooted in a Marxist tradition (I BH and I WH). In addition and often mixed up with the latter, 'communal', 'free', 'new' or 'other' cinemas (Figure 8) were established in various cities and were soon transformed into an early kind of programme cinema (I DS).

Figure 8: Political cinema, Kino im Kopf Nuernberg © Prinzler and Seidler, Kinobuch, 1975.

From 1969–1970 onward, these 'new cinema initiatives' started to emerge in a more pronounced way out of former film clubs, youth clubs, people's academies and private initiatives, transforming existing urban situations into various kinds of cinemas or cinema-like events. They ranged from 'film-ins' – open film screenings where local directors could show and discuss their productions – to cinema pubs, political film clubs, student cinemas, communal cinemas and early forms of programme or art-house cinemas.

A study conducted in 1972 within the framework of the Deutsche Film- und Fernsehakademie (German Film and TV Academy) mentioned the following as the most important of these initiatives throughout the FRG and West Berlin: the Arsenal (Berlin), Cinema Ostertor (Bremen), Kommunales Kino (Frankfurt/Main), Filmforum Duisburg, Cinemathek (Cologne), Zelluloid (Essen), Abaton (Hamburg) and xscreen (Cologne).[11] These initiatives confronted the 'old', 'bourgeois' and 'dying cinema' and, in particular, the former tradition of *Filmkunsttheater* (film-art theatres) or *Gildekinos* (guild cinemas) with a 'cinema of the future'. This kind of cinema was defined as 'independent' and 'emancipatory' in the sense that it 'helped emancipate the individual or particularly interested groups from the restraints of mass culture or the heteronomy of industry and capital' (m. t. Jansen 1972: 17). Its main goal was to once again 'transform isolated consumers into communicators. It has to provide the opportunity to be confronted with more than the image on screen or the own loss of self' (m. t. Jansen 1972: 12).

Around 1974–1975 particular emphasis was given to the fact that, in contrast to TV and commercial cinema, these new initiatives were able to expose cinema's language to doubt and dispute, and the notion of *Kino der Alternative* (cinema of the alternative) also started to be used as an umbrella term for these initiatives (Jansen 1975: 9). Parallel to these new forms of cinema, special interest groups and lobbies such as the Arbeitsgemeinschaft Kino (Working Group Cinema) in Hamburg, the Arbeitsgemeinschaft Gemeindekino (Working Group Community Cinema) in Frankfurt/Main or the Koordinationsbuero Film (Film

Coordination Office) in Munich also began to emerge, as well as new and independent film distributors and film editors such as the Filmverlag der Autoren or the Hamburger Filmbuero (Prinzler and Schwarz 1972: 4).

Also in Yugoslavia, in cities such as Novi Sad, Belgrade, Kranj or Zagreb in the 1960s, non-conventional cinema activism began to enter the scene of the urban stage. But in contrast to the cinema activism emerging at the same time in German and Austrian cities, the Yugoslav novi film tendencies, also known as Crni Talas (Black Wave), and art-film groups like OHO began inside a single structure provided from 'above', that is, by the one-party system. They formed as a network of kino clubs, that is, amateur film clubs, which were part of a state programme called Narodna tehnika (People's Technique) founded by Yugoslav state-socialist authorities as an imitation of the Soviet system of youth education. The aim of this programme was to provide the institutional framework, locations and economic support necessary to create spaces that – like the photo clubs, chess clubs or radio clubs – outside of school and other already established educational facilities, separated the youth from their families and extended families and thus led them towards the production of a socialist 'new world' (Babac 2001: 74f.).

The events around some of these kino clubs – for instance, the kino club Belgrade (Figure 9) or one of the clubs in Kranj, Slovenia – soon showed the uncontrollable momentum latent in such initiatives. With the setting up of these clubs, the socialist system in Yugoslavia was

Figure 9: Kinoclub Beograd, 1960s © Jugoslovenska Kinoteka, Belgrade.

again trying to use the power of cinema with regard to socialization. But in doing so it was providing young people with meeting and representation spaces as well as with equipment and the opportunity to articulate their viewpoints. Diverging from the intentions of the one-party system and its cinema apparatus, some of the young film-makers and cineasts in these kino clubs started making films and started cinema initiatives that showed feelings, observations, a constellation of figures and aesthetic forms that were incompatible with official ideology.

With this, the young film-makers and cinema organizers at the beginning of the 1960s at first often involuntarily and later in a more conscious and playful way, entered into conflict with state-socialist authorities. These conflicts resulted in the banning of several films, censorship and imprisonment, driving some of the film-makers to an inner or de facto emigration (to France, the United States, West Germany). What soon was to be known as Crni Talas started first in the Belgrade kino club and the Novi Sad kino club, but connections were also maintained with various clubs in Ljubljana, Zagreb, Split or Sarajevo as well as with some film critics, curators of art spaces, scriptwriters and journalists all over the country who soon began to support the film activists.

In both the FRG and Austria and Yugoslavia these cinema initiatives emerged against a background of a 'dying' cinema: with cinemas closing down and becoming transformed into parking houses, shopping centres and beat taverns and with a sharp decline in cinema attendance. Whereas at the beginning of the 1960s in the FRG there were 7,000 cinemas, by the end of the 1970s there were only 3,500. And whereas in 1960 605 million ticket sales were counted, in 1970 there were only 167.4 million (Jansen 1972: 11).

In former Yugoslavia these developments were more contradictory but still showed a similar tendency. Due to the proliferation of republican and regional centres of film production in the late 1960s, more films were being produced now, with some ups and downs, than ever before. But simultaneously here, too, the number of film viewers declined, most strongly in the late 1960s and early 1970s. Whereas the highest number of attendances was counted in 1960 with 130.1 million, this number had fallen to 80.8 million in 1971 (Goulding 2002: 64).

At first the rise of TV culture was mainly held responsible for this decline, but in the late 1960s the phenomenon started to be reconsidered. For example, in the FRG, the Film Subsidy Board commissioned an opinion poll, known also as the 'Dichter Study', which pointed out that cinema's enemy was not television but a certain kind of cinema itself that did not fulfil a desire for social contacts, culture and self-education, the experience of emotions and possibilities of regaining a sense of the world (Dichter 1971). Activists involved in the new cinema initiatives picked up on this to redefine a new pronouncedly public function of cinema that crystallized around the concept of a 'communal' or 'political' cinema. In this way film and certain urban situations were presented as being in a process of becoming 'emancipated' from old notions of 'cinema' and being transformed into 'film work' or into a 'means to do political work' (Jansen 1972: 13f.).[12] In Yugoslavia, too, despite the 'crisis' of mainstream film culture, the 1960s were one of the most prolific periods of novi film and cinema tendencies – which was sustained by a general spirit of innovation and experimentation within the framework of the newly installed self-management system, but also by 'new wave' tendencies in other socialist countries such as in Czechoslovakia and Poland (Goulding 2002: 66).

In the various accounts of memories related to cinema, the former activists usually give the name of the place and localize it on the city map – as, for instance, Marko Babac, former member of the kino club Beograd, does when he says: 'This first contact (for me), for example, with Russian directors, was in the Kinoteka, Kinoteka Jugoslovenska, in Kosovska Street, a famous cinema, and it was free' (I MB). At the same time, they sometimes describe a clash between the cinema spaces they experienced themselves and the surrounding city life.

Gottfried Schlemmer, a cinema enthusiast since the 1950s and a founder member of the Austrian Filmmakers Cooperative in the late 1960s, remembers a particular viewing situation in the early period of his cinema fandom in Vienna: 'I'm watching a John Ford film in the Weltbiograph [...] That was still a small cinema and the way it was built, the first row was above the exit and the screen was over the top of the exit. I am looking at the screen, and underneath someone opened the door and the people [in the street] were walking past. It was really like that. They went out onto the street from a room that was wonderful. Everything that made life difficult was gone there, and they went out, outside it had been raining, you slipped; inside everything was perfect, the happy end or the perfect catastrophe, but everything went without a break. [...] Wonderful. You had been in a machine, you came out and you had missed the tram' (I GS).

Similarly, Marko Babac also describes a moment of surprising encounter between everyday urban life and the 'world' they used to construct in their Belgrade kino club, where they not only showed their homemade films, but also played jazz. At a certain point, he remembers, the young people in the club opened the window and the music could be heard in the streets. There was a 'meeting between ordinary people, who were waiting for the tram, with progressive jazz [...] it was not only Louis Armstrong, it was progressive jazz, completely atonal and arhythmic music, [you should see these] faces, meeting, at this moment, this social moment, political moment and physical place, you know, for me that was a fantastic feeling'(I MB).

These quotations show that a questioning of the status quo and an experience of transition in relation to the cinema setting is often linked to some perceptual events sticking out of the usual smooth viewing processes. Sometimes, however, as the narration by Marko Babac emphasizes, the significance was also located in the enthusiasm, the socialization around a certain kind of film and music created and the clash this produces with the usual flow of everyday life. Events of this sort seemed to develop a kind of persistency and supported the construction of 'different' cinema settings which one could inhabit, the production of images and texts that represented an imagination and a perception of the world one could believe in and that could be disseminated further through such spaces.

Hence, despite all the various strategic efforts that in both multiparty and one-party types of society strongly used the cinema setting and tried to calculate what was happening in it, the viewers followed that which they encountered in themselves in the course of the viewing and socialization processes. In both political systems the cinema thus repeatedly acted as a space where viewers could descend in times of profound political change exposing themselves to the strange and unfamiliar, trying out various identifications and the ambivalent feelings connected with them. In this way, transformations in everyday life – from fascism to a multiparty-democratic society or to various kinds of socialism, from Soviet-type socialism to self-managed socialism, and/or from adolescence to adulthood or from being an 'average' cinema consumer to being a politically attentive cinema activist – could be negotiated, reflected, rejected, disavowed and transmuted.

2.2. To become cinema-makers: expanded and other cinemas, the Crni Talas and OHO

The various forms of 'other', 'free' or 'communal cinemas', the Austrian or German Expanded Cinema, the Yugoslav novi film tendencies (also called 'black wave' or 'open cinema') and related cinema initiatives can be called 'cinema as a movement' in the sense of a political movement, because the cohesion inside the collective bodies named in this way – by themselves and/or others – was primarily established through the public activities of their members. This means that the participants did not come from one institution but had various backgrounds and institutional bonding[13] – they usually were brought into being by interactions of networks, individuals, organizations and collective projects. The collective bodies forming around cinema situations in the late 1960s were open, at least to some extent, to attracting new members, cinema enthusiasts or follow-up groups. Besides, the deeds of activists involved in these entities were directed towards a contesting of reigning allocations and viewing options and a seeking of hegemony in the symbolic realm.[14]

Cinema as a movement came about with what is known as the student movement of 1968. Like other new social movements, cinema movements emerge through interventions into particular social spaces where deeds co-acted and struggled not only with those of adherents and constituents of the groups and movements themselves but also with all actors, organizations and institutions to whom they are connected, from whom they distance themselves or who are otherwise present in the same environment. These interventions also occur through an occupation of space, an alteration of existing spatial structures and the constitution of a public-sensible presence. Besides, the deeds, statements and aesthetic productions of these movements generate what Nick Crossley calls a 'movement discourse and culture; that is, norms, identities, symbols, frames, typifications and a range of stories and sacred texts which identify heroes, villains, promised lands etc.' (Crossley 2006: 19 and 27).

The cinema setting was, as already pointed out, particularly suited to assemble various individuals within an entity that is also emotionally charged and that then – through a squatting of particular urban spaces, the screening of films and direct action – could gain public visibility. At the same time, and initially most pronounced in the pluralist democratic political setting, as I will show later on, a 'narcissism of minor differences', as Sigmund Freud (2005: 114f.) called it, was strongly effective, which means that even small differences between how groups saw and made film and how they inhabited the cinema setting were often experienced as insurmountable and could lead to a closure of groups vis-à-vis each other. This led to a strong diversification of cinema initiatives in this context: there were, for instance, the transnational Expanded Cinema or Underground Cinema movement, the more explicitly political or 'red' cinema clubs, the communal cinema movement, as well as film-makers in the rather narrow sense of the word, such as Wim Wenders and the social networks he was part of, which however also viewed themselves as creating '1968' and cineaste culture at the same time.[15]

Expanded Cinema and other cinemas

In retrospective narrations, cinema activists usually present the cinema as a space that divided them from the communities they were born into and their traditional ways of ordering the world and led them to gather in new constellations, with shared judgements, taste, emotional intensity, interest or identification playing an increasingly important role. The cinema is described as a setting able to generate feelings and imaginations bringing people together, without the need to define experiences explicitly or to make clear assignments of one's belonging. Here affiliations such as those of birth – the family, class, craft or local communities – can become less important in respect to new bonds that can be established vis-à-vis what is shown in films, for example by unforeseen encounters that may happen in the cinema spaces themselves.

Gottfried Schlemmer, for example, later co-founder of the Austrian Filmmakers Cooperative (in the late 1960s) and the film-institute Synema (in the early 1980s), remembers the excessive cinema visits which for him characterized the passage towards adulthood and the varying cinema worlds he entered in afterwards: 'In 1948 [...] I went to the Kärnterkino after school. This was my first conscious cinema visit. There I saw *Calcutta,* and I can only remember a black knife flying through space. [...] And then I went to the cinema intensively, three or four times a day' (I GS). In this early period of enthusiasm for the cinema, he saw 'only Hollywood', but soon, he explained, 'I bought a book on film history, the first was *Knaurs Filmgeschichte* [...] and looked out for what was on in Vienna. There was the film archive, run by Gesek, and films were shown there and then at the university; there were the *Filmwissenschaftliche Wochen* [film festivals]. Vagn Boerge showed all of Dryer's films, and so I watched all the art films. This was the second phase. Vagn Boerge showed these in the Palais Lobkowitz. [...] In parallel, I never completely gave up the other cinema, but I now saw it in a broader context. [...] And the third phase began with the *Nouvelle Vague,* there the cinema public was a bit disturbed, the early Antonioni or *Außer Atem (À bout de souffle).* [...] From the point of view of classical cinema, it was full of errors, and that began to interest me very much. I started to be concerned with cinema in a theoretical way at the beginning of the 1960s. Then I stopped watching other films apart from the avant-garde or the *Nouvelle Vague*, and at the end of the 1960s, we founded the Austrian Filmmakers Cooperative. This was directed against classical cinema and everything. It was the liberation from this "opium"' (I GS).

As a sign of these changes in situating himself in the urban environment (and the world in general) triggered by film perception, he also altered the way he dressed. Referring to the late 1960s, he says: 'You can look at old photographs and there you can see that we all went around in ties. [… But soon, A. S.] I was one of the first to go around in blue jeans' (I GS).

Gottfried Schlemmer most liked going to the cinema alone: 'Otherwise I would have felt disturbed; and this way I was mobile too and I could exactly plan how I could get to the next screening a few minutes later' (I GS). Nevertheless, he described himself as being in conversation with others in the cinema simultaneously: with film-makers, cinema-programmers and fellow cineastes. In the late 1960s significant viewing (and reading) experiences brought him to participate in the foundation of an Expanded Cinema group in Vienna that 'translated' viewing experiences into new ways of making or showing films, of creating public-artistic actions and of inhabiting the city.

The artists and film-makers of the Austrian Filmmakers Cooperative put on various events in diverse city locations: they showed invisible films running through a projector, staged provocative public performances on squares and streets – for instance, by using female breasts as a 'screen' that could be 'viewed' by hand in the famous 'Touch-Cinema' by Valie Export (1968–1971) – and took part in new kinds of festivals and public 'action-lectures'. Acting in this way, the Expanded Cinema used very different city spaces for their interventions, that is, not only cinemas in the strict sense, but also metro stations, exhibition and concert halls, streets and squares and even circus tents. In addition to Vienna, they also presented such actions in cities such as Munich and Cologne – the latter especially being a very frequent venue and housing some of the most provocative urban interventions.[16]

With this kind of activism the city was transformed into a cultural arena where spectacular events could take place unexpectedly, and the public was addressed as one that could be provoked in various ways. Here Schlemmer explicitly mentions the potential of the cinema to address a large audience as one of the reasons he chose to articulate his viewpoint in the form of cinema activism (I GS) – which stood in stark contrast with the style employed by Expanded Cinema activists, who were quite critical of what they viewed as the ideological dimensions of cinema as a popular art and entertainment and consequently directed their activism towards 'challenging' and even 'interrupting' the public's ideological frameworks.

This is articulated in an even more explicit way by the artists and film-makers Valie Export and Peter Weibel, also part of the Austrian Filmmakers Cooperative, who described the mainstream cinema of their time in a manifesto, published on the occasion of a cinema festival in Munich in 1969 as follows: 'Our event […] declares that the time of visual communications as profane religious image adoration, of the theatre as secular temples, of the cinema as profane churches to be terminated. It calls for the termination of all these institutions as instruments of domination, which bind the individuals to the values, goals, norms of the state

[…] all that mystic, magic and religion of image-thinking as archaic technologies of ecstasy, the symbolizations as technologies of repressive socialization [… it thus declares an end to, A. S.] all this era of homology, of identification, of the relations of representation of that epistemological system, which from the 8th until the 20th century has managed to dominate and repress the consciousness of the people!!!' (m.t., quoted in: Weibel 1973: 62).

Here, the aesthetic style disseminated by conventional cinemas is linked to the manipulation of 'the people', to the submission of the individual to the norms of the state and hence to repression and domination. Their own alternative form of cinema action is directed against this, so that, as stated in another manifesto, '[t]he perception of new relations becomes possible. The conceptions have to be shattered in order to free sensuality' (m.t., quoted in: Weibel 1973: 42).

In contrast to the variety of urban spaces the Austrian Filmmakers Cooperative occupied with their artistic interventions, another cinema-activist group was created during these years in Vienna. They called themselves Freies Kino (Free Cinema) and chose a more stable, single local stage of action.[17] In this case, this was also motivated by the fact that the collective bonding and emotional loading found in the cinema setting was 'calculated' – even more explicitly – for political purposes. Dieter Schrage, co-founder of the Freies Kino (Figure 10), recalls: 'At the university, in the Neues Institutsgebäude, in this very famous auditorium I, there was a cinema weekend about the new revolutionary Latin American film and the new German proletarian film. I went there first as a visitor, but I knew the initiators very well. This was 1972, at the beginning of 1972. And then we got together, and since this was extremely successful, we said we should show political cinema continuously' (I DS).

Several members of these groups were part of the VSSTOE, the student branch of the Austrian Social Democratic Party, but there was also a film-maker, Mansur Madavi, born in Azerbaijan but raised in Vienna, as well as some other film and cinema enthusiasts. And it was again a communal institution with traditional links to the Social Democratic Party, the KIBA (Kino-Betriebsgesellschaft), who agreed to provide a cinema for screenings (I DS).

Since the activists were expecting mainly a student audience, they chose an old cinema, the Rossauer Kino, in Vienna's 9th district near the university, as the location for their cinema activism, even though other locations would have also been available. They painted it and arranged some catering with beer and wine for special events. But in addition to the overall 'political message' they sought to deliver through the films they chose to show, what was most important was the further framing with introductory addresses at the start, with discussions afterwards and with the magazine they published, *Kritischer Film/Critical Film*.[18] Dieter Schrage explains: 'We had discussions with the Austrian Filmmakers Cooperative […] They accused us of being no different from Hollywood […] But this was not true, since we focused on the political message of film' (I DS).

Important reference points for the Freies Kino in Vienna were the Arsenal cinema in Berlin (since 1970) and the Kommunales Kino in Frankfurt/Main (since 1971). Both claimed to present films not in an isolated way but as part of a wider context, that is, as part of a programme, a retrospective or a seminar. The Arsenal, for example, showed retrospectives

Figure 10: Logo Freies Kino (Free Cinema), Vienna, early 1970s © Austrian National Library.

of documentary films and of Soviet silent movies, programmes of Cuban, Latin American, Polish, Soviet, Hungarian, British, Italian, Algerian and New German movies, besides collections of political 'target-group films' as well as of experimental films. In addition, they focused in particular on the confrontation of the old and the contemporary in film culture. In self-descriptions the communal character of this initiative was pointed out, in particular – for instance, by stating that all people involved renounced payment (Prinzler and Schwarz 1972: 23f.).[19]

In these years, however, it was the latter, the Kommunales Kino (Figure 11), that had gained most public visibility due to a conflict with commercial cinema theatre owners who accused the city of unfair competition. This conflict was resolved in favour of the Kommunales Kino, but it produced as a side-effect a more detailed definition of how new initiatives were to serve, educate and entertain the public – in this way, the cinema was redefined as a kind of *Lehranstalt* (academy). At the same time, it was most strongly differentiated from what was called *Konsumkino* (consumer cinema) and *Kulturghetto* (cultural ghetto) (Prinzler and Seidler 1975: 101f.).

The network character of these initiatives shows itself clearly in the fact that they make strong reference to each other and even 'borrow' certain practices or even programmes. Thus the Arsenal in Berlin is not only mentioned by the Freies Kino in Vienna as a kind of forerunner (besides the Kommunales Kino in Frankfurt/Main) but also by the Kommunales Kino, which also refers to an international example: the Museum of Modern Art in New York. The Arsenal, which was one of the earliest of these new cinema initiatives, claims, in turn, in order to consolidate its status as a 'founding' institution, only to have reference points in foreign cities: the Cinémathèque Français in Paris, the Cinémathèque Belge in Brussels and the National Film Theatre in London (Prinzler and Seidler 1975: 23f. and 101f. and IDS) – something that already indicates the transnational character of 'cinema as movement'.

In the process of their constitution, the various cinema initiatives usually vied for viewers and support and at the same time often set themselves off from each other in an explicit way. So, for instance, the film-maker Birgit Hein, who was one of the main exponents of the Expanded Cinema scene in the FRG, described the explicitly politically engaged cinema movements as 'ignorant' regarding 'formal innovative art', and she accused them

Figure 11: Locating oneself in the city, Logo Kommunales Kino (Communal Cinema), Frankfurt/Main © Prinzler and Seidler, Kinobuch, 1975.

of a simplistic 'one-to-one ideology', which, for example, seeks to rouse people against war by presenting a dying soldier (Birgit Hein in Beyerle et al. 1984: 96). Vice versa, the above-mentioned Dieter Schrage of the Freies Kino in Vienna described the actions of the contemporary Expanded Cinema as 'too formalistic'. He and his combatants saw no emancipatory orientation in the destruction of conventional aesthetic forms (I DS).

But despite such strong demarcations, there were similarities in the activities of the opponents, too: in the early 1970s some Expanded Cinema initiatives also transformed themselves into early programme cinemas. From then on, for instance, the alternative xscreen projection space in Cologne founded by various film-makers and cinema activists after the film festival in Knokke, 1967–1968, was run by B+W Hein as a more permanent programme cinema, where on a regular basis they showed a wider variety of underground and non-conventional films, also including some still (until 1975) officially forbidden pornographic movies (Schober 2009b: 254f.).

The novi film movement and OHO

The reference points for such cinema-activist memories in cities in former Yugoslavia such as Ljubljana or Belgrade had less of a temporary character and varying locations, but instead involved more stable cinema set-ups in a narrow sense. Yet they too combined the screenings of film with art exhibitions or music as well as with educational activities. The spaces most often mentioned by film-makers and cinema activists in Belgrade, for instance, are the cinemas of the kino club Beograd and the Academic kino club, the Kinoteka Yugoslav Film Archive and (for the later period) the auditoriums at the Student Cultural Centre and the House of Youth. Like their counterparts in the FRG and Austria, here, too, cinema enthusiasts recount how they put together a new sense of themselves and of the world by consuming films from various countries and from different periods. They also used stimuli found in the course of viewing films in cinema situations in order to create aesthetic productions that in themselves then intervened in urban life.

Some of the Yugoslav cineasts also described 'their' cinema explicitly as a place where it was possible to survive in times of harsh political transitions and to disavow and negotiate change. Marko Babac, an early member of the kino club Beograd (Figure 12), for instance, said: 'My family was very poor, as a nationalist officer my father had no job, after the war he had to work as a building labourer. And in the clubs you could have a warm room; in my home not, it was always cold. [For] two or three years [we lived] without windows, without glass in the windows, after the war, only with paper and the winters were very cold. [...] In the clubs we had warmth, technology and good friends, they were mostly my age, some older, but I was very young, maybe one of the youngest' (I MB).

This is how Babac answered the question about his reasons for joining the club: 'Cinema, dreams, you know, to run away from reality, from rough reality, very poor. [...] This connection with the dark room, with moving pictures helped me to run into another

Figure 12: Poster of Kinoclub Beograd, with Logo of the Kino Savez (cinema association of Yugoslavia), 1960 © Jugoslovenska Kinoteka, Belgrade.

world, not a world of lies such as in reality, but in lies of dreams. This is something very different. I believe in lies of dreams'(I MB).

In this account, the cinema appears to be characterized as a transition space towards something that was diverging sharply from official strategies. He describes that in the cinema he could step from a rough, false reality full of lies, which for him was connected to the cinema of the regime, into another world full of dreams he could believe in, which was again tied to particular city spaces. The main example of this kind of space was the locality of the kino club and the small cinema they had there, called Tesla and then Union (Babac 2001: 44), as well as the already mentioned Kinoteka Yugoslav Film Archive, where they could get 'an education' as the young cinema lovers used to say.

Some of the collective bodies formed this way were quite big. There were, for instance, around 150 people in the Belgrade club, Babac remembers, even if the core was formed by approximately only 25 mostly male members. They came from 'elementary school, high school, and from all different disciplines at the university level: [law], architecture, technical [studies], more from languages, [from the] philosophy department, foreign languages, English, French and painters, students of painting too' (I MB).

Sometimes, however, a very small personal framework, such as the OHO kino club in Kranj (Slovenia), consisting of only two or three people, could also give rise to a connectivity formed by various spectators, who were in themselves sometimes also cinema organizers, film-makers, journalists, artists and critics. Thus, the OHO kino club audience fed itself from the overlapping with a wider OHO community, a circle of artists working in various fields of literature, theatre, performance and film.

Naško Križnar, founder of this OHO kino club, recalls that in the 1960s he went to Ljubljana every day because he was studying architecture there. Since the last train back to Kranj did not leave until around midnight, he would go to the cinema in Ljubljana before that. He remembers especially having seen films of the Nouvelle Vague – Godard and Truffaut – as well as Italian neorealism, in particular Antonioni, Visconti and Fellini, in the regular cinemas. At the same time, he recalls, he got 'an education' at the Kinoteka in Ljubljana. Here, for example, he got to know the films of Luis Buñuel, Ingmar Bergman, Andrei Tarkovsky and Sergei Eisenstein. 'I don't know if it was my own engagement or my own intuition or this education with the help of Kinoteka, but I felt like I was at home watching Eisenstein's films. I understood everything about his theory. [...] I had a few friends I could talk to about these problems of films. But it was more important to grasp it by myself and to understand' (I NK). Together with a few others he then translated this experience of watching films into a particular way of producing films and of inhabiting the city.

The ideas for these films came, according to Križnar, not only from the films he used to see but mainly from music: 'pop music like the Beatles, the Rolling Stones or from classical music' (I NK). Križnar, together with his artist-friends, only made short films, recorded with a handheld camera, mostly in fuzzy focus, fast-paced, with extreme close-ups and unusual forms of montage.

City life played a central role in these films: they were shot in everyday surroundings, which, however, were changed through unusual performances of bodies and objects, such as the handing out of flowers to strangers, exuberant jumping or carrying around an enormous cardboard box; casual gestures, such as strolling through the city, were re-enacted in surprising ways, or slogans and graffiti were painted on walls.[20] Since these films were shot on location, well-known city spaces and ordinary passers-by became – as involuntary 'actors' – part of the shooting. Locations such as main parks and central city streets in Ljubljana (and other cities they occasionally visited, like Zurich) and actions such as surprised gazing or absorbed watching became in this way – medially enlarged – again re-inserted into urban events such as screenings or festivals where people in the audience could compare themselves in relation to the 'actors'.

Sometimes, however, Križnar also made films that showed a playful 'inhabitation' of the countryside – made on the occasion when some friends came to visit him in Kranj. One sees them running and jumping amid grassland and fields, and this contributed to the OHO reputation of being a hippie-like community.

Naško Križnar especially highlights how important it was for him to gain recognition for his productions from others. He said: 'What I felt was that I had a strong desire to make a film and to show it to others. It was an extremely nice feeling watching the film for the first time with other people, not alone […] it is thrilling, it is difficult to explain' (I NK). Through this film-making activity, he established himself as a member of the wider community of OHO who however mainly engaged in performances, poetry and visual arts. In addition he also became closely linked to this community because he filmed several of their public performances.

In his case, the new community formed in this way was not completely separate from the one he was born into: he, for instance, used family ties to get public support for his project of funding a kino club. He recounts: 'My father was a member of a [photo] kino club [in Kranj, A. S.], and he took me with him when they had a meeting, and I went with my father on these photographic safaris. […] Then, when I joined a group, this was an opportunity for me. Everybody knew me in the club and so I could organize a kino section there.

Figure 13: Zurigo, Naško Križnar, 1966 © Naško Križnar.

[…] It was important to have an official seat. When we had an official seat we could apply for programmes, to be given some funds for film, for footage. That is how it started'(I NK). Hence, in his case, the socializing force the cinema exerts not only created a new community but transformed existing bonds, such as those of the family, neighbourhood or school.

This becomes especially palpable when Križnar remembers the beginning of OHO. He compared forming the group between artists working in various fields of literature, theatre, performance and film to a slow process of falling in love: 'We were all friends and school fellows, neighbours, we met everyday and little by little we started to talk more about these activities and tried to understand. There were some older artists there. Franci Zagoričnik, he was a very well-known poet then, and also some other poets and artists from Ljubljana came to some meetings, some evenings, "cultural evenings" we said […] and after that we began to talk and then this idea of Marko Pogačnik's of "OHO" came up […] "OHO" […] is a combination between *oko*, which means eye, and *uho*, which means ear. So two senses are involved: seeing and hearing' (I NK).

In the Yugoslav context such family bonds which were in some way related also to the Communist Party or the army were important for getting the opportunity to establish a new urban spatial linking point. Not only in small cities like Kranj but also in bigger ones like Novi Sad – as, for instance, Dušan Makavejev reports when he remembers the first activities of the circle which later on became the kino club there: 'There was this organization called Narodna tehnika, people's technique association. This was an imitation of this Soviet system [of youth education, A. S.]. […] When I was in high school, I was in Novi Sad, I was 15 or 16 […] we were going gliding. […] I was the head of that technology-club organization. […] At our school we had a son of a general who was an air-force commander. So I went to see him and said, "Look, could you speak with your dad so that we can get a parachute course?" We needed help from the army […] so we got connections. It was part of this technical education. […] There was a photo kino club, the kino section became stronger […] we went to the basement of the school, we found some old projector that had some old films, there were films [about] how to produce a book, how to produce pottery […] it was a technical school. So we watched all kinds of idiotic films about – whatever. Then we went to an American library that had opened and we got films about electrons, about astronomy. Because they were not allowed to have political films, but they were sending us good school films, like the discovery channel […] so we showed those. Then I came to study here [in Belgrade] in 1950, 1951, and then I was a founding member of the Belgrade kino club' (I DM). Hence, Makavejev also describes how family ties could be used to make new initiatives possible.

Nevertheless, even if there was a re-use of family bonds, the communities formed through film and cinema experience did not overlap with older units of families, clans or villages but created ruptures and new collective formations too. This can also be seen in Kranj, where a special taste in films as well as relating to the visual arts more generally and a certain style of aesthetic expression connected OHO as a group and acted as a dividing line towards previously established communities. Because of this, Naško Križnar is eager to make clear that his father, although he was helpful in establishing first contacts and of furnishing him with initial respectability, 'was not a film enthusiast' (I NK) and because of this, did not belong to the same circle.

In the framework of already existing research on Yugoslav cinema culture, it is unusual to mention performance-like art production and films of art groups such as OHO in relation to films made by directors usually counted as being part of the Crni Talas. I included this group, however, in this book in order to show that around 1968, a bigger variety of cinema activism in former Yugoslavia was emerging than is often assumed. Nevertheless, this does not mean that I would advocate subsuming films made by OHO under the label of the Crni Talas.

The most obvious difference between these forms of cinema activism is that the films of OHO did not enter into the same pronounced conflictual relationship with the regime as did some films by the directors referred to at the end of the 1960s as Crni Talas (black wave). Despite this, there are, however, also several similarities between these 'black' authors and OHO interventions. Both OHO and the film-makers usually referred to as Crni Talas were emerging as part of what was retrospectively known as '1968'. They displaced a difference in viewing the world and in relating to one another onto an aesthetic level and thus also confronted official culture through aesthetic style – whereby they constructed similar genealogies by referring, for instance, to Sergei Eisenstein, Dziga Vertov or the French New Wave. They represented issues such as love, passion, alienation or loneliness, which seemed at first sight non-political but acquired in this context a sometimes strong, politically challenging force. And for a while they managed to sustain a certain emotional bond to public collective acting and to urban nodal points committed to the screening and viewing of films.

Association, differentiation and re-articulation

When film-makers and cinema activists in former Yugoslavia as well as in the FRG and Austria speak retrospectively about the networks they have created, they usually relate to one another by mentioning each other's films they have seen as well as some important viewing experiences, talking about their travels or about participating in the various festivals, some of which they organized themselves. Exchange and the emergence of a closely knit network between the various cinema-activist groups thereby seem to have been especially eased in state-socialist Yugoslavia, since costs for train tickets and for stays in other cities were kept low by state allowances. Marko Feguš, president of the kino club Ljubljana between 1966 and 1970, remembers that they had special tickets for cheap travel to other cities and could usually stay there in student hostels (I MF). This ensured the quite lively participation of young people in the various activities – for instance, at festivals or discussions organized by the local kino clubs. These young people in this way got to know each others' work and could discuss films they had seen as well as pass on insider knowledge.

But also in the case of cinema-activist circles in the FRG and Austria, a close network emerged through common activities such as the production of films, the organization of festivals, film series or underground art events, mutual invitations or through joint travel to some of the biggest cinema and art festivals in Europe. Here, again, travelling was kept cheap by putting up guests in private houses or by driving around in private cars and even staying at campsites. The shared cultural events were thus able to develop into forms of shared living, which made such networks especially close-knit but also caused conflicts.[21]

In relating to their mutual works and to these networks, film- and cinema-makers usually give the name of the city their fellow activists lived in. Compared to this – and this was important especially in former Yugoslavia – any mention of religious or national affiliation was secondary. For instance, Marko Babac recalls that '[t]here was, from Split, you know, Lordan Zafranović […] in Ljubljana Boštjan Hladnik, for example […] a member of the kino club Ljubljana, my friend' (I MB). And Birgit Hein speaks about 'those Hamburgers' or 'those in Munich' (I BH). This means that by inhabiting the city and particular cinema locations as well as by experiencing emotional encounters and strong sensual connotations, new formations of connectivity are created. The assertion of taking part in a collective entity usually developed in quite a small spatial framework – in a kino club, a cinema or a festival space – but simultaneously gave rise to much wider, even transnational communities formed by various spectators, who were sometimes also cinema organizers, film-makers, journalists and critics themselves. And even if most of the activists soon established new lines and made attempts to shift the perception of the audience in certain unambiguous directions, they nevertheless also took part in creating urban cinema settings where such multivalent identification processes could happen beyond any restriction to univocal (ethnic or national) self-attribution. Engagement, loyalty and connectedness were experienced without the need to refer to the reigning and unambiguous attributions of (ethnic or national) belonging. The particular socializing force of cinema thus also acts in bringing cities and ways of inhabiting them to the fore and in creating transnational affiliations able to push national divisions back.

At the same time, the very activities that created a bonding between the various activists usually allowed them to view the cinema of the state or of official strategies through new eyes – thus creating new 'bad others' (Dyer and Vincendeau 1992: 8) and separating from them the cinema they created themselves. Marko Babac, for instance, referred to the Yugoslav state cinema in the late 1950s and early 1960s as follows: 'At this moment […] in the city theatres I could see only Russian films and our propaganda, domestic films with poor lies of life and everything. This was too poor in language and too naive for people […] But we had to go as part of school education' (I MB). And Wilhelm Hein described his enormous fascination with the films of Luis Buñuel, as well as how different this was from usual, commercial productions, which he accused of 'saplessness': 'What fascinated us about Buñuel, in *L'Âge d'Or* and *Un Chien Andalou*, or even in the documentary film *Las Hurdes*, was that in contrast to usual feature films, in […] interpersonal relations, between man and woman, there was such violence, such incredible energy […] this fascinated us, the incredible force of these films. What really did annoy me in commercial films was this saplessness' (I WH). As a consequence, the cinema initiative xscreen in Cologne, which he co-founded, was described by the activists involved as 'direct', full of 'adventure', 'improvization' and 'risk' and directed against 'passive consumerism' and the 'consecrated atmosphere of cultural palaces' (m. t. Prinzler and Schwarz 1972: 156).

Parallel to such a self-conscious distancing, divisions that otherwise existed in society also persisted in these 'alternative' cinema settings and were sometimes even non-intentionally re-articulated. Dubravka Ugrešić, for instance, when looking through children's books, remembers the strict division between 'male' working environments and 'female' private worlds that lingered behind the official Titoist equality rhetoric. In these books, she analyses, 'people (men, I see now) are working cheerfully: pilots and tractor drivers, doctors and miners. Women are only mothers. Or little girls' (Ugrešić 1998: 14). Similarly, a strict division between the activities of men and women was also reaffirmed in and around the cinema settings.

Whereas usually both men and women were present at the screenings, the members of the kino clubs were mostly men. Women are retrospectively almost always described as 'girlfriends' or 'would-be actresses' (I NK, I MB). And, especially, those who made films and, in particular, those of them counted as Crni Talas, as well as film critics or scriptwriters, were almost exclusively male.[22] Networks for boys were created in this way, through activities in the clubs, at the festivals and in the more general informal public sphere that emerged around certain cinema settings and which, besides film-makers, also included journalists and critics. They were often also strengthened through the featuring of particular female stars who were regarded as outstanding and were 'shared' as actresses by most film-makers.[23]

A strict gender divide also characterized the cinema activities in Austrian and German cities – even if, in this respect, first provocations and a questioning are also noticeable. In some groups, individual women artists and film-makers took part from the beginning: Valie Export, for example, in the Austrian Filmmakers Cooperative in Vienna or Birgit Hein in xscreen in Cologne. However, here again their participation in these early movements is attributed retrospectively by some former (male) colleagues to their status as 'girlfriends' of male activists.[24] Birgit Hein recalls that during these early years it was an enormous problem to be acknowledged as a woman. She saw herself all those years as a lone fighter. But at the same time, it was also clear to her that taking part in the film and art circuit was only possible together with a man (I BH). And despite the fact that the Freies Kino in Vienna screened *The Women's Film* (San Francisco Newsreel, 1970) in 1972, which – as the accompanying magazine *Kritischer Film* (1972, 4: 2) stated – investigates the social, economic and psychological repression of women, the organizers otherwise almost exclusively showed works by male film-makers and artists. Consequently, in this context, too, most of the groups and networks emerging in the 1960s were strongly male-dominated. This becomes evident also in that cinema manifestos and declarations such as the *Oberhausener Manifest* (1962) and the *Mannheimer Erklärung* (1967) published in West Germany in the 1960s were almost exclusively signed by male film-makers and cinema activists.[25]

At the same time there were urban artistic interventions such as *Tapp- und Tastkino* (1968–1971) by Valie Export, made in order to challenge the ruling gaze-relationship between the sexes – which in those years in the mainstream press, however, was termed, tongue-in-cheek and ambiguously, 'the first real women's film' (Schober 2002). The ambiguity connected to this issue was also highlighted by the fact that the United Nations declared 1975 the 'Year of the Woman', and several cinema initiatives showed special programmes, but sometimes declared their engagement with these issues only because they saw no way of 'escaping' them.[26] But the situation itself was also changing: in 1974 Helke Sander set up (together with others) the first German feminist film journal *Frauen und Film/women and film*, and whereas annual admissions to the Berlin Film Academy comprised only six per cent female candidates in 1966, this rose to 57 per cent by 1979 (Elsaesser 1989: 100 and 187).

2.3. Transnationality: interaction and struggle vis-à-vis official strategies

Until now I have mainly depicted equivalent developments and similarities between cinema activism in pluralist democratic and communist one-party societies. Yet where do the differences exist?

The most striking difference is that the movements in the FRG and Austria emerged in a rather loose bottom-up process of dissemination, whereas the Yugoslav novi film and experimental tendencies created themselves inside an institutional structure provided by the one-party system. But a second, closer look shows that not only the Yugoslav movements but also the ones in the FRG and Austria developed as some kind of response to and in a struggle with other, rather official or even institutionalized programmes or initiatives that were also using film and the cinema space on various levels in order to manage a society in transformation. Hence, in both types of societies, we can see a double move of responding to and struggling with official strategies and grassroots mobilization, even if a further analysis of this will help us grasp the difference between the multiparty democratic and the one-party socialist context in more detail. This interaction and this struggle happened on various national and transnational levels.

The shape of cinema movements in multiparty and one-party societies

As I have shown above, in the 1950s and 1960s in the FRG, Austria as well as in Yugoslavia, various social and political agents intervened in a new way into social space. Manuel de Landa (1991: 5 and 11) has pointed out that the enormous knowledge in marketing and in managing society accumulated by the military in the First and Second World Wars was later widely used by states and transnational entities in such a way that military and civilian sectors in commerce as well as in governmental policies often became indistinguishable. And most often, the strategies developed in various sectors now used images – films as well as photography or advertising – in an enhanced way.

In pluralist democratic European countries governmental strategies encroached far into social space, managing health, education, work and leisure time as well as creating new frames for mobility and for more or less temporary residence. Then there were the conditions for production and the time, space and body training demanded by it, the calculations by commercial entities or political parties, local initiatives by the cities as well as the projects carried out by various other collective bodies – educational institutions, students' or workers' groups but also art and cultural initiatives. Together all these various initiatives created a multivocal public sphere, in which some of these strategies and initiatives converged and mutually backed each other up and others entered into situations of conflict and struggle.

In one-party societies, such as socialist Yugoslavia, one could observe a somewhat similar process. Here, too, there was a huge variety of governmental strategies, local initiatives of cities and regions as well as grassroots mobilization processes of various kinds that included cinema and film in their strategies. And this again led to a vivid interplay between the official strategies and mobilization from below.

Unlike the link-up processes in multiparty societies, where these struggles and the affinities and convergences they produce are not dominated by the image of a single agent in history, in Yugoslavia, however, the interaction of various cinema initiatives was dominated in the end by the Communist Party, which represented the 'people as one'. The party and its head, Tito, were conceptualized as fully mastering this movable and multiple formation and as subjecting it to the one and the same project of creating a new, socialist society. In this way, power and society are fused together, any unpredictability, insecurity and most of the divisions that accompany democratic processes are eliminated or are at least closely mirrored and notions of social heterogeneity or of differences in lifestyle or taste are combated and viewed with suspicion (Lefort 1986: 284f.; Fischer 2013). Whereas any division inside society was rejected, society as a whole was seen as being essentially different from its Other: from old, bourgeois, primitive society or from influences pushed forward by the foreign, imperialist world. Following this logic, all signs of such divisions and all differences coming up inside the social body of the new world 'Yugoslavia' could be attributed to strata deriving from old, primitive society or from the foreign, capitalist and imperialist world.

So even if, especially after the self-management process was implemented in 1950 (Lydall 1984: 71f.), socialist Yugoslavia tried to strengthen collective initiative and collective management at several levels of society, a struggle between various agents and the presence of different positions and of difference as such were to a large extent precluded. They were allowed only as long as neither the 'people as one', the party, nor its head, Tito, were called into question or challenged, and it was of course for the party and Tito to decide if this was the case or not. This led to a situation where on the one hand there was considerable latitude for public action and initiative – of which the kino club activities were a paradigmatic example – and on the other hand there was an absence of a public coalescence from below, an absolute domination by the party and a constant need to deal with its non-negotiable decisions.

In relation to such struggles, various members of the kino clubs emphasized that official censorship organs were particularly concerned with representations of the party, of party functionaries and of Tito (I MB). Dušan Makavejev, for example, recalls that his film

Parada/The Parade (1962) (Figure 14) was first banned and only passed censorship after he cut two scenes. The film consists of a montage of impressions collected in the course of the preparation of an official parade held in Belgrade on 1 May, workers' day. Contrary to officially commissioned representations of such events, which usually show the parade itself mixed with close-ups of Tito and of happy faces zoomed out of the mass of spectators, in this film we only see scenes taking place before the parade started. There are piglets being pulled and sheep carried through the urban space, close-ups of the painting of official portraits and party symbols closely following pre-cast samples, the careful display of flower arrangements, rehearsals of young people, an agitated mother, people waiting with empty chairs and facing the empty streets, a pensive boy wrapped in a flag in front of a shop window, a Roma band and, high up in the air, a poster of Marx alongside floating balloons accompanied by the sound of bells.

When the film was banned, Makavejev recounts, the censors themselves were embarrassed at banning it and at the same time could not discuss the film. Because, if

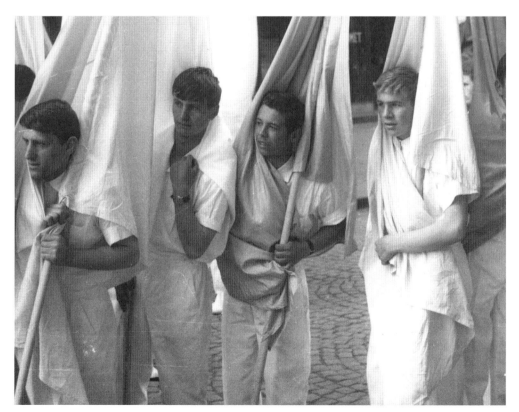

Figure 14: *Parada/Parade,* Dušan Makavejev, 1962 © Dušan Makavejev, courtesy Jugoslovenska Kinoteka, Belgrade.

he, as the author, were to pick out one of the scenes and ask them about their reasons for censoring it, they would have been challenged to explain what they considered wrong with this collection of peripheral fragments of real life. So he decided to choose self-censorship and cut out two scenes, which, after viewing the film again, seemed to him to be the most ironic ones regarding official political representation and therefore the most threatening: one scene showed an enormous portrait of the then minister of the interior being made based on a small postcard as a sample, and another sequence showed a female Roma fortune-teller in the streets, shouting 'happiness for a dinar, happiness darling', followed by a shot of Tito arriving at the scene by car. With these changes, the film finally passed censorship. Makavejev summarizes: 'It was the celebration. And they became nervous, because they discovered that people are joyful without being asked to be joyful, because this was a popular event and not because it was a political event. The main thing was that at a certain point, when you started making documentaries and films, you started getting into this zone, that was a kind of grey zone. […] Basically, as soon as you are in movie-making, you're doing something that is not regular, actually art is not regular, art is offensive in any system' (I DM).

This example shows that the uncertainty connected with the irony and the multiple meanings of such films was something that especially in relation to official politics (i.e., the party and Tito himself) was in a particular way threatening for the one-party system, because here the party and the egocrat were installed precisely to exclude any uncertainty and temporariness, whereas both uncertainty and temporariness are constitutive of democracy. In the field of the arts, this led in one-party societies to the emergence of a 'grey zone' dominated by censorship and self-censorship, where actions, gestures and styles are – without any explicit negotiation – always threatened with falling on either the one (passed) or the other (not passed) side.

Thus, the different political forms in which society in countries such as the FRG and Austria on the one hand (a multiparty, conflictuous society) and in Yugoslavia on the other (a state-socialist society) were recreated after the Second World War also shaped the ways cinema activism emerged. In Vienna or Cologne, groups constituted themselves in a bottom-up process. This bottom-up aspect of cinema activism and its orientation towards involving a desiring public was sometimes explicitly reflected on by those involved. So, for example, cinema enthusiasts who created the xscreen group in Cologne formulated their objectives in a self-description of their activities published in 1972: 'The need for a new form of experience is overwhelmingly large. The viewer wants the adventure of a new situation, the awareness of taking part in a developing process, in which he is able to intervene himself. Here [in the cinema we create, A. S.] we have situations that the usual plugged-in cultural scene is not able to offer because it is run by people who are scared of losing their jobs and do not want to take any risks' (m. t. Prinzler and Schwarz 1972: 156).

But, simultaneously, groups and, to some extent, also individual 'authors' competed openly with other forms of cinema appearance. The Expanded Cinema, for instance, struggled against commercial cinema and the educational films of the 'K-groups' against the socialist-minded Freies Kino as well as against the ideological corsets of everyday life in general (interview with Birgit Hein in Beyerle et al. 1984: 96). 'New' film-makers such as Wim Wenders (1968: 16) accused experimental film-makers who focused on multiple projections, the destruction and disruption of meaning and life events of producing non-original copies of their American, 'imperialistic' oriented role models. And the Freies Kino in Vienna emerged out of cinema initiatives at the University of Vienna undertaken by youth groups affiliated with the Social Democratic Party – even if the group chose a name for their cinema activities that showed it was eager to highlight the fact that it was 'free' of all direct interference (I DS).

In parallel, the new subsidy system that was introduced after the Oberhausen manifesto was published by some film-makers in 1962 forced individual film-makers into a particularly sharp competition with each other. This system introduced from above favoured the director who acted simultaneously as his (or her) own scriptwriter, fundraiser and PR manager all in one, but demanded at the same time that a difference already became visible at the script and project stage of a film proposal. This favoured a strong diversity and individuality of productions – even if there were some recurrent thematic motifs (such as the family, authority and marginal figures) and formal solutions (such as point-of-view shots). Furthermore, it brought film-makers to address journalists and critics who also acted as members of governmental advising boards, in particular, or to travel with their films to cinemas and festivals (or to get otherwise involved in new cinema initiatives), for the sake of self-promotion but also to create and to 'educate' a new kind of public they could then address their next projects to.[27]

This struggle led the emerging groups and movements but also individual film-makers to define their 'own' tactics and to design demarcations and 'enemies', which was expressed, for instance, in declarations as well as in a 'very recognizable' aesthetic style. Sometimes, this style was immediately taken up by the media and so became enlarged, popularized and, to some extent, also 'fixed'.[28]

The Yugoslav novi film movement (later called Crni Talas) also emerged in response to and in rejection of certain appearances of film aesthetic. They, for instance, opposed the conveyor-belt state production of heroic partisan films as well as the home movies made by the average ciné amateur who was 'happy to record flowers and family scenes' (I DM). But the movement did not form in such an open struggle against other groups and movements and through such openly expressed accusations and demarcations, since struggle and conflict was exactly what the state-socialist system precluded. Their cinema interventions were instead shaped by a constant but 'silent' and individual negotiation with the party and with Tito – a negotiation that was displaced very often at the aesthetic level, could take on various styles and had to react to constellations that were, in themselves, changing. At the same time the Crni Talas, like the Expanded Cinema or the Young German Film and the New German Cinema,[29] was a media phenomenon, since it was journalists and magazines that first started to identify various approaches of telling non-conformist stories represented in unusual aesthetic styles as something of 'a movement' and who by representing it also shaped and enhanced it.[30]

So even if the formative processes of cinema movements in both types of societies involved a similar fascination with sometimes the same strands of cinema history and contemporary film-making, a searching for position, an anchoring in the city, delimitations from other initiatives, and a coalescence from below (in response to official strategies and the fixations and popularizations conducted by the media), the multiparty and the one-party context, nevertheless, shaped these cinema movements quite differently: in the FRG and Austria, a search for the 'right' difference in the aesthetic style and political message, the assertion of particularity and originality, explicitly exhibited demarcations, a sometimes belligerent language and the use of – in the cultural context unusual – 'political' media, such as posters, leaflets and manifestos, prevailed. In the former Yugoslavia there were mainly individual and 'silent' negotiations with the party (and Tito) – which were mostly displaced onto the

Figure 15: Kinomobil, Nuremberg © Prinzler and Seidler, Kinobuch, 1975.

level of film aesthetics and were usually not explicitly expressed or declared – for instance, in the form of manifestos, even if some manifestos were published in this context too.[31]

This difference between the pluralist democratic and the state-socialist one-party context shows itself also in the process of naming the various initiatives. In the ways they named and presented themselves in public, the West German and Austrian cinema-makers became the active agents. Often they even vigorously displayed their reference points – most prominently, for instance, with the American Underground Cinema. Analogous with the Film Makers' Cooperative in New York and the Expanded Cinema in the United States, they referred to themselves as 'cooperatives' and 'Expanded Cinema'.[32] Names of other cinema initiatives such as Freies Kino (Free Cinema), Notausgang (Emergency Exit, in Berlin, since 1971), bad movies (in Mannheim, since 1971)[33] or Kommunales Kino also quite explicitly revealed the activists' concerns in the name they choose for their public image, that is, to differentiate themselves from what they viewed as 'un-free', 'closed', 'well-educated or cultured' cinema or from one that affirmed and enhanced social isolation.

In contrast with this, the Crni Talas was, as already briefly mentioned, first identified and named by others, that is, not only by journalists, but also by members of official bureaucracy, by the party and finally by Tito himself. Even if movements such as the Young German Film or the New German Cinema – like the French Nouvelle Vague – were also to a large extent media phenomena (Frisch 2007: 33), film-makers in the FRG or Austria indeed described themselves as taking part in a 'new' and 'other' cinema. In Yugoslavia, however, film-makers at first did not refer to themselves as being 'black'. Marko Babac, for instance, an early member of the kino club Beograd and one of the film-makers usually listed as 'black', recalls that it was '[…] the press, I think, the press, all these negative critics.' It referred to 'not original, it is black, it is only imitating the others, from outside of our country, with strange ideas and subjects. Not original, not domestic, something strange […] but we never said, before others, that we are black. [… This was] never [part of the, A. S.] sense of what I am. I only deeply felt that I expressed myself, subjectively, expressively, like a foreigner' (I MB).

Želimir Žilnik points out that film-makers in Yugoslavia – like their colleagues in other European countries at that time – preferred to use the term 'novi film' or, in reference to the French New Wave, 'New Yugoslav Cinema' when referring to themselves (I ZZ). His film *Rani radovi/Early Works* (1969) and the controversial discussion that followed from its success at the Berlin Film Festival in the same year, however, got the newspaper *Borba* to publish an article by the journalist Vladimir Jovičić about the 'black wave in our cinema'. In this text Jovičić (1969; Goulding 2002: 79f.) related Yugoslav film-makers to the 'black' Polish documentaries of the 1950s and Czech dark-wave films, it accused film-makers of a 'distortion of the present' and even attacked some of the most influential film critics for being blind vis-à-vis the nihilism, horror and misery of these films and of supporting film-makers in overstepping the limits of freedom.

By using the term 'black wave', however, quite different actions and styles of making films were identified and unified into one 'movement'. This also created a kind of label that started to replace the previous, rather self-coined name of 'novi film' and could then be picked up by cinema enthusiasts themselves – sometimes also ironically. So, for instance, in 1971 the then very young film activist Želimir Žilnik made a movie called *Crni film/Black Film* for which he adopted the classification from outside and tongue-in-cheek countered it, since in this film he was depicting a group of homeless people – and so exhibiting a problem that in the official public discourse in Yugoslavia was usually presented as 'resolved' and 'non-existent'. In this respect, in the Yugoslav context OHO stands out, since like the various kinds of 'new', 'other' or 'free' cinemas or the Expanded Cinema, this group quite explicitly and self-consciously called itself into existence, named itself and managed also to remain identified with its own self-designation.

Transatlantic alliances

Through significant encounters with – in their context – 'foreign' films accompanied by film theory, literature and various strands of modern music (jazz, beat, rock), young people in both the FRG or Austria and Yugoslavia were encouraged to get actively involved in film-making and the staging of cinema situations themselves. This included also imagining themselves as being part of a new cultural 'revolution' that transcends national boundaries – something that was supported also by the fact that activists were inspired by each other's productions and work and that they were able to meet at newly installed and sometimes also at self-organized festivals, conferences and more informal urban events. In this way, encounters with US films, literature and music were particularly formative. So, for instance, Wilhelm Hein from the xscreen group in Cologne remembers and recalls that 'America was the only country, all the Beat literature that came over that was our influence' (I WH).

Young people in the FRG and Austria as well as in former Yugoslavia appropriated US underground, avant-garde and counter-cultural styles in order to reject the reigning cultural and political positions in their environment. Thus 'America' was never adopted in a 'pure' way but mixed and merged with a variety of other inspirational sources, which included avant-garde culture from before the Second World War as well as French New Wave, Italian Neorealism or the aesthetic approaches of Leni Riefenstahl, Sergei Eisenstein or Dziga Vertov. In doing so, the work of these cinema activists in part affirmed other strategic interventions, those, for example, set out by US institutions in order to 'democratize' political culture in Europe after fascism and the Second World War.

Austria and the FRG as well as former Yugoslavia played a particular role in the formation of these transatlantic alliances emerging in the 1960s. The former two because the presence of US institutions and re-education efforts after the NS regime resulted in an exceptionally close political, economic and cultural association with US institutions during the Cold War (Klimke 2010: 6). The latter because after Tito's 'No to Stalin', Yugoslavia assumed a particularly important strategic position between the Eastern and the Western blocs. In both cases, however, 'Americanization' from above and 'grassroots Americanization' collaborated as well as entering into a struggle with each other and so produced strongly ambivalent aesthetic productions and political activities.

Already in the 1950s, amid the heated propaganda competition with the Soviet Union known as the 'Cold War', American political attention focused on youth and youth interests in a particular way.[34] Dušan Makavejev remembers the following incident that sprung from this orientation: in July 1959 as a young cinema activist and cadre of the Yugoslav Communist Party, he stayed with some fellow young intellectuals for a few days in Vienna in order to take part in the *VII World Festival of Youth and Students for Peace and Friendship* organized by international communist youth organizations (*World Federation of Democratic Youth* and *International Union of Students*) in the formerly Soviet-occupied part of the city. He remembers a colourful mixture of young people gathering on that occasion: people from Latin America (Chile, Brazil, Argentina) as well as from Africa mixed with delegations from Eastern Europe in their greenish (Hungarians) or brownish (Poles) outfits. The highlight of the festival, according to Makavejev, was a concert by Paul Robeson, the 'old, communist, black singer'. But simultaneously, as he narrates, there was another big concert nearby organized by the Americans bringing on stage no one less than Ella Fitzgerald. Unlike other delegations, which were taken by bus to the various events without being able to decide for themselves where to go, members of the Yugoslav delegation were attending only as 'guests' and he remembers discussing which concert to attend. According to Makavejev, the 'Eastern and Western world were competing for the hearts of the youth with two black singers, both of them fantastic' (I DM).

Besides music, theatre and discussions, film and cinema played an important role in this event. One of the two major locations was the Metro cinema, where scientific and educational films were shown as an integral part of workshops and discussions. An international multipart seminar of students of the film arts was also held at the festival.[35]

With the rise of the US student protests and the emergence of anti-Vietnam War activities, which started to turn the American SDS (Students for a Democratic Society) into a mass movement in 1964–1965 and also triggered a variety of responses among European student organizations, this orientation towards youth and mass culture became more pronounced (Klimke 2010: 40f. and 52f.). In July 1964, for instance, the Secretary of State Dean Rusk communicated a personal address to American ambassadors worldwide, stating the significance of dealing with the young leaders now so present on the public stage: 'Young leaders have risen and are rising to power, political change is occurring, and the events with which the traditional arts of diplomacy must deal are moving at breathtaking speed. We must broaden our horizons if we wish to gain the initiative against a resourceful and ruthless competitor in the Communist bloc and in the face of considerable disarray in our own ranks' (quoted in Klimke 2010: 150).

In accordance with this, there was a 'promotion of American culture' through modern art and mass media in which various foundations, institutions and programmes were involved. The public library in the America House in Vienna, for instance, acquired books about avant-garde writers, such as Gertrude Stein, film theory, the New American Cinema, film and cinema history, film anthologies, statements by US film-makers, the history and theory of jazz, new art forms such as happenings, kinetic environments and mixed-means performances, art theory, public art, television, computers and photography, etc., as well as magazines about art and cinema.[36]

At the same time some of the young cinema activists in Europe started with enthusiasm to discover the 'other America' in cinema and film productions. So, for instance, in October 1963, Peter Konlechner, who together with Peter Kubelka in 1964 founded the film museum in Vienna, organized a Western American Experimental Film Festival at the Technical University, where they screened films from the Canyon Cinema in Berkeley, California – which also had links to the emerging New American Cinema Group in New York. Under the headline 'The Discovery of America' he described the 'creative' and 'vital' film production of the United States as the antithesis of the usually known 'trash films' and 'false commercial productions – often celebrated with the Oscars (m. t.)'.[37] With these activities, transatlantic networks started to emerge – with international festivals acting, as I will point out in more detail later, as nodal points where first encounters and initiations could happen but also where networks could be maintained or even tightened.

In parallel, the tactics of US avant-garde film-makers, too, became heavily focused on extending their radius of action. They oriented themselves on and were supported by fractions of the American elite who might be called 'business liberals' and promoted the avant-garde in visual arts, music and film as a kind of incarnation of progressive American culture (Orton 1996). The New American Cinema Group, which held its first meeting in September 1960, stated, for instance, in its *Constitution And By-Laws* that besides encouraging the development of a 'new cinema' and the combat of all forms of censorship, the main objectives of this group were 'to encourage and organize international film festivals and to introduce the work of the new generation of film-makers in every part of the world.'[38] In the *Introduction to the International Exposition of the New American Cinema* (1961–1963), Jonas Mekas, the spokesman of the group, states that in America, the most interesting things have been happening in poetic, non-narrative cinema. 'It is this cinema that we want to show to the world. [...] The young American film-makers represented in this exposition feel that the official film festivals that are mushrooming all over the world have become commercial projects – they no longer show what's really going on in cinema [...] There is too much emphasis on dramatic narrative cinema. This emphasis has become damaging. The young American film-makers are sending this exposition as a sort of artistic protest and manifesto. We are taking a stand for modern cinema.'[39] This was followed by an open letter written to address the public at the Pesaro Film Festival in 1966, where Mekas made an explicit call for 'the independent film-makers of the world, anybody who sees life is cinema, who is making and must make films, to create film-makers' cooperatives of their own, in their own countries.'[40]

The first of these Expositions of New American Cinema was presented at the Festival Dei Due Mondi in Spoleto, Italy (1961), and at the experimental film festival in Knokke-Le-Zoute, Belgium (1963–1964); exhibitions in other European cities, such as Bergamo,

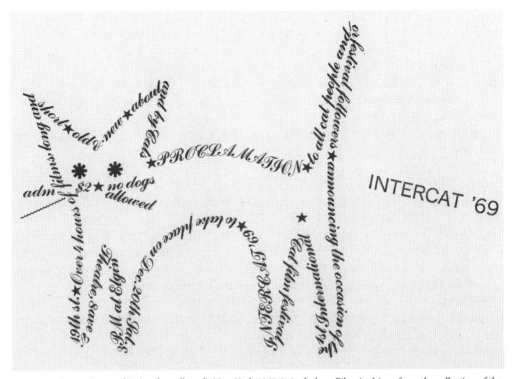

Figure 16: Poster *Intercat '69 (no dogs allowed),* New York 1969 © Anthology Film Archives, from the collection of the Austrian Film Museum.

and a series of other small Italian cities, Stockholm, Munich, Brussels (1964), Turin, Rome, Naples, the film festival in Pesaro and Zurich (1967) followed.[41] Branko Vučićević remembers that in 1967–1968, a member of the group, P. Adams Sitney, travelled with this exhibition through Yugoslavia – after he had got into contact with Yugoslav cinema enthusiasts at the Pesaro Film Festival (I BV). The New American Cinema was presented at the film festival in Pula and in winter 1967–1968 in Belgrade, Zagreb, Sarajevo and Ljubljana (I BV). And in July 1970 Jonas Mekas and the American underground cinema participated in the Forum des Jungen Films (Forum of Young Film) in Berlin, which was held as a counter-festival to the Berlinale (de Valck 2007: 66). As a result of this expansionist exhibition activity and the declarations that accompanied them Jonas Mekas was described as the 'experimental cinema's own minister of propaganda' (Banes 1993: 173) – a description he sometimes also used self-ironically for himself when signing memorandums for the group (Arthur 1992: 32).

Some of the policies of the New American Cinema group were to develop a creative and very flexible system of financing and distributing movies and to reorganize knowledge about avant-garde film in the form of services to colleges, universities, film societies, art theatres, art galleries and museums.[42] Furthermore, Jonas Mekas and his colleagues also published the *Film Culture* magazine and maintained The Millennium Film Workshop.[43] Besides applying for federal grants and support from private foundations, this system was intended to rely mainly on film rental fees and donors, called 'Circle of Angels of the New Cinema'. In order to generate PR for joining this circle, the Film Makers' Cooperative repeatedly talked about its expansionist activities. For instance, in an invitation to join the circle in 1967 it is mentioned that 'its cooperative system has had a worldwide influence on New Cinema. There are now film-makers' cooperatives in London, Canada, Rome, Mexico City, and San Francisco.'[44]

After 1966, with the growing politicization of young people all over Europe and the rise of criticism against the US war politics in Vietnam, this expansionist activity of US film-makers was seen by some fractions of the emerging student movement as highly problematic. During the Experimental Film Festival in Knokke-Le-Zoute, 1967–1968, for example, students from Ulm, Berlin, Brussels and Paris protested against 'American imperialism in experimental film'. They demonstrated with banners and chants and even became involved in fist fights (Reitz 1968: 18). But at the same time it was exactly this growing festival scene that worked as a catalyst for the formation of European Expanded Cinema groups.

The chain of cooperatives founded in the 1960s throughout central European countries, but also through the United States and Latin America shows that the film-makers and critics, who formed the core of the New American Cinema, such as Jonas Mekas, Stan Brakhage, Stan Vanderbeek or P. Adams Sitney, offered a certain alteration in film-making and in staging the cinema setting as well as a discursive framework that gave other film activists, who were attracted by details or particular concepts of the American productions and theories, the possibility to create their own, related positions in response to their particular milieus.

In this way the encounter with the US 'underground' set a strongly emotional process in motion through which some aesthetic styles and concepts have been passed on further. Important for this was that Jonas Mekas managed to unite the handling of the Film Makers' Cooperative and the Avant-Garde Film Travelling Library, as well as editing the *Film Culture* magazine and being a film critic for *The Village Voice* in a one-person unit. The *Film Culture* magazine, in particular, was formative for some young European cinema-makers. So, for instance, Wilhelm Hein recalls: 'First we were into painting, but that didn't satisfy us […] We [Birgit and Wilhelm Hein, founding members of the xscreen Expanded Cinema group in Cologne, A. S.] started to make films in 1967. In 1962 or in 1963 we bought our first *Film Culture*, this New American Cinema magazine and […] this way of Stan Brakhage, Gregory Markopoulos and all that stuff that interested me incredibly. […] In the end we knew more, even if we had not seen anything yet' (I WH). The movement created in this way staged a cultural and at the same time aesthetic difference in its situational context by adopting a cinema from an 'other America' that in itself strongly distanced its 'revolutionary' cinema 'with multiple projections and multiple sound system'[45] not only from commercial cinema but also from West- as well as East-European art film festivals such as Cannes (France), Pesaro (Italy) or Karlovy Vary (ČSSR).

Nevertheless, the Expanded Cinema movement created in West Germany and Austria transformed what they encounterd, and through their actions they created a response to what in their view was at stake in their environment. In contrast to the US neo-Dada film activities, which were often inclined to contain references to Zen Buddhism, Hinduism or esoteric rituals, they were inspired more strongly by the practices of the Living Theatre, which sought to provocatively challenge its audiences. Thus they developed a 'shock aesthetics' that was more aggressively directed towards challenging and even physically attacking the audience. This aesthetics, characterized by gestures of destruction and a demonstrative exertion of sex, the body and its fluids and excrements, was introduced in order to reject not only capitalism and bourgeois, moral and religious values but also to fight a repression of sexuality that was seen as standing in continuity with Nazism. Hence Expanded Cinema activists in the FRG and Austria presented their activities not only as 'liberating' but simultaneously also as 'anti-fascist' (Schober 2009b: 156f. and 277f.).

At the same time, this transatlantic love affair was not a solely one-dimensional process: Expanded Cinema networks and shared film tastes were also shaped by film-makers from Europe – for instance, Peter Kubelka who in 1966 travelled to the United States to present some of his films and was then on the jury for the first screening of the Anthology Film Archives in New York in 1970 (Kubelka in Jutz and Tscherkassky 1995: 35f.).

In the local context, Expanded Cinema adoptions were usually severely contested by emerging young film-makers or cinema activists who had other 'film visions'. Wim Wenders (1968: 16), for instance, called the experimental cinema scene a 'conformist school that is already delivering its own plagiarism'. Simultaneously, however, he too produced films that exhibited a strong fascination with US culture – albeit in another variation. In 1968–1969 Wenders made two films that reflected on US pop music and visual culture: *Alabama: 2000 Light Years from Home* (1968–1969), a film for which he invented images paralleling a Bob Dylan song and which showed references to US gangster movies and Film Noir; and *3 amerikanische LP's/3 American LP's*, which he made in 1969 where he 'translated' songs from LPs by Van Morrison, Creedence Clearwater Revival and Harvey Mandel into images showing himself and a co-driver (the writer Peter Handke) as if in a road movie, roaming the suburbs of Munich by car and discussing the covers of the LPs.[46]

Simultaneously, Rainer Werner Fassbinder, who around 1969 started to shift from theatre to film-making, stated in an interview made in 1971: 'American film is the only one I can take seriously, because it actually reaches its audience. German cinema before 1933 also accomplished this and of course there are also some directors in other countries who have contact with their audiences' (m. t. Braad Thomsen 2004c [1971]: 221).[47] His film and cinema vision was strongly nourished by the place he lived in during those years – Munich – a city which offered a particularly broad range of cinema initiatives in those days: besides commercial cinemas and *Eckenkinos* (corner cinemas), there were various kinds of 'new cinemas' and 'art house cinemas', the city museum cinémathèque, an underground cinema initiative, a 'red' student cinema and a cinema pub. One of these cinemas, located in the trendy nightlife and entertainment district of Schwabing and called 'Leopold'[48] programmed exactly the 'other' Hollywood movies Fassbinder was so fond of – besides European films that had somehow 'digested' Hollywood like François Truffaut, Claude Chabrol or Rudolf Thome. This indicates that for various 'new' film scenes emerging around 1968 'America' was, similar to the role it had already played during the Weimar Republic (Schober 2009b: 217f.), again functioning as an ambivalent 'other' that was able to support and nourish quite distinct and sometimes even conflicting world views.

Yugoslavia's ambivalent position between the Western and Eastern blocs

From the beginning, these transatlantic cinema networks included Yugoslavia in a particular way. As the above-narrated story by Dušan Makavejev about his travelling to the *VII World Festival of Youth* in Vienna in July 1959 shows, members of the Yugoslav delegation were accepted to attend as 'guests' and could pick what interested them most from both the Eastern and the Western blocs (I DM). In this respect, Makavejev, too, singles out encounters with US film culture as particularly formative. He, for instance, especially remembers the educational films he found in the American library at the beginning of his kino club activism in the 1950s – which was what got him interested in including fragments of scientific discourse into his later feature films. Besides, he broadly recalls that already in the early 1960s Gideon Bachmann from the Film Study Group in New York (where he collaborated with Jonas Mekas; see MacDonald 1992: 86) stayed in Belgrade and showed a huge programme of New American films at the Kinoteka Yugoslav Film Archive (including *Shadows* [John Cassavetes, 1959], *The Connection* [Shirley Clarke, 1961], *Hallelujah the Hills* [Adolfas Mekas, 1963] and *The Brig* [Jonas Mekas, 1964])[49] – although he was already familiar with some of these films from the film festival in Oberhausen (FRG) in 1962 (I DM).

Around 1968 the transatlantic underground and protest cinema relations between the United States and former Yugoslavia became more intense. After the 'French' May of 1968 and as an expression of a redirection of the attention of the US student organizations (in particular the SDS – which until then had focused mainly on Third World issues) towards (East-) European movements,[50] Yugoslavia was selected to host a working meeting in the summer (August 25–28) of 1968. This meeting was organized by The International Confederation for Disarmament and Peace (ICDP) and the German SDS and involved representatives from West Germany, France, Finland, Spain, Switzerland, Canada and the United States, was held in Ljubljana and was advertised as a 'working meeting of leading student and youth activists who wish to cement their links of solidarity with their comrades in other countries' (quoted from Klimke 2010: 100f.). And in 1967–1968, the American Avantgarde Film Travelling Library was shown, as already mentioned, at the Pula film festival and in most major cities all over former Yugoslavia (I BV).

In parallel, films from young Yugoslav film-makers started to be shown in the United States, Latin America and Canada (I DM; I JJ). These contacts forged emotional and spiritual bonds across the Atlantic and stimulated follow-up activities by some film-makers:

Dušan Makavejev, for example, shot parts of his next feature film *WR: Misterije organizma/ WR: Mysteries of the Organism* (1971) in the United States and also used this film to portray anti-Vietnam War activism and the emerging transnational student movement.

In spite of these mutual transatlantic exchanges, film-makers such as Dušan Makavejev, Želimir Žilnik, Marko Babac or Živojin Pavlović usually mention a very broad mix of international films available to them in the 1950s and 1960s. Since they did not as programmatically form movements that were split up into a variety of sub-movements and groups as their counterparts in the FRG and Austria did, they were also not so eager to distance themselves from each other strongly through references to other film-makers and film paradigms. Consequently, their work was quite accessible to process a broad range of stimuli.

Furthermore, due to their activism in the kino club and the amateur film circles and, in several cases also the youth organization of the Communist Party – from which, however, they were periodically (informally) expelled or from which they resigned – some of them had the opportunity to travel to the most important national as well as international film festivals. This allowed them to acquire, as Želimir Žilnik states, 'a cinema repertoire that was very rich: everything new from the East and from the West' (I ZZ). Besides, Dušan Makavejev, for instance, mentions that he had the opportunity to participate as a Yugoslav delegate in a series of UNESCO meetings about film and education since 1960, where he encountered people from French, British, Norwegian, Italian and German cinema institutions (I DM).

In contrast, film-makers from the same generation like Jovan Jovanović, for example, who were not members of the party and their extended networks and were known for holding oppositional, even anti-communist views, were to a large extent cut off from these opportunities to participate in such official international networks. This was the case even when, as with Jovanović, some first films provided them with a reputation of being talented. After his feature film *Mlad i zdrav kao ruža/Young and Healthy as a Rose* (1971) in which he represented the gap between the everyday lives of young people and what he calls an 'Orwellian world of Titoism' – he got no further opportunity to make films (I JJ).[51]

What kino club activists and other kinds of cinema enthusiasts have in common, however, is that one institution in particular – the Kinoteka Yugoslav Film Archive – functioned as their 'school' in respect to film history and to the broad range of film styles emerging on both sides of the East-West divide. Marko Babac mentions having seen American films quite early. 'In the beginning', he says, 'it was not allowed, it started really slowly.' But he especially remembers having seen the Japanese film *Rashomon* (Akira Kurosawa, 1950). (These films came) from European festivals, Venice and Cannes' (I MB). For Jovan Jovanović the only relevant films were American movies from the 1930s to the 1960s and especially B movies (I JJ). Karpo Godina remembers that Agnès Varda's first film *La Pointe-Courte* (1955) had a particularly strong and long-lasting effect on him and his fellow cineasts (I KG). And Dušan Makavejev recalls having already seen some interesting 'black' Polish, Hungarian and Russian films as well as Italian documentaries in the mid-1950s. For the early 1960s he recalls in particular the already mentioned encounter with the New American Cinema (I DM).

Besides, most of the young Yugoslav cineasts mention that quite early, 1954, Henri Langlois from the Cinémathèque Française showed some 'packages' of already classical French films, including also films from René Clair and Jean Vigo (I DM and I KG).

Želimir Žilnik, who is about ten years younger than most of these cinema activists and used to live in Novi Sad, highlights another urban space as most formative for his development as an artist: the Tribina mladih (Youth Forum), where new and progressive tendencies in literature, art, performance and cinema were exhibited and discussed. Between 1961 and 1964 he was invited as an 18-year-old student to act as a programmer of this space, which in this way was 'the best education he received'. By showing programmes by young film-makers from the kino clubs in Zagreb, Split or Belgrade as well as by travelling not only to the national film festival in Pula but also to the various amateur film festivals held all over Yugoslavia (in Split, Zagreb, Novi Sad, Belgrad, Niš, Skopje), he acquired detailed knowledge about contemporary film-making trends in Yugoslavia. He particularly remembers also going to 'normal cinemas' and seeing 'early Soviet Expressionism' (Alexander Medvedkin, Vsevolod Pudovkin and Sergei Eisenstein) as well as the French Nouvelle Vague, New York independent film-makers (in particular, John Cassavetes' *Shadows*, 1957–1959) and avant-garde films from the New York Film Makers' Coop. These viewing and programming experiences also contributed to his shift from being a painter and a law student to becoming a film-maker and cinema activist (I ZZ).

All these stories, but in particular the one narrated by Želimir Žilnik, show that in Yugoslavia the internationalist dimension that had been part of cinema since its beginnings was in a particular way employed by the regime in order to create a new transnational culture that went beyond the old nationalist borders and put cities, networks and certain cinema spaces in the foreground. Through film-making, travelling, programming each other's films, organizing discussions and gatherings as well as through writing about films, young cinema activists were encouraged to participate in a 'planet cinema' that pushed the older national and regional separations into the background. In this way, however, official party politics also tried to use film culture to create a new political order that was devoted to the celebration and even production of a new Yugoslav 'people as one'.

Yet the viewing events and transnational bonding emerging inside these new cinema and cultural circles exceeded this and entered, as already described, into tension with these efforts to create a univocal 'Yugoslav' culture. Young cinema enthusiasts were brought into contact with a quite extraordinarily diversified knowledge about national and international movie scenes, which pushed them to articulate a pronounced 'different' film language that portrayed issues (such as homelessness, village life, criminals, Roma culture) as well as aesthetic styles that were judged by official culture as 'already conquered by communism', 'bourgeois', 'anarchistic', 'decadent', 'black' and soon also as in fact or potentially 'anti-communist' (Jovičić 1969: 22f.; I ZZ).

After the first student protests in Belgrade in 1968, the considerable latitude for creating provocative image-worlds and discussions around film that characterized Yugoslavia in the 1960s was sharply withdrawn. With slogans such as 'Against the Red Bourgeoisie' or 'Down with the Dukes of Socialism' – as *Lipanjska gibanja/June Turmoil* (1969), a documentary made by Želimir Žilnik about the student protest in Belgrade in 1968 shows – young people started to articulate a difference and an oppositional will that in the climate of Russian tanks crushing student protests in Prague were seen by leading fractions of the official bureaucracy as threatening the very national 'unity' they used to proclaim. The tensions resulting from this were augmented by the fact that, as I will show later in more detail, around 1968 film-makers from former Yugoslavia started to receive extraordinary attention and success at international film festivals. Želimir Žilnik, for example, remembers that he started to experience serious working restrictions after his first feature film *Rani radovi* won the Golden Bear at the Berlin International Film Festival in 1969.

These examples show that in their struggle over the 'right' difference to be made film-makers and cinema activists in both West Germany, Austria and Yugoslavia took part in the constitution of the broader transnational movement of 1968. These movements and groups picked up and even expanded the internationalist dimension that had been part of cinema since its beginnings, created new opportunities for further contacts and thus acted as a catalyst for a further 'globalization' of cinema.

In this process 'America' was perceived and represented in a pronounced, ambivalent way: as being both a United States of racial suppression and imperialist warfare as well as another 'America' full of utopian and counter-cultural inspiration. The struggle and adoption that resulted from involvement with this ambivalent opponent as well as from processing a broad range of further adoptions of 'other' cultural inputs triggered efforts to furnish public presence for new political and aesthetic differences that could exceed the rigid frames of Cold War politics (cf. Klimke 2010: 241).

Film festivals as a risk and as recognizing gazes from outside

(International) film festivals were particularly important arenas where films could be identified as taking part in a 'new wave' or where directors could receive recognition as 'authors'. At the same time film festivals provided very emotionally intense encounters and forged an initial bonding between film-makers, critics, cinema activists and the public which was then developed further, for instance, through mutual invitation, further festival visits, local screenings of films or film-theory readings. The student movement of 1968 was closely entwined with a transformation of the international film-festival circuit: before the events of 1968, film festivals were national showcases in an international competition, with them they became specialized, thematic festivals that presented authors, new waves and rare 'discoveries' and staged a political difference (de Valck 2007: 27f. and 112f.).

In order to grasp these transformations and the effects they had on the local level of cinema activism, it is necessary to briefly review the history of international film festivals. The first European festival was held in Venice and was set up during fascism as a kind of 'Olympiad' for national cinemas. Here films were exhibited prestigiously in the film-like setting of an old spa outside the commercial chain of distribution and screening in order to 'sidestep' Hollywood cinema standards. Most of the other European festivals founded immediately after the war were conceived as counter-festivals in respect to already existing ones: the Locarno Festival in Switzerland and the Cannes film festival in France both opened in 1946 to counter the Venice film festival and its fascist legacy. The Karlovy Vary festival in Czechoslovakia was founded as an Eastern counterpart to these events, that is, it was founded in 1946 as a platform for exhibiting socialist films and confronting capitalist film production (cf. Elsaesser 2005: 82f.).

In 1951 this scene was expanded with the Berlin International Film Festival, which again had been established as a special arena for exhibiting Western and in particular US films in close proximity to East Germany and the Soviet bloc (Fehrenbach 1995: 234f.).

All these festivals staged films as 'national' artefacts taking part in an international competition, whose successes could contribute to a reconstruction of a new world in stories and the proud recognition of one's own cultural achievements – something that after the shattering of former worlds by the Second World War, fascism and the Holocaust was extremely pressing and was manifested in varying degrees of accentuation and traumatic experiences in various European countries. At the same time, however, these festivals functioned as places of transnational diplomacy and struggle and held the potential for contact with other film and cinema cultures as well as the risk for conflict on a transnational but also on a local scale. Hence, film festivals again highlight the already-discussed role cinema is able to play as a part of modern efforts of creating order, and at the same time they expose very visibly that such efforts usually only work in increasing ambivalence.

Around 1968 the cinema events that were most visible in the international media and which in this way contributed to the constitution of the student movement were the upheaval and the occupation of the Festival Palace by young film-makers and parts of the public in Cannes in 1968 (which, for instance, in 1969 inspired the Pesaro Film Festival in Italy to focus on 'cinema and politics') and the scandal around the film *OK* by Michael Verhoeven during the Berlinale 1970 and the organization of a counter-festival in respect to it, Die Woche des jungen Films (Week of Young Film) in the same year (de Valck 2007: 62f.). These events, however, already had a history. They took up and reinforced a festival practice that had already been emerging since the early 1950s at smaller specialized festivals focusing on experimental and avant-garde cinema as well as on short films. The most important of these 'innovative' festivals which also caused the most intense discussions were the EXPRMNTL festival in Knokke-Le-Zoute, Belgium, as well as the Kurzfilmtage in Oberhausen, FRG.

The earliest editions of the EXPRMNTL festival were held in 1949 and then in 1958 as part of the World Exhibition in Brussels.[52] Some initial avant-garde film networks were already formed here.[53] With the next edition at Christmas 1963–1964 the festival relocated to Knokke-Le-Zoute (again a spa town) and gained enormous international attention due to a scandal caused when the film *Flaming Creatures* by Jack Smith was censored by the festival although it had originally been invited (I JM). Since this scandal further enhanced public visibility of the avant-garde cinema scene worldwide, the festival was even better attended in 1967 – it was here that most of the younger Expanded Cinema film activists would meet who later founded several cooperatives and film forums, for instance, also in the FRG and Austria modelled after the New York Film Makers' Cooperative (Hein 1971: 133 and 136f.).

At the EXPRMNTL political engagement and formal experiments were in the foreground, and in respect to this a sense of national belonging of the films and film-makers turned out to be less important. This was also enhanced by the fact that transnational encounters made possible by the festival also caused conflicts and demarcations. The US Expanded Cinema group was, as already mentioned, criticized by some of the European cinema enthusiasts as being 'imperialistic' and some of the European disciples of Expanded Cinema were attacked for being 'epigones'.[54] Nevertheless, the festival coined a new form of festival practice that was based on emotional and sometimes conflictual relationships between cinema activists of various kinds (film-makers, writers, journalists, critics, etc.) driven by a strongly diversified aesthetic taste.

The second of these festivals, the Kurzfilmtage in Oberhausen, showed even more clearly that film festivals did not only embody potentialities for transnational affiliation, but were also locally perceived as a risk: in this case, the risk of an encounter with films from behind the Iron Curtain. Like another similar festival that was held in Mannheim for the first time in 1952, the Oberhausen festival started in 1954 as a *Kulturfilm* (culture film) festival.

From the beginning, both festivals were closely linked with the Young German Cinema that also grew out of dissident voices raised by student activists of the film club movement of the 1950s. These voices started to oppose the then dominant *Heimatfilm* in German cinema and stated provocatively in the form of a 'manifesto' published in Oberhausen in 1962 *Papas Kino ist tot!/Papa's cinema is dead* (see Fehrenbach 1995: 213). Edgar Reitz recalls the formation of the Oberhausen group as follows: 'It was neither a politically cohesive group nor a group with specific aesthetic principles. What united us was simply the rejection of what was showing at the cinemas at the time and the fact that we were outside looking in. We saw that the "New Wave" was possible in France, that there was a Young Czech and a Young Polish Cinema. We were depressed because of our own situation but optimistic enough to believe that something similar could also happen in Germany' (Reitz in Koch 1985; translated into English in Fehrenbach 1995: 225).

Reitz also mentions the main reason why the festival in Oberhausen soon started to gain more national and international visibility than its 'sister' in Mannheim: it was the first German festival that programmatically invited films from socialist countries. Even if the second edition of the festival only included a few animated cartoons from Czechoslovakia, the third edition in 1956 was already presenting films from such diverse state-socialist countries as Poland, Hungary, Romania, Yugoslavia, the Soviet Union and the German Democratic Republic. Headlines such as *Roter Mond über Oberhausen/Red Moon over Oberhausen* (*Der Abend*, 3 December 1957) and *Unter unserer Würde/Beneath our Dignity* (*Berliner Zeitung*, 12 February 1958) indicate the conflict and discussion caused by this exposition of films from state-socialist countries in both West and East Germany.

At the same time, however, these headlines also demonstrate the public attention that was drawn in this way toward this public event. Oberhausen became an arena where all those who were interested could get a glimpse of the variety of films being produced in Eastern Europe (Fehrenbach 1995: 222). For cinema activists from various European countries as well as from the United States or Canada, Oberhausen became a 'gateway to the East in both cultural and economic terms' (Fehrenbach 1995: 223). But simultaneously it was a place where film-makers from Eastern Europe, and Yugoslavia in particular, became more involved in the international film-festival scene and could foster personal contacts they could also use later on for the transnational production of further films (I DM and I ZZ).

This public visibility caused by the screening of films made behind the Iron Curtain also started to focus discussion on the programming practice of other festivals held in West Germany, in particular that of the Berlinale, which was characterized by the exclusion of films from state-socialist countries (de Valck 2007: 52). Already in 1963 a group of cinema enthusiasts, the Freunde der Deutschen Kinemathek (Friends of the German Cinematheque), began to organize alternative screenings which relied on aesthetic criteria and innovative styles rather than on Hollywood stars, something which challenged the programming practice of the Berlinale even further. This increased public visibility of various types of 'other' cinema slowly led to an inclusion of some films from Eastern Europe (from Czechoslovakia and Yugoslavia) in the main programme of the Berlinale from 1966.[55] But only in 1970 did a more profound upheaval occur: *OK*, a film by Michael Verhoeven, transferred a 'found' story that took place during the US war in Vietnam to a Bavarian context and caused a major scandal and a further critique of the US influence over the festival.

The public visibility of these events was enhanced by a more explicit 'counter-festival' to the Berlinale organized in the same year, the Woche des Jungen Films (Week of Young Film). This festival showed a retrospective of films by Rainer Werner Fassbinder as well as other films that explicitly dealt with homosexuality by Rosa von Praunheim, besides productions from Cuba and the American Underground Cinema (de Valck 2007: 66).

These various cinema events between the late 1950s and early 1970s backed each other up in their objective of bringing to the fore a 'different' kind of cinema, a mix of challenging aesthetic and political films, young authors and new waves, and expanding the gap vis-à-vis older festival styles that mainly relied on stars and on the competition of films as national products. Almost immediately, various institutionalized festivals reacted to this challenge and reorganized their festival structure. Already in 1969 the Quinzaines des Réalisateurs was established as a parallel section of the festival in Cannes and in 1971 the Forum des jungen Films (Forum of Young Film) was set up as a quite similar venue, that is, as a platform for young, radical and marginal cinema, as part of the Berlinale. At the same time, new thematic festivals were inaugurated, such as the film festival in Rotterdam (1972), and older festivals started to select films based on thematic and aesthetic rather than national criteria, as the Viennale, which had already existed since 1960, did around 1971.

As a result of this, festivals were opened up to films from a variety of countries and in particular to films made behind the Iron Curtain, in Third World countries and marginal regions of 'world cinema' and were changed into institutionalized places for cultural, aesthetic but also political intervention. Through these festivals the films selected for prizes or special programmes were also communicated to activists involved in setting up 'new', 'other cinemas', 'free' or 'communal' cinemas which created their programmes and retrospectives out of these pre-selected offers and in this way distributed some of these films throughout the country and over the whole year. For instance, the Kommunales Kino in Frankfurt/Main declared in 1974–1975 that it was engaged in the 'systematic care of Young German Film' as well as determined 'to keep cinema of third world countries continuously present' (m. t. Prinzler and Seidler 1975: 85 and 229). In parallel, festivals also had the role of acknowledging a selection of film journalists as 'writers' and 'film experts' who were soon also involved by the various cinema initiatives, which started to establish advisory boards composed of these experts for the programming of their screenings[56] – something which consolidated the emerging knowledge elite in respect to film and cinema even further. Since most of these initiatives, as part of their 'mission', experimented with showing films in their original-language versions (often with subtitles),[57] they also contributed to a rising presence of various languages in the national public spheres but also to a wider acceptance of English or French as new 'international' languages.

These examples show that the reorganization of the international film festival circuit went along with redefinitions of the relationship between 'self' and 'other'. Films from Eastern Europe, but also from Third World countries or films bringing up the question of *Gastarbeiter* (migrant guest workers) in the FRG (Rainer Werner Fassbinder) or of sexual difference (Rosa von Praunheim and Rainer Werner Fassbinder) achieved a public presence at festivals as well as in the newly established cinema initiative networks. In this way they triggered significant viewing events opening up an interrogating relationship with 'the other' (in ethnic, gender or sexual orientation terms). At the same time these films were also regarded as 'discoveries' and evidence of a 'subculture' or 'another culture', which fixed them into a quite homogeneous and not further differentiated exoticism. Besides, the rediscovery of national cinemas as expressed by 'authors' also had the effect of providing a distinct and 'individual' profile for the new state-funded film production emerging throughout Europe.[58] In a similar double-edged way, films challenging the reigning worlds in stories about their 'own' past led to events that threw these stories into crisis and could trigger curiosity and persistent research (cf. Schober 2004: 122f.) but could, at the same time, also cause a framing of these stories as 'barbaric' counterparts of a basically progress-oriented modernization process.

In this process, and in particular in re-defining the relation between 'East' and 'West', Yugoslav cinema held an exceptional position. There was a particular success of New Yugoslav cinema at international film festivals at the end of the 1960s, which was an effect of these transformations but which also worked in pushing them further. This, however, had very different consequences for film activists in the various countries on both sides of the divide between the pluralist democratic and the one-party communist setting.

In Yugoslavia the ambivalent effects of national as well as international film festivals became visible in a very pronounced way: festivals participated in creating a new 'Yugoslav' and at the same time communist order capable of pushing the older national, ethnic and religious divisions into the background, and simultaneously augmented the visibility of various kinds of differences. The most important national cinema event was the Pula Film Festival, which was established in 1954 and started to distribute national awards in 1957. Besides, the annual calendar was filled with amateur film festivals organized regularly in all bigger Yugoslav cities. The most important national amateur film competition was again held in Pula one week prior to the main Pula Film Festival – thus attracting a huge group of cinema amateurs to the main national cinema event too (I ZZ).

As already mentioned, travelling to these festivals and watching, programming and discussing films by cinema activists from other regions created a close network of young cinema enthusiasts but also a shared taste and new standards in film-making. This taste and these standards were nourished by a variety of encounters with foreign films from both sides of the Iron Curtain – which was all the more important since there was only an extremely small, almost non-existent body of indigenous 'Yugoslav' films from before the war available to the young cinema-makers (Kosanović 1986). Through circulation in this network, some cinema activists were recognized as 'authors', their films were viewed as aesthetic models for further film production and usually they were also promoted to take part in the juries of national competitions or to act as film critics.[59] Young cinema enthusiasts thereby experienced themselves as part of something 'new' that was just in the process of becoming. As Dušan Makavejev stated: 'We were part of a culture that didn't exist yet' (I DM).

The creation of new image-worlds and narrations in relation to the communist state of 'Yugoslavia' in the making was also exposed to enhanced control, which in some cases caused conflict and even exclusion. This becomes particularly visible in relation to productions made by film-makers later classified as 'black' who circulated in the most important national and international festivals. In 1962, for instance, the film *Kapi, vode, ratnici/Raindrops, Water, Warriors* made by three members of the Belgrade kino club, Živojin Pavlović, Marko Babac and Kokan Rakonjac, already experienced some censorship problems, but nonetheless won a special prize at the Pula Film Festival of the same year. Because of the public attention caused by this, the next film made by the trio one year later, *Grad*/The City (1963, Živojin Pavlović, Marko Babac, Kokan Rakonjac, Figure 17), did not pass censorship and was even brought before the general court and convicted of being a threat to socialist society. Marko Babac remembers: 'As authors, we had a big problem back then. [...] We were put in the 'bunker' [...] we were not allowed to continue working. Živojin Pavlović started to work in Slovenia. Kokan started to work as an amateur again and to sell his ideas to producers, but it was very complicated for him to continue to work. And I started to work as an editor' (I MB).

The participation of young film-makers at international film festivals posed an even bigger risk for the one-party state – since in these arenas such control and exclusion could not be executed. But at the same time international film festivals could also act as occasions where the Yugoslav independent way of socialist cultural production could be recognized and acknowledged. This double-edged role is also highlighted by a story told by both

Figure 17: A 'convicted' film, *Grad/The City,* Živojin Pavlović, Marko Babac, Kokan Rakonjac, 1963 © Courtesy Jugoslovenska Kinoteka, Belgrade.

Dušan Makavejev and Marko Babac about travelling in 1957, at a time when there were still travel restrictions, to the amateur film festival in Cannes, which was always held there during the winter. They remember that during Christmas in 1957, five members of the kino club, among them Makavejev, Babac and his then girlfriend, went there with a tent (but in the end preferred to sleep in the big Festival Hall) authorized by a special travelling permit for this trip. Makavejev participated in the competition with his short film *Antonijevo razbijeno ogledalo/Antony's Broken Mirror* (1957), which was selected for special reviews and in this way gained initial international recognition for the author. Their female co-traveller, however, used this trip to France as an opportunity to 'run away' and never came back – something that led to detailed investigations of the kino club and even of Marko Babac's family (I DM and I MB).

One decade later, at the end of the 1960s, travelling restrictions were to a large extent abolished, and the tensions produced by international film festivals manifested themselves in a different way. There was an extraordinary success of productions by film-makers coming from Yugoslav amateur film circles at international festivals which initiated a change in the recognition of the 'Yugoslav New Wave' movement. From 1967, some films made by novi film authors started to win the most prestigious international awards. Here I will mention only the most important ones: in 1967 Aleksandar Petrović, for instance, won the Special Grand Prize of the Jury in Cannes as well as the FIPRESCI (International Federation of Film Critics) prize with *Skupljači perja/I Even Met Happy Gypsies.* Afterwards the film toured for several years in the by then emerging art-house and community cinemas all over Europe (I DS). A year later, in 1968, Dušan Makavejev's film *Nevinost bez zaštite/Innocence Unprotected* won the Silver Bear at the Berlin International Film Festival as well as the FIPRESCI Prize and Želimir Žilnik won the Grand Prix at the Oberhausen Film Festival with

Nezaposleni ljudi/ The Unemployed (1968). Again, in the following year Živojin Pavlović's film *Zaseda* won the Golden Lion at the Venice Film Festival 1969, but was put in the 'bunker' at home in Yugoslavia. In 1969 the Berlin International Film Festival programmed a 'Week of Yugoslav Films' and a special selection of Yugoslav short films. At the same time, the winner of the Golden Bear of this edition of the festival was another Yugoslav film-maker, Želimir Žilnik with his film *Rani radovi* (1969) – a film that again started to cause serious problems for the film-maker at home. And in 1971, Dušan Makavejev won the Interfilm Award Recommendation at the Forum of Young Cinema at the Berlin International Film Festival with *WR: Misterije organizma/ WR: Mysteries of the Organism*.

These successes of Yugoslav film-makers were made possible by the above-mentioned transformation of the international film festival scene towards more politically active interventions, younger and more radical aesthetic styles and a new interest in films from countries that had until then been marginalized in the West, in particular the films from communist countries. Around 1968 some of these films were chosen for screenings or prizes in order to highlight the political agenda of a festival or to feature a special thematic section. Due to their pronounced experimental, avant-garde and non-conventional aesthetics, however, the films made by Aleksandar Petrović, Živojin Pavlović, Dušan Makavejev or Želimir Žilnik in turn pushed these transformations further.

Some of these international successes of novi film-makers were also reflected in the national competitions: Živojin Pavlović, for instance, won prestigious awards at the Pula Festival almost three years in a row for *Buđenje pacova/ The Rats Woke Up* (1967), *Kad budem mrtav i beo/ When I Am Dead and White* (1967) and *Rdeče klasje/ Red Wheat* (1970). This again highlights that the 'difference' communicated by young, non-conventional Yugoslav film-makers worked in a particularly double-edged way: the regime used the transnational recognition of film-makers and artists featuring a pronounced experimental, avant-garde aesthetic language as a 'business card' (I BV) in order to prove its distance from the Eastern Bloc and its open-mindedness vis-à-vis new and 'Western' phenomena. The participation (and success) of Yugoslav films at international film festivals turned out to be an effective means of gaining international distinction and recognition as an independent player between 'East' and 'West' – and was 'mirrored' in the prizes some of these film-makers won at home. The international visibility of the difference staged by these films enhanced the importance of difference as such and put it, so to speak, 'on a tableau'. In this way it could also be interpreted in other terms, for instance, in national, ethnic, religious or class terms or based on 'high-versus-low-culture' value. Hence, the visibility related to these successes also held the potential of exposing a difference that was closely controlled at the national level since it was viewed as bearing the potentiality of undermining the very unity of the 'people as one', which the Yugoslav regime had identified as representing the essence of the new state.

Towards the end of the 1960s when national tension started to rise and communist one-party states experienced a general and enhanced legitimacy crisis after the events in Czechoslovakia in 1968, such tensions and conflicts around non-conventional films became more intense. Thus, these tensions around novi film authors were also enhanced by the fact that Yugoslavian films were particularly successful at the Berlinale – a festival that was, as already mentioned, founded as a place for confronting communist Europe.

Activist and political film styles and expanded cinema initiatives in the FRG and Austria also began establishing themselves – as already described – through international film festivals such as the EXPRMNTL in Knokke-Le-Zoute or the International Underground Festival in London in 1970. Through this 'gateway' they too gained recognition in the newly emerging (avant-garde) or media art festival and cinema networks, venues of art museums or, in some cases, women's film festivals. In a similar way, the New German Cinema – a bit later, since the mid-1970s – also gained enhanced visibility through international festivals and reviews in the foreign press, for example, at the New York Film Festival of 1974 and 1975 with films from Werner Herzog and Rainer Werner Fassbinder (Elsaesser 1989: 29 and 290f.). And already, from the early 1970s on, through embassies, cultural missions, Goethe Institutes, and other official entities, governments had started to promote new and avant-garde cinema and film tendencies as kinds of 'art ambassadors' and as proof of 'another', 'more liberal', 'internationalist' and 'vanguard' Germany or Austria.[60]

In summary it can be said that the transnational circulation of films and urban cinema actions staging aesthetic as well as political differences and employing new forms of production yielded quite diverse effects in multiparty, democratic states such as the FRG and Austria and in Yugoslav one-party state socialism. In the case of multiparty states – even if competition and struggle occurred there too – such articulations were seen by some fractions of official politics as a confirmation of a democratic, pluralist spirit and were sometimes used as forces for producing change – particularly in some, until then, quite restricted and regulated areas such as pornography, urban event culture and adult education (cf. Schober 2009b: 288f.). By contrast, in the case of Yugoslav one-party socialism these articulations soon started to be viewed as serious threats to the proclaimed national unity and were answered with more rigid controls and even with attempts to inhibit the most prolific and provocative of the young film-makers from further production.

2.4. Difference, privatized ambivalence and the (informal) public sphere

Art cinema and the event city

Around 1968 aesthetic and politically challenging films were featured prominently at festivals, film series and individual cinema screenings. As a result, film was recognized as art, formal experimentation and political provocation rather than as popular culture. Directors were presented as 'authors' and an individual stylistic signature and distinction replaced national affiliation as the main criterion for the selection of films. This was accompanied by a growing critical discourse around film and cinema, to which most of the authors also contributed. Some festivals published extensive documentation, and seminars and exhibitions were organized alongside the screenings, which started to disseminate an international cinema discourse (de Valck 2007: 208).

In parallel, activists of the various cinema movements too started to publish articles and to edit magazines, fanzines or documentation of their interventions. In West Germany and Austria, cinema activists to some extent published in magazines such as *Film* or *Filmkritik* – even if these media were soon viewed by some activists with scepticism or were terminated – but they also edited various kind of programme journals, collections of their essays as well as detailed documentations of their activities and work.[61] In former Yugoslavia, magazines such as *Ekran, Sineast, Film danas* and *Filmske Sveske* supported new film trends (I ZZ). Also here, authors such as Živojin Pavlović, Dušan Makavejev or Želimir Žilnik acted as writers and film-theorists themselves and used to publish in these magazines, but also produced editions of collected writings (Makavejev 1965; Pavlović 1969).

This shows that the cinephilia that accompanied the film practice of the author produces, as Paul Willemen (1993: 239) puts it, 'the institution of the magazine/fanzine which in its turn helps recruit future cinephiles'. In this way, writing and collecting statements or reviews written by others seem to have been more important than reading, that is, more important than the audiences themselves. This kind of cinephile writing was directed at conveying responses to film experience; it is more a 'gestural outlet' (Willemen 1993: 239) than criticism or information. At the same time, it actively constructs 'new traditions' – usually situating the authors and activists firmly inside a genealogy of 'ancestors' and like-minded people.[62]

In this way the film author emerged in the FRG, Austria as well as in Yugoslavia in the 1950s and 1960s as an aesthetic and promotional 'auratic' category and as a distinguishing feature of cinema and film in relation to other, less 'noble' forms of mass media such as television (Corrigan 1991: 102).[63] Around 1968, however, auteurism and cinephilia reached a culmination, where they started to transform into something else (Willemen 1993: 227; Maule 2008: 21). Some activists then claimed to be involved in a transition from the cinema setting to multi-media platforms, from individual film-making and film-criticism to production and discussion collectives and from art to life. Simultaneously, however, these activists usually still posed as artists, albeit as artists engaged in 'new' and 'mixed media'. And, in parallel, the film-festival circuit also institutionalized, as already mentioned, politically provocative film-making as 'new wave' and productions of 'authors'.

This ambivalence is also highlighted by the 'bad others' that were redefined as part of this cinema practice. Though new, avant-garde and political cinema was addressing a mass audience, activists usually did so only in order to challenge the visions of this broader public. They usually defined their own styles against what they viewed as 'consumer cinema', 'bourgeois cinema' or 'cultural ghetto' (in the FRG and Austria), 'party cinema' (in Yugoslavia) or against certain despised indigenous popular traditions. Examples of the latter in the FRG and Austria were the *Heimatfilm* (sentimental films with regional backgrounds), but sometimes political or avant-garde films that often only minimally differed from their own positions[64] were also mentioned. In former Yugoslavia in contrast, the 'bad others' were partisan movies and conventional cinema-amateur-productions (I MB and I DM).

'New' or 'other' cinema initiatives strongly distanced themselves from the old art-cinemas. So, for instance, the cinema Ostertor that had existed in Bremen since 1969 claimed to reject everything 'luxurious' and 'extravagant' that could be associated with 'first class' cinema such as red velvet curtains, cinema gongs, violin music, differentiated prices or usherettes. Instead, they praised themselves for their good technique, special equipment for showing films made by experimental and underground film-makers, a monthly printed programme and 'good contact to the visitors due to discussions after the screenings with directors and film-makers' (m. t. Prinzler and Schwarz 1972: 67f.).

In spite of such a distancing, however, and as a consequence of the above-mentioned redefinition of film practice, in the FRG and Austria the cinema situations created by activists of the 1960s usually established themselves in the form of 'program cinema' or 'art-house cinema' as a more permanent element of the urban calendar – and this holds true for avant-garde cinema as well as for the more explicitly politically active leftist cinema interventions.

Wilhelm and Birgit Hein, for example, 'institutionalized' the cinema situations created by the Cologne Expanded Cinema group xscreen after the first one-and-a-half years of collective activism in the early 1970s (I WH). In the course of this, they first rented spaces in an already existing art-film cinema, the cinema Lupe, followed by another cinema, and after

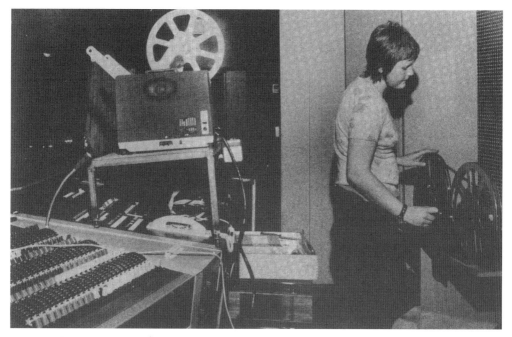

Figure 18: Cinema initiative Bochum © Prinzler and Seidler, Kinobuch, 1975.

the Lupe was closed down, they took it over and ran it, later together with a second closed-down cinema (located nearby, at the Ring in Cologne), as art-house cinemas with a daily programme. They first showed a mixed programme composed of art and underground films as well as (officially forbidden until 1975) pornography, but later on, as an art-house cinema, they also screened a range of feature films but not 'Hollywood in the narrow sense'. In the late 1970s they sometimes also used the cinema space for Punk concerts and so re-affirmed their fame as a 'counter-cultural establishment' (I WH and I BH).

Similarly, the Freies Kino in Vienna, which at the beginning of the 1970s started as a place to show 'socialist-minded' films, very soon became a kind of art-house cinema. As such, it presented a quickly changing programme and two and (on weekends) sometimes three screenings a day, which in some cases were accompanied by public discussions or the invitation of selected authors. In order to develop a programme, the Freies Kino oriented itself on existing programme cinemas, in particular the Arsenal in Berlin and the Kommunales Kino in Frankfurt/Main. The films shown were procured through an also emerging system of 'progressive' German and Swiss distributors, which pre-selected their films at international festivals as well as through various cultural institutes of embassies of communist countries (the Hungarian, Polish, Soviet, Yugoslav, Korean embassies, for instance) (I DS).[65]

These various initiatives created a circuit of art-house cinemas and distributors that continued to be nationally subsidized but which nevertheless operated transnationally and were closely linked to international film festivals. It was there that the films entering this circuit received attention and distinction through prizes, scandals or news coverage that featured them as 'discoveries' (de Valck 2007: 94). This circuit also included films from behind the Iron Curtain and the until then marginalized regions of World Cinema – which blurred the strict divisions established during the Cold War and increased ambivalence between the reigning 'we' and 'them' groups. At the same time, as I will point out later on in detail, it was now the individual viewer who was entrusted with the charge of dealing with this ambivalence and the tensions emerging from this transformation.

This re-classification of movies as 'politically challenging' and as 'art' led to a multiplication and diversification of places where films were shown and consumed. In West Germany and Austria, cinema activist groups started to present films in museums, art galleries, at the universities and in adult education centres. New urban situations emerged that combined communication, education and entertainment in a more self-conscious way.

An example of this is the Abaton cinema in Hamburg, which has a particularly close relationship with the student movement of 1968. It grew out of a 'film-in' organized in 1967 by film-makers in Hamburg in a studio in Bruederstrasse, where they showed their own film productions (films by Hellmuth Costard, Werner Nekes, Thomas Struck) combined with silent films and old Frankenstein movies.

Activists remember (Prinzler and Schwarz 1972: 125f.) a 'new cinema feeling' due to this mix of films, the massive audience of up to 300 people and the possibility of getting something to drink from the pubs nearby. When a group of people decided to start a more permanent cinema initiative in an old garage, they wanted to be as close to what they experienced in Bruederstrasse as possible. This meant that they included a pub – where a South American cook made pizza – as well as a shop where you could buy books, journals and music (records). In this way a new kind of cinema-restaurant-shop unit was born that could attract pizza-lovers to watch a film and film enthusiasts to trying a new kind of food.

The activists involved described such activities as 'learning by doing.' Reacting to new kinds of desires and needs they were observing in their own life milieus, they were creating a new urban unit that in turn contributed to the rising entertainment character of the city. This 'learning by doing' did not just inform the creation of the spatial outline of the Abaton, but the PR-work of the activists as well. Also, in this field, they reacted in a new way to what they found in their surroundings. For example, they described how they learned to relate cinema programming to other cultural events staged in the city. They stated: 'When there is a pop concert in Hamburg or a music festival, we play the corresponding film' (m. t. Prinzler and Schwarz 1972: 129). In this way they created particular synergies between various cultural events and enhanced the public visibility of their own activities as well as that of others. At the same time, they were very conscious about 'emphasising differences', that is, engaging in cinema activities that distinguish themselves from the usual 'cinetheater-nasty-programmes' (m. t. Prinzler and Schwarz 1972: 130).

In parallel to the emergence of such new urban units, the city as such was also discovered as an arena for aesthetic and political action: urban squares and streets, markets, circus tents and newly constructed metro stations or construction sites of metro stations were used for aesthetic intervention and so connected with 'underground' and 'progressive culture'. Expanded Cinema activists transformed film into new ways of inhabiting the city and vice versa, architectural collectives, such as Haus-Rucker-Co, Coop Himmelb(l)au, Missing Link or Zünd-Up started to present projects in the form of Expanded Cinema-like urban events. Several of these groups directed their actions to counter what they called a 'neutralization of the senses' and to feature the 'impure', 'the surprising' and a 'concurrence of the senses' (see, for instance, Schober 2009b: 253; Schober 2003).

Such city-interventions created a change in how the political and the cultural was practised locally: cultural arenas like the cinema, concert spaces and festivals or new cultural forms such as multi-media and live happenings were brought into the foreground of urban spectacle culture and were directed at simultaneously producing a local interruption of everyday-life flow as well as connecting the viewer to a wider, international or even global fan community. For some sections of the urban public it was now no longer the traditional spaces of politics, such as parties or unions, but these newly created cultural spaces of cinema, music and happening that were functioning as arenas of politicization. Film as well as music, art and literature were thereby 'merged' with new forms of lifestyle often borrowed from marginalized subcultures.

In the student movement in the FRG and Austria around 1970, for instance, an identification with and an adoption of protest symbols of the US Black Panther movement became very fashionable – an adoption that sometimes was represented in ways of staging oneself in public (Klimke 2010: 108f.). Birgit Hein, for example, recalls that after the Underground

Festival in Munich in 1968, she no longer wanted to look the way she normally did and changed her appearance to an Afro look. During the Underground festival in Munich, she still had 'honest hairdresser curls', but shortly afterwards she adopted the Afro look – as a statement, however, not a very provocative one since this was already in fashion at that time (I BH).

Yugoslav movies were part of this emerging new cinema culture. Certain films such as *Skupljači perja/I Even Met Happy Gypsies* (1967) by Aleksandar Petrović were shown for years in the spreading new art-house cinemas (IDS). At the same time, in Yugoslav cities in the 1960s, one also witnessed similar developments towards an 'event city' such as in West Germany or Austria, even if this process was closely monitored by party bureaucracy. Also here, there was a multiplication of spaces where films were being shown and discussed or where they were connected with other components of emerging youth lifestyles.

In Belgrade, for instance, the members of the kino clubs used to organize jazz parties alongside screenings and festivals in the 1960s. Marko Babac remembers that they organized Saturday-night parties, featuring 'not only Louis Armstrong – it was progressive jazz, completely a-tonal and a-rhythmic music' for the Belgrade kino club. He recalls further: 'In the cinema club we had pirate copies of modern music and at the time we were [famous] in Belgrade [...] Full of young men, each Saturday evening we had parties where we only played modern music, free' (I MB). Besides these screenings by the local cinema club in Belgrade, you could watch art films at the Kinoteka as well as the Akademski kino klub (Academic Kino Club). Since 1964 their spaces were joined by those of Dom omladine (House of Youth), where new and sometimes politically challenging cultural events were also staged, in particular in the field of music.

In Novi Sad, which at that time was one of the 'most liberal places' (I ZZ) in former Yugoslavia, but where the kino club at that time was 'at a standstill' (I ZZ), spaces like the already mentioned Tribina mladih (Youth Forum) were set up for the presentation and discussion of innovative culture and avant-garde art in cinema, music, literature or theatre. There were amateur film festivals all over Yugoslavia and between 1963 and 1970 the GEFF festival (genre film festival without genre) was held in Zagreb on such diverse issues as 'Antifilm', 'Research by Film', 'Cybernetics and Aesthetics' and 'Sexuality as a Possible Way to New Humanism' (Daković 2003: 478f.). In Ljubljana and Zagreb, art collectives such as OHO or individual artists such as Tomislav Gotovac (Figure 19) transformed theatre and film into urban action similar to the transnational Expanded Cinema scene. And as some of the photographs and films, for instance by Želimir Žilnik or OHO members, show, in Yugoslav cities performances of the self oriented on the beat generation appeared – for example, long-haired men in flowered trousers and casual outfits.

Despite this considerable latitude for screening and viewing a whole range of non-conventional movies from various 'Eastern' as well as 'Western' cinema worlds and for adopting new lifestyles, any use of urban space in socialist Yugoslavia had to involve (usually implicit and 'silent' instead of explicit conflict-ridden) negotiations with official authorities. Similar to other state-socialist countries[66] space was – in addition to any activity

Figure 19: Tomislav Gotovac, *Pokazivanje časopisa Elle/Showing Elle,* 1962 © Tomislav Gotovac, courtesy The Art Collection of Erste Group.

that otherwise happened in it – claimed by the state on behalf of the 'people as one' and as a public arena for the formation of the new Yugoslav citizen. This means that cities were strictly hierarchically and centrally organized whereby the city centre was staged as a main locus of state power. This became most visible in Tito posters and slogans such as 'Živeo (Živio) naš voljeni drug Tito' (Long live our beloved comrade Tito) that covered the main buildings. In this way the fantasy of an egocrat, representing and incorporating the love of the 'people as one' as well as of a 'transparent text' expressing the vision of this people and this egocrat was set against the dynamics of urban life, characterized by diversity and contingency (Rouvillois 1984: 318).

In parallel, private uses of space were pushed back or were strongly controlled by the state, which adopted terms closely linked to privacy such as 'love' or 'fatherhood'. As the slogan shows, Tito claimed to possess the love of the Yugoslav people or was presented as their 'father'. Through their participation in parades or even in the writing of poems or the drawing of pictures, individuals and in particular young people or children were called upon to express their love for the new nation and its leader – something young film-makers and cultural activists were provoked to react to. The already mentioned film *Mlad i zdrav* kao *ruža/Young and Healthy as a Rose* (1971) (Figure 20) by Jovan Jovanović, for instance, opens with a sequence showing a young man in a car speeding though the Belgrade city centre, passing by various structures covered with Tito posters and slogans. This is accompanied by a radio programme, broadcasting a love poem that a young female student is reciting to Tito. In combination with the young man clad in a shirt featuring the British flag and using a rather harsh language and brash conduct, the various indications of publicly expressed love for the leader were on the verge of being overexposed and of unmasking their hollowness.

Dušan Makavejev recalls a very similar public *mise-en-scène* initiated by some people working at the local radio station in the 1960s. They had the idea of publicly inviting children to come to the city centre in order to draw flowers for Tito's birthday and announced this

Figure 20: *Mlad i zdrav kao ruža/Young and Healthy as a Rose,* Jovan Jovanović, 1971 © Jovan Jovanović.

on the radio several times a day. Thousands of children came, and the police had to block the streets because they could not stop the children from pouring in, nor could they arrest children for creating public disorder. According to Makavejev, this action was also an exaggeration of this officially prescribed, staged love for the leader that was on the verge of creating disorder and confusion. The next year, however, the same action was repeated by the official party bureaucracy, but then everything was organized: the children came as part of a nursery school or school field trip and certain spaces were assigned to them (I DM).

As already mentioned, even more pronouncedly than other arts the cinema was mobilized by the one-party regime in order to involve the public in a highly emotional experience of what being a 'Yugoslav' means. Besides art films and 'new wave' in the 1960s, there was a broad range of films from the United States as well as from various European countries being offered in Yugoslav cinemas and certain spaces emerged that were exclusively dedicated to 'new tendencies' in the arts. Despite this, the proclaimed 'oneness' of the Yugoslav people was not allowed to be questioned and the use of space remained closely controlled. In this respect, '1968' in former Yugoslavia was a turning point of a different kind than in the FRG or Austria. In the years following the student upheaval, the regime started to eliminate certain key Yugoslav actors in the film circuit and to watch the activities developing in cultural spaces even more closely.

The explicit or implicit redefinition of 'bad others' inherent in the cinema practices of the various kind of 'new cinemas' emerging in the 1960s thereby contributed to the tensions some of the films experienced in their local environment. Particularly in this respect, the difference between the multiparty context in West Germany and Austria and the one-party context in Yugoslavia becomes very visible.

In the FRG, for instance, an 'art film' was often considered as 'elitist' by the broader public as well as by the politically engaged activist. The 'Forum of Young Film', for instance, which after the scandal and the counter-festival of 1970 was included into the Berlinale as a regular venue for art cinema, avant-garde, explicit political movies and experimental productions, was soon judged not only as a 'barricade battle-cry' but also as an 'ivory tower' (de Valck 2007: 67). Conversely, more politically explicit movies were usually viewed by avant-garde film-makers as 'no different than Hollywood' (I WH, I DS).

'Hollywood', however, thereby functioned as a very ambiguous notion – it could simultaneously indicate a rootedness in popular traditions of cinema culture as well as 'mainstream movies decorated with Oscars'. So, for instance, the above-mentioned xscreen group in Cologne, which was founded around the notion of avant-garde and experimental film, distributed membership cards featuring Mickey Mouse. At the same time, members distanced themselves from other 'new cinema' trends such as the French New Wave or films made by Alexander Kluge more than from Hollywood cinema (I BH).

In Yugoslavia, by contrast, the tensions resulting from this re-classification of film as 'art' were much stronger and touched the essence of the self-definition of the new state. Cinema was viewed by party officials as having a particular duty with respect to 'the people' and to popular traditions. A cinema that in one way or another staged difference in a pronounced articulated way – be it aesthetic, sexual, regional or ethnic difference – was seen as putting this duty at risk and consequently as threatening national unity. Hence the definition of cinema as 'art' also entered into opposition to the official view of cinema's grounding in popular 'culture as one'. Even if film-makers such as Makavejev or Žilnik did not strongly support such redefinitions of cinema as art themselves and adhered more to a view that depicted cinema as popular culture rooted in a Marxist tradition (I DM, I ZZ), the recognition of their films at international festivals that supported such a distinction was enough to blur the strict boundaries erected by the one-party state and to enhance the tension around film-making at the end of the 1960s.

As a consequence, the way in which official strategies interacted with grassroots cinema culture with respect to urban event culture was quite different in multiparty and one-party states. In cities like Cologne, for instance, the urban interventions created by cinema activists concurred – besides all conflicts – with various official initiatives. In the late 1960s, the city experienced a new kind of demand for cultural activities since it had to make a difference inside a diversified leisure and culture market and had already started to reconfigure the environment in an eventful and explicitly modern and cosmopolitan perspective. Since the Contre Festival (1960), featuring among others Nam June Paik, this redesigning of Cologne had an explicit avant-garde, neo-dada character. This was accentuated also by the dense variety of 'other' cinema initiatives that emerged in Cologne around 1970: the Bambi-cinema, the Cinemathek and xscreen (since 1968) (Prinzler and Schwarz 1972: 140f.).

In continuation of this, in the late 1960s the city started to offer artists and film-makers opportunities to organize public performances and spectacles, for instance, in 1968 in a still incomplete subway station. The newly formed cinema-activist group, xscreen, exploited such occasions. Nevertheless, they were not doing exactly what was expected of them, but somehow surpassed the expectations of the city and heightened public provocation by presenting films by the Austrian actionist Otto Mühl, which, due to 'obscene' acts, produced a widespread scandal (Hein et al. 1971: 116). Together with further cinema situations staged by the xscreen group, the other cinema initiatives, the performances of the Living Theatre, the establishment of the art fair and several newly founded galleries, this subway event worked to promote the later fame of the city as a metropolis of avant-garde art.

But also at the level of (adult) education, official strategies and grassroots organization started to coincide. In German and Austrian cities film was slowly discovered for educational activities: it was used for teaching, for popularizing science, but also as an investigation

Figure 21: *Male Nude Film*, xscreen poster, Cologne 1969 © xscreen archive berlin, courtesy Wilhelm Hein.

object in its own right. At universities, film seminars were held, art galleries and film museums began collecting films and cinema libraries were founded. Young film-makers and cineasts interacted with these strategies (I BH and I WH). They were among the first to present films in arenas of high culture, to show films in their original language, to use citations from educational films in their work and to give the academic investigation of film a different political edge. So, for example, in the FRG and Austria in the late 1960s, classic US Westerns were analysed emphatically and by several groups as carriers of ideological meaning (I DS) or as exposures of the 'international society game' (Alexander 1967).[67]

In former Yugoslavia the interrelation of official strategies and mobilization from below was very close from the outset, since alternative film practices developed inside institutionalized structures provided by the one-party state. Nevertheless, around 1968 a change occurred in this respect which augmented the tensions between official politics and some of the most publicly visible cinema activists. As a survey made in Yugoslavia in the 1960s shows, mobility and the transformation of lifestyle had led to the broader dissemination of a feeling of taking part in a transnational culture, even if basic value structures of society (such as marriage preferences or the choice of where to live) often continued to be informed by ethnocentrism (Bertsch 1973: 5f.). At the end of the 1960s, however, in some elite-political arenas such as party organizations but also cultural institutions difference was rearticulated in national terms, as can for instance be seen in Albanian claims for autonomy in Kosovo in 1968 as well as Croatian criticism of Belgrade centralism between 1967 and 1971, known also as the 'Croatian Spring'. This new visibility of national difference was then taken by the communists as a trigger-point to reorganize, re-centralize and consolidate themselves as a party, which went along with the expulsion of thousands of its members accused as 'anarcho-liberal' or 'anti-socialist' but also with the divestiture of sectors that were operating particularly transnationally. (Bieber 2005: 50 and 63f.)

The very publicly visible cinema networks known to articulate difference on various levels were especially affected. Starting in the summer of 1969 but more strongly later on towards 1972–1973 prominent figures such as Želimir Žilnik or Dušan Makavejev experienced several 'warnings': apartments were searched by the secret police, films were not shown, there was no opportunity to work and to earn money, the party sent letters to the official press telling them not to mention names of their films or their own names in public except in cases of death. Žilnik recalls that in 1973, after they saw in the news that Lazar Stojanović, another film-maker accused of being 'black', had been arrested,[68] both he and Makavejev followed advice telling them 'to disappear' (I ZZ and I DM).

In parallel, national cultural organizations such as the Croatian institution Matica Hrvatska were closed, but – since transnational networks were dissolved in particular – various types of cultural 'dissidents' remaining in the country now became increasingly enclosed into niches which often were precisely 'national' niches. In this way, despite employing a rhetoric of countering nationalism, the party started to create structures in favour of nationalism (Bieber 2005: 83). In parallel, new urban cultural places were inaugurated – such as the Student Cultural Centre in Belgrade (SKC) in 1971, where artistic tendencies bound to '1968' such as happenings, conceptual art or underground film now became 'institutionalized', that is, they could be performed but were at the same time even more closely monitored than before.[69] In this way, unconventional events continued to be staged in a selected location of the capital city even if key cultural players were sent abroad and the niches for those remaining were strongly controlled (and played increasingly on national terms).

The viewer as a 'montagiste', other bodies and changes in the reference frame

The cinema activism of the 1960s demonstrates also how media shape collective sensorial experience and self-culture.[70] It shows, for example, that contours and choices of the cinemagoers' own responses to what is offered as visual culture became more important – ranging from a silent immersion into the crowd, to the translation of significant viewing experiences into new styles of living, but also into elaborate political and aesthetic positions. With this, viewers turn into users and sometimes even become cinema-makers or other public actors. As such, they try to gain public recognition for the particular aesthetic-political position they articulate – which contributes to the emergence of an (informal) public sphere.

This is again closely linked to the body, which in this way is affirmed as an instance not only for selecting images but also for providing them with particular colours, tastes, temporary structures and even shapes. The transformations happening in art and popular culture around 1968 can thus be read as indications that the image is always already an image in-formation. It exists only in and through the body of the perceiver and its affective responses.[71]

Some Expanded Cinema actions such as 'Movie Movie' by Jeffrey Shaw (which was created for the experimental cinema festival in Knokke-le-Zoute in 1967) make this particularly evident. For this event he used an inflatable structure in the form of a cone with an outer transparent and an inner white membrane functioning as a soft and undulating ground. In the space between the two membranes performers entered and played with the movable surrounding, whereas film slides as well as liquid light-show effects were simultaneously projected onto the surface of the whole structure. This created a situation in which the changing movements and actions of the performers who acted inside the dome, and of some people from the audience who joined them, visibly affected how images and light materialized (Duguet et al. 1997: 70f.).

In this way, perception seems to be guided by the affective responses of the viewers' bodies and confirms and authenticates vice versa a self-experience of being an acting and perceiving entity. Simultaneously, however, perception is in an enhanced way seen as being fragmented and distracted. In urban spaces there are usually various and contrasting visual stimuli on offer ranging from the news to advertisement, from movies to medical photographs or from window shopping to religiously inspired image worship. Paradoxically, however, an effect of this was that it is again the individual viewer who is pushed back onto him- or herself in order to act as a *montagiste* and to gain and make sense out of these various fragments.

Such a fragmented, distracted and at the same time subjectified experience had already started to disseminate in certain geographical contexts with the turn towards modernity. But in the 1960s it emerged in certain vernacular alterations where even more emphasis was put on the image as a process and as a public action, on viewing as a montage of phenomena that usually do not show up with each other and on the tendency towards a dissolution of hierarchical relationships between those who present and those who consume.

Thus, the various visual fragments and image-worlds circulating in the public sphere increasingly seem to be of equal value, which means that existing validations, for example of high and low, important and unimportant, beautiful and ugly, are called into question. This becomes evident in various Expanded Cinema actions where everyday objects such as a Nivea plastic ball or T-shirts with meaningful messages such as 'the rebel' are used to produce high-art statements. But it also appears in movies by novi film-makers such as Dušan Makavejev where city surfaces are not only shown as being 'decorated' with enormous Tito and Lenin posters but are also covered with beautiful girls smiling from advertisement

Figure 22: *Nivea,* Expanded Cinema Performance, Peter Weibel, 1967 © Peter Weibel.

panels, showing some similarity to the female protagonists of the films roaming the city too.[72] This levelling of the value attributed to images was again particularly provocative in socialist Yugoslavia where it was able to call the officially attributed importance of party symbols and the egocrat Tito into question.

One effect of this throwing the single viewer back onto her- or himself as a sense-creating entity is that the tensions of collective life and the ambivalences that come up with the various changes in living conditions also increasingly become 'privatized', that is, they have to be resolved as part of the inner activities of the individual. With this – as Zygmunt Bauman has shown – the self has to take over tasks that previously were solved collectively and has to rebuild sense and sustain the creation of imaginative frames for belonging and to integrate them. This 'burdens' the self in a new way as Bauman (1993) maintains, but also opens new possibilities for the imagination and for change.

The cinema setting is able to play a particular role in this since it is a place in which the individual viewer confronts him- or herself in an extraordinary way, a place that makes room for the imagination, but also allows for an experience of connectivity, an immersion into a group of other people that also includes strangers. Hence the cinema pushes these conditions of perception further but also provides a space and a cultural horizon in which effects of these transformations can be reflected, disavowed, transmuted or negotiated.[73]

This ambivalence was enhanced with the media-consciousness that developed as part of the politicization of broad groups of young people around 1968. A kind of militant public started to emerge that expected cinema and culture in general to set agendas and to restage the sense of being in the world (Elsaesser 1989: 155).

But in the 1960s it is not only the ways images appear and become effective but what they represent that changes as well. This, for example, becomes graspable in several photographs reproduced in the programmes of the Freies Kino in Vienna in the early 1970s. One of these photographs, reproduced in luminous orange and in landscape format on a single page, depicts a densely packed mass of people inside a big auditorium, enthusiastically stretching their arms upwards, slightly moving and turning more or less in one direction. The image does not show what the audience sees or hears – it might be a group of speakers or even performers – but provides us with a view inside this mass of bodies from a slightly elevated position, which, however, is still part of what is going on. With some hands and arms waving and dark shadows in the foreground between us as viewers and the bodies of others, the photograph somehow includes us in what is happening and gives us the impression of being enclosed by bodies in affective motion – something to which the warmth of the colour orange in which the photograph is reproduced contributes. The caption of the photograph reads *Studentenrebellion 1968* (student revolt 1968) and gives the name of the photographer, Michael Ruetz.

This image, which is representative of a whole range of pictures in which protagonists of the student movement stage themselves as an enthusiastic crowd, testifies to a particular kind of desire in which the depicted students, the cinema activists of the Freies Kino, but also the photographer and possibly also the viewers of this photograph meet: a desire for immersing oneself into a mass of others and for the bodily pleasure that is experienced through the emotional sharing of a collective event. This photograph links the cinema activism of the Freies Kino visibly to the student upheaval of 1968. In doing so it, however, also indicates that it is the bodily immersion into a mass of similarly affected people where '1968' and cinema enthusiasm overlap.

A cover of another programme published by the Klub Kritischer Film (club of critical films), the official operators of the Freies Kino, shows a further important feature of the collective visual experience that emerged with '1968'. Headed by the title Revolutionärer lateinamerikanischer Film (Revolutionary Latin American Film, Figure 23) the cover again shows a close-up of a rather orderly mass of people in a huge space that fills up the photograph. In the foreground there is a big, dark-skinned, barely clad figure in a straw hat, who has climbed up to the top of a lamppost and is swinging a sword. The man at the top of the lamppost is backlit and thus appears in a rather schematic way and not very rich in detail. At the same time he functions as an 'everybody',[74] that is, a projection figure alongside which everyone in the crowd but also we as viewers of the image are able to reflect onto ourselves and the sense of the world. The 'everybody' on the cover is identified by the title of the programme as a 'Latin American'. Other figures mentioned in a similar function inside the programmes of the Freies Kino are, for instance, the Gypsy, the 'black' Native American or the new woman.

But not only such images, cinema programming too was focused on 'other' everybodies in the late 1960s, early 1970s. The Freies Kino, for example, showed anti-Vietnam-War movies – for instance, Joris Ivens' *17th Parallel: Vietnam in War* (1968), 'critical' movies from the GDR, Yugoslavia, Czechoslovakia or Hungary, several examples of Italo-Westerns, a few films on women's liberation, 'leaflet films' (Ciné Tracts) and other short films produced by political groups and young film-makers, some older films by Eisenstein and others about the Russian Revolution and films about fascism. Quite often 'revolutionary' movies from Latin America were shown, as well as some films fraternizing with political struggles in Africa or with the conflicts between the authorities and Afro-American liberation groups in the US. From former Yugoslavia the Freies Kino screened the 'Gypsy-film' *Skupljači perja* (Aleksandar Petrović, 1967) over a particularly long time span, as well as *Ljubavni slučaj ili tragedija službenice P.T.T.*/Love Affair, or the Tragedy of the Switchboard Operator (1967) by Dušan Makavejev.[75]

By showing films from state-socialist countries such as the GDR, Hungary or Yugoslavia and by simultaneously stating 'we would never have shown anti-communist films' (I DS) any strict demarcation between the two 'systems' that was so typical of the period of the Cold War was blurred. And, in parallel, there was an emphasis on the filmic examination of imperialism and colonialism and films dealing with Vietnam, Latin America or the Afro-American liberation struggle were especially prominent.

These examples show that in the 1960s the central figures alongside which the men or women immersed in the crowd reflect about themselves and try to make sense of had changed: such figures were no longer 'the worker' or 'the proletarian' as they used to be

Figure 23: Revolutionary Latin American Film, Cover Magazine Kritischer Film (Critical Film), 1972 © Austrian National Library.

in the main emancipation movements before and immediately after the Second World War, but are now other figures, usually ones considered 'marginal' and 'repressed' like the 'Third World inhabitant', the 'black activist struggling for emancipation', or the 'new women' fighting not only for the right to vote but also for individual self-realization.[76] As previous figures of this type such as 'the worker', these figures address 'all of us' in the public. But at the same time they seem to incorporate features of an affective life and a desire that is not kept in official representations which are perceived as 'mainstream' visual culture. For some cinema activists these figures embodied an 'authenticity' and a 'truth' linked to a political sensibility that they otherwise experienced as missing in their everyday surroundings.[77]

As part of non-conventional film and cinema culture, new 'everybodies' who show a similarity to the figures coming up in multiparty political settings were also appearing in socialist Yugoslavia around 1968. Novi film-makers such as Dušan Makavejev, Želimir Žilnik, Živojin Pavlović or Karpo Godina often choose protagonists who expose features in sharp contrast to what official representations are showing and who could thus act as a kind of 'counter-figure' vis-à-vis the officially promoted socialist 'new man'. These are sometimes 'problematic' figures such as homeless people or criminals who in standard party rhetoric are usually regarded as having been 'overcome'. But often these are also protagonists of a world that Socialism claims to have pushed back, such as villagers proudly presenting their regional costumes, people adhering to local and even national or religious particularities, Gypsies, prostitutes or youths surviving in the streets or driven by non-channelled passions.

Especially telling in this respect (Figure 24) is a scene in Želimir Žilnik's film *Rani radovi*. Depicted is a fight between village men and the protagonists of the film – young people with

Figure 24: Mud, *Rani radovi/Early Works*, Želimir Žilnik, 1969 © Želimir Žilnik.

modern clothing and hairstyles – during a trip to the countryside on a muddy, wet street lined with peasant houses. The fight happens after the young female protagonist announces over a megaphone that the young people, entering the village in their fancy Citroën ('R4') have come to form an alliance with the poor peasants: 'We are with you, be with us!' Immediately after that, one sees how the villagers, as a response to this request, violently attack the young visitors on the muddy ground. One young man manages to run away, but the others, a boy and a girl, are pushed down, rolled around and pulled through the mud until they are completely soaked and exhausted. Several close-ups show details of these two struggling bodies being dragged through puddles and pushed about on the slimy ground as well as the heavy 'labouring' bodies of the village men. The scene ends with a shot of two men dragging the young female protagonist, struggling and soaked, to the side, throwing her onto a pile of straw and violently starting to undress her, evoking rape. Then the film cuts to the next scene, where she, sitting at night at a campfire says ironically: 'I am glad that there are no peasants in communism.'

With this scene Želimir Žilnik offers us figures who have been brought up in socialist Yugoslavia but are nevertheless confronted with and bound to all the things most city dwellers, according to official propaganda, should have left behind – something that is somehow concentrated in the image of the mud and the rurality, backwardness and violence associated with it. These young guys are – despite their socialist upbringing – represented as being 'stuck in the mud' (in the village) so to speak.

According to the writer Slavenka Drakulić, the presence of mud in photographs, films and narrations of various (even urban) environments in former Yugoslavia indicate the enduring dependence of the city and of modern life on the village and rural economies that never stopped haunting the proclaimed new socialist life.[78] Consequently, the representations of young, mud-sodden men (quoting several scenes from Karl Marx's *Early Works*) violently received by villagers in *Rani radovi* were seen as a strong provocation and as a symbol of opposition to the socialist, officially promoted notion of the 'new everyman' constructed to confront the old, bourgeois, decadent and primitive society: the proletarian stepping out of the factory into the new city, clean and purged of all regional particularities.

As an expression of this official view, the journal *Filmska Kultura*, which was most critical of novi film tendencies, showed a still from exactly one of these mud scenes in *Rani radovi* linked to the article 'Crni film' ili kriza 'autorskog' filma ('Black Film' or the Crisis of 'Authors' Cinema), part of the series *Tri pogleda na novi jugoslavenski film* (Three reflections on new Yugoslav film). The still (Figure 25) shows the face of one of the young men, Marko (Marko Nikolić), looking into the camera earnestly and with squinting eyes, and in the background one sees the muddy streets and old peasant houses of a village. The face of the young man is covered with mud, which makes him somehow part of the village and its muddy ground, even if he also seems to be just a visitor here. In the article which is linked to the photograph, Milutin Čolić declares that the Crni Talas is a blind alley in the development of Yugoslav cinema. Further, he states that these film tendencies express ideas in an 'inadequate, confused and contradictory way' and 'are anti-conformist either

Figure 25: Village Habits, *Filmska Kultura,* 1970 © *Filmska Kultura* and Želimir Žilnik, courtesy Slovenksa Kinoteka, Ljubljana.

without a clearly defined intellectual position or by way of an anarchist and nihilist attitude of everybody against everybody.' Then, even more closely linked to the film, '[t]he former protagonist, the so called positive hero, is more and more often replaced by a man full of problems, crisis, defeats, alienation, despair, death [...] Often this is the result of pure imitation and pose' (m. t. Čolić 1970: 14 and 16).

In the case of novi film-making, such figures running counter to the socialist new man are – similar to the new everybodies discovered in 'alternative' cinema in the FRG and Austria – usually again linked to an experience of authenticity: the playful handling of sexuality and bodily needs (such as collectively performed defecation) or of violence and body force linked to the tactile experience of mud in *Rani radovi* can be interpreted as expression of youthful authenticity, sometimes enriched by a ironic twist in relation to socialist 'collective' customs. In several films, emotions, excess, extravaganza or even intoxication are linked to the figure of the Gypsy, which is particularly often represented in novi film productions as a lead character carrying the argument (for instance in *Skupljači perja* [Aleksandar Petrović, 1967]) or as rather peripheral characters (for instance in *Čovek nije tica. Ljubavni film*, 1965, and *WR: Misterije organizma*, 1971, by Dušan Makavejev). Other films link the experience of strong authentic feelings, such as sexual desire, hate, tensions between inhabitants of different regions or even nations or loneliness and a feeling of abandonment to the figure of male or female grown-ups (such as *Mali vojnici* [Bahrudin Čengić, 1967] and *Nemirni* [Kokan Rakonjac, 1967]) or at least to young people (*Ljubavni slučaj ili tragedija službenice P.T.T.* [Dušan Makavejev, 1967] or *Kad budem mrtav i beo* [Živojin Pavlović, 1967]).

And again, as in the FRG and Austria, other (and especially the 'expanded') movies directed the focus of discussion away from the centres of the First World. Also here, the war in Vietnam in particular was often turned into a subject of public discussion. In *Eve of Destruction* (1966, Figure 26) by Naško Križnar, for instance, we as viewers are drawn into

Figure 26: *Eve of Destruction*, Naško Križnar, 1966 © Naško Križnar.

a process of painting anti-Vietnam War slogans, flowers and other drawings on Ljubljana city walls to the sounds of the eponymous song by Barry McGuire and are at the same time prompted to observe the surprised looks of passers-by, which are also featured in the film.

Another example is the film *Jutrišnje delo/The Morning Paper* (1967) by Jože Pogačnik from the kino club Ljubljana. Revolving around the story of a young boy selling the daily paper in the streets of Ljubljana, this film shows a jarring montage of TV footage and newspaper photographs about the war in Vietnam, US pop and folk songs, advertisements for various consumer goods or sequences from local news portraying official public life. In several scenes *WR: Misterije organizma* (1971) by Dušan Makavejev mocks the 'joy of soldiering' that left the theatre of war in Vietnam behind and entered everyday urban life in the United States.

In socialist Yugoslavia there was a broad gap between the ordained discourse of public power and the experience that people had of their situations. This also implied that an experience of authenticity and incontestability lingered in large parts outside the official stories provided by the socialist regime (van de Port 1998: 48; 2004). Besides, there were competing and often contradictory stories from the outside about the 'Balkans' or the fate of self-managed socialism, which, however, could not be easily adopted by 'real existing' Yugoslavs either – because in terms of emotional resonance these stories had little to offer, or because any appearance of alternative stories about past, present and future inside Yugoslavia was so closely controlled.

In this situation, films of novi film-makers offered figures and opened an imaginary space in which contact could be made with an experience that was not officially accounted for. These figures not only allowed for but were constituted by particularity, difference and an experience of authenticity and incontestability. Alongside such figures, the cinema-goer could expose him- or herself to elements of what officially was marginalized, forbidden or taboo and could again access an incontestable 'truth' and a particularity of experience constantly denied by the exposure to an official language that veiled most differences through repetitive talk about equality, brotherhood and unity or the classless society linked to visions of linear progress.

This means that with '1968' new projection and mirror figures appeared in both multiparty capitalist and in one-party socialist societies in the shape of those who were excluded, marginalized, oppressed or downplayed by the narrations offered by official or mainstream culture. By adopting inputs from a variety of countries on both sides of the Iron Curtain, by focusing on outsiders and marginalized groups in their own environments and by relating to struggles like those against the Vietnam War or the anti-imperialist battles in Latin America, these cinema-makers and film activists, like other 1968 movements, participated in the fabrication of a new transnationally disseminated frame of reference, which displaced the previous east-west polarity by one in which differences were multiplied, and thus a North-South opposition emerged (Klimke 2010).

These novel everybodies featured in films and accompanying visual materials allowed for viewing events towards the other and that which was excluded from legitimate culture. In this way they made current asymmetries and repressions evident despite the flaring up of official emancipation or modernization rhetoric and so triggered further negotiation, stirred up adoptions, research or even political action. But at the same time these figures also allowed for a new fixation of the other as the 'other'. As such, these outcasts and marginal figures could be 'swallowed' by the perceiver to reflect about him- or herself in a novel way and discover other 'authentic' features of this new self.[79] Or their otherness could be amplified, coloured and romanticized in order to bring the contours of a 'self' more pronouncedly to the fore – something that leads to a ghettoization of the other and allows for ample re-invention of the national, the folkloric and the ethnic.

These everybodies in the shape of the marginal or the repressed are thus in a particular way linked to ambivalence – an ambivalence the spectator is now requested to resolve as part of his or her viewing activity. In this way the cinema works as an agent of 'privatization' and 'internalization' of ambivalence and uses difference in order to re-position the self. At the same time it also opens possibilities for renegotiating this by creating a public sphere together not only with friends and locals but also with strangers and passers-by.

Difference and the (informal) public sphere

Cinema activism around 1968 goes beyond the classical cinema setting, as some of the legendary Expanded Cinema happenings of this period such as *Movie Movie* by Jeffrey Shaw (1967), *Tapp- and Tastkino* by Valie Export (1968–1971) or the filmed wall-painting event *Eve of Destruction* by Naško Križnar (1966) described above demonstrate. At the same time, this activism re-invents cinema and so also reaffirms the role of cinema as a stage for setting agendas and for challenging the status quo. Thus old cinema boxes were sometimes conserved in an only slightly brushed-up way such as in the case of the Freies Kino in Vienna – and a lot of other newly emerging art-house cinemas which also co-exhibit the nostalgic charm of past cinema cultures. At other times, however, the central elements of the cinema setting are re-assembled in always new combinations in exhibition halls, museums, metro stations or people's universities.

This perseverance of the cinema setting as a spatial frame for gathering in the city has to do with the particular socializing force and the qualities it holds for constructing a public sphere. As already described, these qualities include, for example, the darkness of the space which opens the imagination and the mutual closeness of the bodies of strangers assembled in it; the relaxed deportment of the spectators vis-à-vis images blown up on the enormous screen; the mingling of bodies and the potential to be challenged and carried away by some of the images flashing-up; the standardization, adaptability and low-cost of edificial construction in combination with the potential of reaching a big group of people.

The desire to make films or to organize a particular cinema situation often emerged in response to viewing events that made a difference – usually occurring in already established cinema settings. For instance, Wilhelm Hein from the xscreen group in Cologne describes it thus: 'We were at the universities [...] at that time part of the film club scene [...] and they played the Mexico film by Buñuel and that was the first time that I got off my seat and said, "That can't be true! Such an incredible film" [...] that was completely trivial but had incredible vitality and emotional force' (I WH). Rainer Werner Fassbinder remembers having seen one of Godard's earlier films, *Vivre sa Vie /It's My Life* (1962), 27 times, while explaining that Godard's films after he had made *Bande à part/Band of Outsiders* (1964) no longer interested him (Wiegand 2004 [1974]: 278). In relation to the former he summarizes: 'This along with *Viridiana* [Luis Buñuel, 1961] was one of the two most important films to me.' And Dušan Makavejev (in Cowie 2004: 104) recalls the perseverance that such experiences could have: 'I liked the dancing camera in Claude Chabrol's *A Double Tour*. To me he was probably more important than anyone else in the early days. Some of the images from *Les bonnes femmes* have stayed with me for forty years.'

This indicates that some films, but also some scenes or a particular image could enter into significant relations with the viewers, hold and nourish their attention and trigger a renegotiation of sense. In such statements the cinema again appears as a transition space: by way of certain kinds of film experience, the perception of the world could strongly be affected and could kick off the beginning of something new. And sometimes it was literature, music, the visual arts or the city and the everyday environment itself, which, besides films made by others, opened the imagination and triggered the 'transformation' of a spectator into a film-maker or cinema-organizer.

Those affected then tried to 'transfer' or 'translate' (Schober 2004: 122f.) the significant force experienced into the most diverse kinds of activity that in themselves stated a difference: film-making, writing about films, organizing festivals and public discussions or creating new and different cinema situations. These perceptions, deeds, provocations, stimuli and films as well as artworks and the newspaper coverage and discussions they triggered constituted a plural and conflict-ridden public sphere where diverse groups and individuals made themselves and their projects visible and audible for each other, but where they also contested reigning allocations or ways of looking at the world and were struggling for hegemony in the symbolic realm.

The public, political sphere that was created in this way was closely bound to these various forms of appearance of difference – an appearance of difference that could happen at the levels of perception, of explicitly expressed judgement, of aesthetics, of provoking and challenging the reigning visual regime, of featuring novel everybodies or of inhabiting the cinema setting. And it was exactly this dimension of producing difference, of provoking unexpected activities, of challenging the reigning visual regime and of offering fragments for producing alternative worlds in stories that caused certain kinds of cinema activities to produce conflicts and triggered a public renegotiation of things – something that was problematic in different ways in multiparty and one-party societies.

In West Germany and Austria the *mise-en-scène* of difference played a constitutive role in the formation of the various cinema-activist groups around 1968; usually groups called themselves into existence or individual actors tried to gain position by distancing themselves more or less explicitly from other forms of cinema or film-making – for example, from productions featured by fellow cineasts, even if they might have had only slightly different ways of working, from *Heimatfilms* or Hollywood movies, from TV productions and the conventional cinema settings. The Expanded Cinema activists in particular presented their work as oppositional and as interventions that challenged and attacked what they called 'instruments of domination that bind the individuals to the values, goals, norms of the state' (m. t., Weibel 1973: 62).

In this process, the city and its surface seem to have been particularly important for opening and nourishing the imagination and for triggering unusual forms of inhabiting it. In 1969, for instance, with the action *Notstandsbordstein* (Emergency Curbstone), Wolf Vostell realized a 'street film' in Munich that referred to the heated discussion about a new law accepted by the Bundestag (lower house of the West German parliament) on 30 May 1968, which envisaged a *Notstandsverfassung* (emergency constitution). This law was formulated in a way that gave government bodies the ability to take exceptional measures in order to prevent an interior or exterior state of emergency and, in the midst of the student protests of 1968, was seen by several fractions of the protesting students and trade unions as an attack on the democratic foundations of the state.[80] With this street film, Vostell extended the practice of *dè-coll/age*, which he also used otherwise for artistic creation, to rearrange the interplay of city and cinema. From a moving car he projected a 16-mm film loop featuring just the notion *Notstandsbordstein* onto house walls, billboards, parked cars and passers-by. By moving the projector and creating new 'collages' composed of the film and the urban surroundings, he reverses the screening situation usually used in the cinema. He employed the notion of *Notstandsbordstein*, which indicates such diverse phenomena as 'exceptional circumstances', 'danger', 'crisis', 'designation' and 'delineation', as a kind of commentary on the recent discussion. Simultaneously, and in quite a crude way, he directed the gaze of the viewers to the city environment as a contested area where both state control as well as public, political action are potentially able to take place.

In the 1960s and 1970s the Austrian experimental filmmaker Kurt Kren also made several short films – for instance, *4/61 Mauern pos.-neg. und Weg/4/61 Walls pos.-neg. and Path* (1961) or *33/77 Keine Donau/33/77 No Danube* (1977) – for which he used 'found' elements and locations of the city such as crumbling walls in a park or a backyard in Vienna. He took photographs, filmed them (*4/61 Mauern pos.-neg. und Weg*) or exposed the same piece of film and same frame to light multiple times (*33/77 Keine Donau*) – creating layers of possible time relations (Palm 1996). In another short film, *30/73 Coop Cinema Amsterdam* (1973), he filmed the projection room of a collectively set-up cinema of the same name over the course of three weeks in individual shots and temporal shots. The scenery was modulated through various kinds of activity on the part of the audience (meeting, talking, milling around, sleeping) but also through daylight entering through an open door or darkness when the lights were turned down. In all these films the images appear in multiple veils lying on top of each other or side by side and must be seen several times in order to grasp their interventionist nature into the field of visibility and how it is structured by our everyday movements. Once this happens, however, they guide our gaze towards an assessment and an inquiry concerning the ways images are linked to how we perceive the world and how both images and perception can be used for various types of intervention.

Besides these pronouncedly experimental works, film-makers in a more narrow sense of the word, like Wim Wenders, who used to distance himself strongly from Expanded Cinema procedures, also began focusing on the city and its perception in order to position their work inside a broader field of debate. In *Silver City* (1969, Figure 27), for example, Wenders presented eight long shots strung together all taken from windows of sometimes different, sometimes unvarying apartments situated in the upper stories of high buildings. These shots depict streets and crossings from high above, very early in the morning in shades of a bluish light that is only broken by the traffic signals or late in the evening, so that one is able to observe the absence or increase of traffic. In this way he presents a contemplative appropriation of the city, which is underscored by the mood music that accompanies the whole film. Also in this case the music in combination with the long shots that continuously repeat similar views during the cycle of a day encourages us as viewers to look at ourselves

Figure 27: *Silver City,* Wim Wenders, 1969 © Wim Wenders, courtesy German Filminstitut, Frankfurt.

gazing on this and to acknowledge that there is no objective or absolute 'outsider' position from which to synthesize all views. It is through this refusal of a coherent, easy-to-grasp story and this challenging and redirecting of our attention to the processes of viewing and image-making on the one hand and the use of other media such as music on the other that lets us judge films like these as 'political'.

By contrast, another film made by Wenders almost at the same time, *Polizeifilm/Police Film* (1968), makes the explicit oppositional position Wenders took up against the ruling powers more immediately graspable. This film consists of shots observing the Munich police and their tactics of dealing with the student situation in 1968. This gives the film its pronounced political character since it also places the public in a position of observing these practices of controlling public space and encourages them to take a position towards it.

These various ways of stating a political difference by way of inhabiting the city and making our gazing an issue were joined by the set-up of urban meeting places exclusively dedicated to the screening of 'political' films. Besides, the public sphere involving film and cinema created in the course of the 1960s and the early 1970s was also constituted by the already mentioned conflicts and scandals in these places – such as the dispute around the showing of films from behind the iron curtain at the festival in Oberhausen or the conflicts around the anti-Vietnam film *O.K.* by Michael Verhoeven at the Berlinale in 1970. These conflicts and scandals created pronounced public visibility of the political dimension of cinema and film – which in turn led to a reorganization and transformation of the film scene, to a further differentiation of cinema worlds and to the institutionalization of new cinema initiatives such as thematic film festivals or the programme cinema.

Similar to what happened in the course of the incorporation of film and cinema into official strategies, attempts were also made on the side of the 'alternative' cinema scene to create new kinds of orders and to direct the perception of the viewers through speeches, addresses, information folders, banners and flags as well as guided discussions.[81] Simultaneously a new interest in the discussion of the public function of cinema started to disseminate. Most prominently this discussion was triggered by the film-making and writing activities of Alexander Kluge who, for example, coined the notion of the cinema as an 'alternative public sphere' or 'counter-public' (Negt and Kluge 1972)[82] – something which, however, again establishes an kind of clear and unambiguous distinction between 'we' (counter-cultural) and 'them' (mainstream) groups. But at the same time there were also always other positions and different films and ways of urban dwelling present in cities such as Munich, Cologne, Vienna or Berlin that held the potential of causing encounters with the strange and unfamiliar. It was not mainly the will to politicize but the co-presence, multiplicity and struggle of such positions and unexpected events that constituted the public political sphere.

As in the FRG and Austria, cinema activists in Yugoslavia also staged a difference by representing a view on their urban environment that diverged from the city depicted in the officially sanctioned world in stories. In this respect, films produced in the surroundings of the kino club Beograd are especially significant. For instance *Lice/The Face* (1962, Figure 28), a short film made by Ivan Martinac[83] combined shots showing a gazing out of a window that captures prefabricated slab constructions so typical of socialist countries in the 1960s as well as a Belgrade square with close-ups of strange, clownish, ugly, inexpressive, mirrored or long-nosed masks of faces made during a makeup course taught by a makeup artist. Serving as a surrogate audience of the film, a man and a women in the film are shown looking at these faces, city surfaces or objects randomly lying around, and the misunderstanding between these two spectators 'in the picture' that already emerges at the beginning of the film is not resolved but rather increased by this use of masks, things and spaces. In this way, the city, as well as the self as 'other', appear as objects of an alienated gazing that is shown as dominating everyday life.

In a similar way *Grad/The City* (1963, Živojin Pavlović, Marko Babac, Kokan Rakonjac), the first film that, as already mentioned, entered into explicit conflict with state-socialist authorities and was brought before court (I MB), opens with a long sequence that also depicts aimless strolling though the city and the playful roaming of the gaze through reflections in big shop windows or through lace curtains which allow a glimpse into the interiors of bars and cafés. This depiction of an individual delivery of the self to the superficial allures of the city can again be read as a representation of an alienated state of mind – whereby the 'decomposition' of self and environment was underscored by the free jazz music that accompanied these sequences. This potential of being perceived as 'alienated' was also the main reason why the authorities regarded these films as 'black' and 'dangerous' – even if, as in the case of *Grad*, this happened after it had first won an award.

Besides alienation, other features of urban life or certain living areas that were officially threatened as 'outmoded' and 'obsolete' (because they are seen as part of 'bourgeois' or 'primitive' society) were also depicted in films by novi film-makers. *Buđenje pacova/The*

Figure 28: *Lice/The Face,* Ivan Martinac, 1962 © Ivan Martinac, courtesy Jugoslovenska Kinoteka, Belgrade.

Rats Woke Up (1967) by Živojin Pavlović, for instance, showed Belgrade as being a place full of deep, wet mud into which one was constantly in danger of sinking (Figure 29). And *Skupljači perja/I Even Met Happy Gypsies* (Aleksandar Petrović, 1967) represents housing areas on the outskirts of Belgrade where – among other places – members of a Roma community live and make their living begging and singing in the streets of the city centre, collecting garbage and engaging in prostitution.

At other times, films asserted a difference by showing evidence directed against the actual means the regime used in order to control the public sphere. Naško Križnar, for instance, recalls such an occurrence as follows: 'There was a big political struggle against a magazine, a cultural magazine called *Perspektive*. […] At that time [1964, A. S.] this magazine was [banned] discontinued. In this first film [by myself] we see [the actor] Marko Pogačnik running along the streets when this magazine falls out of his pocket, it was precisely this magazine. We were all very worried about this situation. […] This was perhaps, as I can remember, the only explicit political involvement, after that I never

Figure 29: *Buđenje pacova/The Rats Woke Up,* Živojin Pavlović, 1967 © Courtesy Jugoslovenska Kinoteka, Belgrade.

thought of myself as politically involved through my activities. [...] Though [today] looking back I think that [...] perhaps our public activities opened a political space, little by little' (I NK).

The 'difference' of these novi film or OHO productions was underscored by their aesthetic appearance. Contrary to what was shown on TV or to the new indigenous light entertainment productions characterized not only by conventional thematic perspectives but also by naturalistic aesthetic styles, closed narrative structures and happy endings these films featured an enhanced montage technique using sometimes quite disparate images, handheld cameras, parody and satirical commentary, complex and sometimes dissolving narrative structures, and they were usually shot in everyday urban locations using non-professional actors and 'found' stories.

In former Yugoslavia the motivations for producing such pronounced and in multiple ways 'different' representations could be quite diverse. Dušan Makavejev, for instance, points out that he as a film activist 'fought for differences in order to make the party be truer to what their programme claimed' (I DM). Others, in contrast, were more concerned about developing an essayistic, existentialist style in order to oppose totalitarianism on the aesthetic level (I MB). And again others, such as Naško Križnar and the OHO community, were more concerned with integrating art and life and thus realizing alternative lifestyles beyond what they saw as consumer and mass society.[84]

The double-edged character that films made by novi film authors or experimental film-makers conveyed to party officials consisted of the fact that for the latter self-representation and the representation of a greater whole merged in these films, that is, representation appeared on the one hand as clearly authorized through individual fabrication and an original style but on the other hand it still remained related to the allusions of being made in accordance with the state and the party that authorized it. Some film activists such as Dušan Makavejev or Želimir Žilnik supported such a view by defending their productions publicly and by demonstrating that the films they made were, even if a bit unusual, still representations in accordance with Marxist ideology and its realization in Yugoslav state socialism (I DM and I ZZ). Others, such as Marko Babac or Naško Križnar, at least had to abstain from explicitly questioning this.

This merging, however, made it quite difficult and arbitrary as to where to draw the line between the legitimate representations of the 'people as one' and the illegitimate deviations from it. At the same time the representing subject could be seen as simultaneously being an accomplice of state power and its antipode – which tended to enforce the role of the official authorities, since they were the ones who decided and controlled the boundaries between the legitimate and the illegitimate. At the same time, however, this displaced struggle and conflict into the inner worlds of the artists (and film viewers).

In spite of this, and by representing on several levels what in the reigning regime of visibility was excluded, banned, neglected, played down or ignored, these productions allowed for a flashing-up of difference – often, as already mentioned, linked to an experience of authenticity and truth. However, this potential of cinema to provide a touching experience of difference and to potentially involve viewers in creating alternative worlds in stories was regarded by Titoism as being problematic and threatening in a particular way.

One-party systems are, as described, concerned with suppressing the emergence of non-authorized difference and precluding political struggle. In former Yugoslavia, since 1950, a self-management system had been adopted that strengthened initiative and collective action – for instance, in the form of the workers' council. Simultaneously, however, the party was very careful not to let such action and initiatives accumulate into political opposition. This way, the identification between power and the 'people as one', between this people and the party, between party and leadership and between leadership and the body of the egocrat Tito which, as Claude Lefort had shown, was very typical for totalitarian states tended also in this context to eliminate any form of difference that did not overlap with the officially established division between the people and its enemies (Lefort 1986: 299f.). All that could create a vivid public, political sphere (Arendt 1958; Rancière 1999) was suppressed or at least closely controlled – that is, any emergence of a plurality of distinguishable positions that made themselves visible and audible for others, challenged each other or fraternized in an unpredictable, contingent way were closely mirrored, and diverging political positions tended to be pushed underground. Nonetheless, for a certain time span the above-described activities of novi film-makers or of groups such as OHO triggered an appearance of difference and a renegotiation of sense and caused a series of events linked to film and cinema that to some extent created a visibility of diverging positions and a challenging of the status quo.

This public and political dimension of their activities is remembered vividly by some of the members of the kino club Beograd. Marko Babac for instance recalls that, after they had delivered the first non-conventional own production and some collectively made films like *Grad* (1963) had gained public attention but were also being attacked and put 'into the bunker', the regime started 'to see our clubs with completely new eyes. They [party officials, A. S.] said: "We wanted them to be separated from their families, but then they constructed a family we didn't want"' (I MB). As he explains in more detail: 'When we started making films we organized meetings and little festivals, and journalists, the papers, started to write about us. It was now a public problem [...] an affirmation of some different kind of movie-making. It was something that had become public, it was completely different from official film production, which was very conservative and very administrative' (I MB).

This public sphere, however, was not so much constituted by explicitly articulated political positions but rather by ways of inhabiting the cinema setting and of making and viewing films, that is, by a representation of a series of phenomena, experiences and perceptions that were excluded, downplayed or ignored by the official representations and by a challenging of how things and the common world are seen, spoken about and dwelled on. The representation of other everybodies such as villagers, homeless people or non-conformist youth could, as already pointed out, exhibit difference just as much as the filmic representation of a banned magazine, a depiction of city spaces covered with mud or composed of Roma dwelling sites or a montage of light-impressions reflected on a city café on a sunny day accompanied by jazz music (as in the case of the film *Život je lijep/Life is beautiful* by Ivan Martinac [1966]).

These expositions of difference and the further public and plural negotiation they were able to stimulate call into question the strict distinction advocated by Claude Leford between democratic and totalitarian societies (Garcelon 1997).[85] Since, however, an open contest of diverging positions and an explicitly articulated opposition towards the ruling power remained impossible, this particular public sphere emerging in Yugoslavia in the course of the 1960s and early 1970s can be called an 'informal public sphere.'[86]

The cinema setting was particularly suited to be involved in the constitution of such an informal public sphere since it functioned as a space that was occupied by intimate sensations – by feelings, memories and inner pictures evoked by film – but also by experiences of being anchored in the city and by the possibility of accessing a mass public and for involving it into processes of stating and exploring the sense of being. In summary, the cinema functioned as a space where the public was able to retreat from the world and, simultaneously, out of which a struggle to make sense of this world could be initiated. The public sphere thus created, which involved cinema and film, can be called 'very private', that is, it is a sphere for which the dichotomy of public-private is not really fitting. In cinema, privacy and intimate feelings are involved in a special way, but it has, at the same time, the potential to intervene into the realm of perception and to represent the common world, thus it becomes involved in the construction of a politically relevant sphere.

This double-edgedness of being simultaneously private and public, a shelter and an action space, is also repeatedly mentioned by cinema activists from both former Yugoslavia and Austria or West Germany. This becomes graspable when Marko Babac describes his motivation for joining the kino club, saying, as already quoted, '[T]his connection with the dark room with moving pictures helped me run into another reality, not a world of lies such as in reality, but of lies of dreams' (I MB). And when he says that he went to the kino club in order to meet his friends he depicts the cinema as a place for being with others – for discussions, screenings and parties and as a space where one could learn how to make films by producing them. A similar narration is conveyed by cinema activists from West Germany. The film-maker Wilhelm Hein, for instance, retrospectively recalls the search for a place of refuge which at the same time could function as a laboratory: 'It was as if we were in a vacuum. In Germany we were the only ones making such films. Given that, you're helpless and you have to find a place. First you find such a place in literature, then in the past and then it started with England;[87] we went there and located ourselves culturally, but that was not the starting point' (I WH).

The role of the cinema as a space for public intervention was thereby often strongly promoted by cinema activists and sometimes even made into a programme. The Expanded Cinema activist Peter Weibel, for instance, declared 'action' as the central means of a new art practice and presented it as a 'world art and an independent genre […] able to claim it could repatriate art from the alienated and false circulation spheres (from the studio directly into the museum) to its roots, namely life and people, hence it may claim it has a direct influence on the vital needs of the population, on human reality, on politics' (m. t. Weibel 1972: 50). This quotation however also shows that the spectre of a 'new' but unitary world involving a notion of 'the people' and linked to a desire for revolution and for a 'good society' is not only a characteristic of one-party societies but continues to haunt the pluralist democratic ones too (Lefort 1986: 272). And even if, as already pointed out, in the case of cinema activism emerging in pluralist democratic political settings in the 1960s, a narcissism of small differences prevailed and there was more emphasis on cinema as a space for explicit political positioning and agenda-setting, here again film-makers such as Wim Wenders, Rainer Werner Fassbinder and Kurt Kren were also concerned about intervening into the inner worlds of the public, provoking and challenging their perceptions and making their desires and emotional relationships an issue.

The simultaneous private and public dimension of cinema was brought to the fore in particular by the activities of Yugoslav film-makers since they used to operate – especially in the early 1960s – with rather restrained actions that seem at first almost inconspicuous because they concentrate on the mis-en-scène of love, alienation, sexuality and loneliness and relate film-making and film viewing to the consumption of jazz music. Nevertheless they created representations that entered into conflict with party bureaucracy since they exhibited differences that were seen officially as 'decadent' and bound to a society the new socialist world claimed to have left behind. In parallel, film-makers transferred their struggle with the ruling elite mainly to the level of style. Marko Babac recalls: 'I learned a very useful lesson from this totalitarian cinema, from NS Germany and communist Soviet Union. It is [about the] fight for artistic freedom, to be free in creation. How to be free? With language, with style, with film design, a specific artistic style – for example, Leni Riefenstahl or Sergei Eisenstein' (I MB).

The differences in how the cinema is experienced as a private-public space in the FRG, Austria and former Yugoslavia also have to do with the fact that the meaning and handling of 'private' and 'public' was not the same in multiparty capitalist and one-party socialist societies – and the meaning of 'private' was renegotiated strongly in both types of societies in the 1960s. In pluralist democratic and capitalist societies, the notion of 'private' is usually associated not only with the spheres of families and intimate relations but also with private markets and individual economic initiatives.

In the late 1960s several of these meaning clusters were seriously questioned by the student movement, and emerging feminism, which stated that 'the private is political', made sexuality and the body a highly discussed issue,[88] challenged the 'nuclear family' and often struggled simultaneously for a collective grassroots democratic control of production and distribution and for communality in general. In parallel, the welfare states extended their area of influence and management far into the 'private' realm of family, sexuality, health, childcare or the body and in doing so, subjected these areas to new regulations and attempts to create order too. In this way several formerly private and intimate areas of life have become politicized and opened up to discourse by state attempts to manage them – something to which various collective grassroots agents are now also responding, stating divergent political positions. Simultaneously, however, as shown above, cinema enthusiasm in the 1960s contributed to a further 'privatization' since it affirmed the individual as an acting and problem-resolving entity – which means that the privatization of the public sphere as well as the politicization of formerly private matters were further points in which actions from various sides coincided.

In state-socialist societies such as Tito's, by contrast, the private sector and privacy were regarded by the authorities with general suspicion and were subjected to repression, increased control and even destruction. The regimes tried to push back the influence of the churches and of families and clans in general, especially in the field of education (Pomian 1990). They transferred private estates to state property and in official discourse 'love' became, as already mentioned, closely bound to 'the people', 'the party' and the egocrat himself (Garcelon 1997: 311). It was precisely because of this general suspicion hanging over anything 'private' that the importance given to love, sexuality, intimacy and sensuality by some novi film-makers had such a politically explosive force. And vice versa, the enormous importance that the regime invested in everything public and the over-visibility of the party and its leader, Tito, made the 'private-public' space of the cinema very attractive to young people searching for meaning. But simultaneously in this context too, the cinema setting contributed to a burdening the self with the obligation to handle problems that could not be solved or even addressed publicly. This led to a further widening of the gap between the official world in stories and the meaning that 'real existing' inhabitants gave to their situation as well as to a 'privatization' of conflicts and of how to negotiate difference and ambivalence.

In the 1960s the public sphere on both sides of the divide between multiparty-democratic and one-party communist societies was not only in an enhanced way private, but was in addition strongly bound to urban settings that were conventionally seen as 'cultural' rather than 'political'. Hence the various activities of film-makers, artists, cinema organizers, spectators, members of the crew of film festivals, but also of editors, film critics or journalists converged in shifting 'culture' toward the centre of society, to a place which had previously been occupied by 'the social'. Furthermore, the (informal) public sphere emerging around these cultural spaces is characterized by the mingling of entertainment and political engagement, a focus on the aesthetic level and the individual psychic involvement and self-reflection processes that gave rise to rapidly changing and often overlapping communities (Featherstone 1995: 15f.; Reimer and Gibbins 1999: 76f.). The arenas of politics in a more narrow sense, such as traditional political parties or the parliament, looked rather old-fashioned by comparison and in the long run were only perceived and dealt with if they somehow fitted in with the measures established by these cultural pressure groups.

Moreover in film productions and various kind of 'alternative' cinema programming, new projection and mirror figures appeared in the shape of bodies that were marginalized, oppressed or downplayed by official representations – be it the villager, the Gypsy, the prostitute, the homosexual, the 'Black power' activist, the migrant 'guest worker' or the Third-World inhabitant. By bringing these bodies and the new aesthetic languages connected with them into the foreground, cinema movements of the 1960s managed to break away from the rigid geopolitical division of the Cold War and participated in the constitution of a public sphere in which instead a North-South dualism started to emerge and the staging of differences multiplied.

In this way cinema-makers in both multiparty and one-party societies of the 1960s sustainably contributed to transforming the conditions and main characteristics of what being a public sphere means. Nevertheless, a few years later – at the end of the 1960s, beginning of the 1970s – a process of back-peddling concerning the political role of cinema and film could be witnessed in both former Yugoslavia and central European countries such as the FRG and Austria, even if this was motivated by different circumstances and events.

In Yugoslavia, the long year of 1968, as already mentioned, marked a change in how the regime viewed and dealt with the non-conformist activities of film enthusiasts. Even if Marko Babac recalls discovering upon hearing about the events in Paris in 1968 that he was 'part of one global kind of thinking, of [one] will', (I MB) others retrospectively have a stronger recollection of the restrictive measures that followed these events. Naško Križnar, for instance, describes that in 1968 the occupation of Czechoslovakia was emotionally much more important to him than what happened in the United States or in Paris. He says: 'The occupation of Czechoslovakia made us aware that it was a real danger to live in a communist country. But at that time in Yugoslavia there was [still A. S.] a kind of liberation. […] Later on in the early 1970s we suddenly realized that the situation was changing and that these political forces of communism were becoming stronger and stronger again. There was stronger pressure. It was evident in the 1970s' (I NK). After the events in Czechoslovakia, the difference film-makers and journalists used to articulate was seen by official bureaucracy as a threat to the unity of the 'people as one'. Consequently, these activities were stigmatized as 'distorting' Yugoslav reality and as deriving from 'old' and 'barbaric' or 'foreign' and potentially 'threatening' influences (Jovičić 1969: 22f.).

An incident in 1969 can be read as indicating two tendencies that at this point started to take on momentum: after the Pula film festival in 1969 the film critic Slobodan Novaković started a discussion in the well-known journal *Filmska Kultura* about national film languages and different aesthetic traditions in various regions of former Yugoslavia (Novaković 1969). He was immediately stopped by the party from discussing the topic and was even asked to publicly recant the theses he had developed on this subject (I DD). On the one hand, this shows that any emergence and negotiation of difference was now subjected to stronger control. On the other hand, however, it also demonstrates that difference started to be articulated more explicitly in regional and even national terms. A few years later, non-conformist cinema networks were, as already described, broken up by 'eliminating' key figures such as Želimir Žilnik, Dušan Makavejev or Lazar Stojanović and by prohibiting the remaining ones from pursuing exactly the transnational cooperation that had been nourishing them. Contrary to the intentions of the regime, however, this also opened the path to a re-invention of new stories accommodating difference, authenticity and incontestability – experiences that now increasingly became linked to pronounced national and ethnically 'pure' fantasies concerning the self and the other. In this process in the 1990s the Crni Talas was also sometimes defined in national univocal ways, that is, the movement was 'Serbianized' especially by some protagonists of film institutions and younger critics.[89]

Both in Austria and West Germany '1968' was linked to the above-described transformations of political arenas and in particular to a strong transnationalization of political culture as well as to a strengthening of democratic forces. Nevertheless, the student movement also triggered quite distinct long-term effects in both countries. In Austria, politicization processes of the youth encountered more rigid structures in the form of a frozen system of established parties and federations. Here a new linkage of politicization, youth and cinema first emerged within these structures as the Freies Kino and its connection to the youth organization of the Social Democratic Party shows. But the initiatives of students, artists and young cinema enthusiasts in this context, too, managed to go beyond these structures by widening the gap between parties and political mobilization, the youth in particular, and by bringing to the fore cultural arenas such as cinemas, but also concert halls, urban art happenings and theatres. At the same time, the Social Democratic Party in Austria was able to use and integrate issues and actions brought forward by the student movement to gain an extraordinary long-lasting political hegemony that would not be called into question nor start to decline until the 1970s to the 1980s (Pelinka 1993).

In the FRG in 1969 a social-liberal model first emerged under Chancellor Willy Brandt. It was characterized by a new approach to Eastern European countries under the label of *Neue Ostpolitik* (new politics towards the east) but also by the more visible activities of the Außerparlamentarische Opposition (APO, extra-parliamentary opposition), left-wing terrorism and a drastic economic crisis. By 1974 this led to a conservative turn that manifested itself in restrictions of civil rights (for instance, the occupational ban on political activists) and an extension of the powers of the executive branch (Elsaesser 2001: 31f.).

In parallel an *Anwerbestop* (recruitment ban) for foreign workers in 1973 in the FRG and in 1974 in Austria fuelled public discussion on migrants 'as a problem' (Friedrichs 2010), but it also prompted initial efforts for creating public and also filmic visibility and for re-narrating the world in stories from the margins (Götürk 2000). Tensions and conflicts in terms of difference started to increase in connection with the activities of the women's movement and the initiatives of making sexual difference a public issue. Since the 1980s this converged not only in nodal points of discussion such as 'multiculturalism' and a 'new politics of difference' but was also restaged in various interventions into urban spaces – with several of them again being carried out in the form of film or new cinema set-ups. For instance, there were films by Turkish film-makers and ethnic film festivals, women's film series, and gay-film nights – public interventions that soon acquired a more permanent presence as niche cultures and neatly separated and existing side by side, they created a social space that was often defined as a 'multicultural' one. Nevertheless, in both former Yugoslavia and countries like Germany or Austria, the cinema setting – albeit today often in a rearranged form – still functions as an important arena for challenging the reigning regime of visibility and for regaining sense.

Notes

1 In 1933 the Reichsfilmkammer was created in order to control film and cinema. In 1934 a new law on film-making was established that enabled the exclusion of films that could be seen as questioning NS ideology and formulated the education guidelines for filmmaking as well as cinema programming in such a way that 'non-Aryans' were excluded (Naica-Loebell 1996).

2 In April 1934, the last cinema in Berlin, the 'Camera', in which, despite official warnings, 'unauthorized films' were shown, had to close (Naica-Loebell 1996: 182).

3 Press photographs, for instance, show usherettes hired by the company Pez distributing goodies to children in Viennese cinemas in the 1960s.

4 In British cinemas, for instance, the national anthem was played at the end of every screening. On this, see http://www.britmovie.co.uk/forums/british-films-chat/94046-playing-national-anthem-cinema-shows.html (4 June 2009).

5 Austria and the FRG are characterized by similarity but also some divergent political developments after 1945. Since the focus of this part of the book is on the transnationality of cinema movements and a comparison between how they constituted themselves in pluralist democratic and one-party societies in several places, Austria and the FRG will be sometimes named linked up to each other – but this should not eliminate distinctions between cinema culture in both countries and of their distinct political, sociological and economic contexts. On similarities and differences between German and Austrian developments, see in particular the essays by Manfred Prisching, Günter Bischof and Hans-Jürgen Schröder, and Anton Pelinka in Böhler and Gehler 2007.

6 For Claude Lefort modern democracies arising from the revolutions of the eighteenth and nineteenth centuries are characterized by the fact that power is on the one hand linked to the people, but on the other hand it remains an empty place that is occupied only temporarily, whereby the ones elected to occupy this place for a certain time span depend on others who can also re-elect different ones. Totalitarianism picks up on the foundation of power in the people but tries to eliminate any unpredictability, temporariness and insecurity linked to the democratic process by fusing power with the 'people as one' and by excluding any division between state and civil society and inside society itself (Lefort 1986: 297 and 301).

7 The implementation of self-management was aimed at decentralization and a gradual withering away of the state and installed worker's councils as basic economic units and local governmental bodies of the commune as central political units. Nevertheless, the commune remained a central party organ through which the Central Committee of the Communist Party could exercise control. Harold Lydall on the processes of forming a new elite, which happened immediately, stated: 'The local party members, who control the communes, soon tended to identify themselves with the managers running the local enterprises', something, which 'gave rise to what the Yugoslavs call "localism", or "particularism"' (Lydall 1984: 71f.).

8 The notion of 'egocrat' was coined by the Soviet writer and dissident Aleksandr Isayevich Solzhenitsyn (Lefort 1986: 287).

9 These deeds question the 'passivity' Richard Sennett (2003: 125) postulates in respect to the dominant behaviour of 'spectators' in public spheres since the turn towards

Modernity – even if the research I will present at the same time also confirms the 'privatization' he is also addressing. An account of and investigation into 'expressive' behaviour in the public sphere (and an implicit critique of Sennett's views) can be found in Reimer and Gibbins (1999: 58 and 141f.).

10   These notions are used by various cinema initiatives to describe the 'bad others' they wanted to distance their own cinema creations from (Prinzler and Schwarz 1972: 16f. and 102f.).

11   This study collected self-descriptions of the various cinema initiatives emerging during the 1960s and early 1970s (Prinzler and Schwarz 1972).

12   Thomas Elsaesser pointed out that by the mid- to late 1970s, cinema attendance figures again started to rise and the press was proclaiming a new cinema-going boom. Besides the new cinema initiatives, the popularization of new film tendencies by TV was mainly responsible for this (Elsaesser 1989: 32f. and 36).

13   On this definition of aesthetic-political movements, see Greenberg 1979: 78f.

14   On the use of 'political movements' for new protest activities in areas usually seen as more 'social' or 'cultural' than 'political', see Crossley 2006: 19f. and Crossley 2007.

15   Wim Wenders and some of his former colleagues speak about film viewing and early film-making activities in Munich around 1968 in the documentary film by Marcel When, *Von einem der auszog – Wim Wenders' frühe Jahre* (2008).

16   This was also because several of the activists were banned from performing in public in Austria over longer periods. For more detail, see Schober 2009b: 253f.

17   In 1973 in other Austrian cities such as Linz and Graz, further critical film clubs were set up, orienting themselves to the Viennese model. See a note in the magazine *Kritischer Film*, 2, 1973: 5.

18   The magazine appeared between 1972 and 1975. It introduced the films but also disseminated general statements about the political role of film. In relation to the press coverage of the Freies Kino, Dieter Schrage recalls: 'We were treated very favourably by the Viennese press, especially by the Kronen Zeitung, but also by Kurier, AZ and others. We were covered by the press on a regular basis [...] soon there were also other spaces like the Filmmuseum, the film club Action and a film series at the Technical University. [...] But we were clearly the number one because we had our own magazine, we had daily screenings and we had a continuous PR work for our public' (I DS).

19   This was perhaps a strategic argumentation at that time or these modalities soon changed. In self-descriptions published only two years later, the Arsenal is said to have a staff of eleven people, all of them paid (at least part-time) (Prinzler and Seidler 1975: 39).

20   For instance, in the films *Zurigo* (1966), *Eve of Destruction* (1966) or *19. Živčni Zlom* (1966) all by Naško Križnar depicting other OHO members.

21   On this see, for instance, the documents and photographs reprinted in Habich (1985: 3ff.) and various statements in the documentary film by Marcel When, *Von einem der auszog – Wim Wenders' frühe Jahre* (2008).

22   Bojana Marijan-Makavejev, the wife of Dušan Makavejev, however, was part of the novi film scene. As a member of the kino club Beograd, she made one short film, *Vesela Klasa/The Cheerful Class* (1969) and later worked for the radio.

23 Milena Dravić, for instance, played leading roles in several films by Dušan Makavejev, Kokan Rakonjac, Puriša Đorđević, Boštjan Hladnik, etc.

24 Hans Scheugl describes Valie Export's activities before 1968 as those of a photo model, script girl, tapestry designer and girlfriend of Peter Weibel (Scheugl 2002: 40).

25 These declarations are reprinted in Prinzler and Rentschler (2001: 29f.). It was not until 1979 that a manifesto by 'women film workers' was made public as a feminist reaction to the *Hamburger Erklärung* published in the same year (Prinzler and Rentschler 2001: 32f.).

26 For instance, the *Kommunales Kino* in Frankfurt/Main (Prinzler and Seidler 1975: 90).

27 On the effects of the Oberhausen manifesto, the new subsidy system that was introduced afterwards and the 'cultural mode of production' encouraged by it, see Elsaesser 1989: 40f. and 154.

28 Important for this were major magazines, for example, *Der Spiegel*, as well as the local press; television too was very influential, since it showed special programmes on the Expanded Cinema movement.

29 Thomas Elsaesser (1989: 24 and 290f.) proposed 'Young German Film' for films made up to ten years after the Oberhausen manifesto was published, characterized by a revolt against commercial film industry and its main product – narrative film. He then uses 'New German Cinema' for slightly later productions by authors that openly acknowledged an influence by Hollywood and had a more optimistic view regarding the public such as the today classic films by Rainer Werner Fassbinder, Werner Herzog, Wim Wenders or Hans Jürgen Syberberg of the 1970s and 1980s.

30 In 1969 the magazine *Borba* published a supplement on the Crni Talas and articles on the movement regularly appeared in *Filmska Kultura*.

31 For example, by OHO (reprinted in Đurić and Šuvaković 2003: 553f.)

32 See the conversation of W+B Hein with colleagues in 1967 and 1968 (in Habich 1985: 3f.). The Viennese group called themselves the 'Austrian Filmmakers Cooperative' (1968) and referred to themselves as 'Expanded Cinema' (Hajek 1968: 3).

33 Auto-descriptions of the bad movies in Mannheim and the Notausgang in Berlin can be found in Prinzler and Schwarz (1972: 39 and 171).

34 NARA 80.4614/6-1351. Quoted in Kotek 1996: 201.

35 RFE (Radio Free Europe) Background Report, 15 July 1959, 'E' Distribution 170. Open Society Archives, Budapest, Box 95-2-174.

36 See the listings 'America House Library, Neuerwerbungen' and 'Bücher – Neuzugänge der Amerikahaus Bibliothek' between 1961 and 1970 in the ÖNB, Austrian National Library.

37 *The Western American Experimental Film, Experimentalfilmschau*, TU Wien, Programme. Austrian Film Museum Vienna, Documentation Department, Anthology archival material, Dossier: New American Cinema, file 2a (1963).

38 See Austrian Film Museum Vienna, Documentation Department, Anthology archival material, Dossier: New American Cinema, file 1 (1960).

39 See Austrian Film Museum Vienna, Documentation Department, Anthology archival material, Dossier: New American Cinema, file 1 (1963).

40 See To Pesaro & World Filmmakers, Austrian Film Museum Vienna, Documentation Department, Anthology archival material, Dossier: New American Cinema, file 1 (1966).

41 A detailed report and listing of these screenings can be found in *New York Film-makers' Newsletter*, vol. 1, no. 1 Nov. 1967. Austrian Film Museum Vienna, Documentation Department, Anthology archival material, Dossier: New American Cinema, file 1 (1967). See also Hein 1971: 72 and 122.

42 In an interview conducted in February 2008, Jonas Mekas stated that the Film-Makers' Cooperative survived because 'in the United States universities and colleges had introduced film classes. In 1960 there were only about fifteen universities and colleges with film departments, in 1970 there were 1,200 universities and colleges […] 22,000 film courses in the States. […] Students demanded also independently made films. So that helped the cooperative. But that did not happen in Europe' (I JM).

43 This system seems to be loosely oriented on the funding system used for establishing the Film Library and its circulation program in the Museum of Modern Art. The establishment of this Film Library in the 1930s was primarily financed by private foundations and had a strong international orientation too. In particular, the Humanities Division of the Rockefeller Foundation diverted 'funds away from universities and scholars considered unfriendly to present-day concerns and socially useful knowledge and towards more relevant and engaged projects […] New communications media such as radio, film, and the popular press were singled out as a crucial part of any such project' (on this in detail, see Wasson 2005: 141f.).

44 See Invitation To The Circle Of The Angles Of The New Cinema (1967). Austrian Film Museum Vienna, Documentation department, Anthology archival material, Dossier: New American Cinema, file 1 (1967).

45 To Pesaro & World Filmmakers. Austrian Film Museum Vienna, Documentation department, Anthology archival material, Dossier: New American Cinema, file 1 (1966).

46 This film showed a similar structuring principle to Peter Fonda's *Easy Rider* (1969) (Coury 2004: 127).

47 The interview was made in July 1971 during the Berlinale.

48 A description of the Leopold can be found in Prinzler and Schwarz (1972: 189f.).

49 These films are quoted in an interview with Makavejev in Cowie 2004: 104.

50 A few weeks before the Ljubljana Festival, the World Youth Festival was held in Sofia (Kraushaar 1998: 350).

51 This film was again shown publicly in ex-Yugoslavia only in 2007, after having been banned during Titoism but also during the various follow-up regimes. Since 2007 his films from the 1960s and 1970s had quite a strong and well-deserved late success especially among a very young audience – for this group these movies now have cult status. Lately, early films by Jovan Jovanović are often included in retrospectives of the Crni Talas – which shows that whoever is counted as being part of the Crni Talas is continuously being redefined. Whereas this inclusion might be justified to some extent in terms of style and subjects depicted – even if his films are much more 'anti-communist' in content than films by other film-makers usually regarded as being part of the Crni Talas – Jovan Jovanović strongly distances himself even today from the movement. He sees himself as a kind of 'victim' not only of the policies of the official Titoist regime but also of the close boy networks emerging around some of the kino clubs (I JJ). Besides his style, the content of his films and the enthusiasm of a younger generation for his productions, the main reason for including him in more recent research

on and in screenings of the Crni Talas is that he is seen as a 'Serb' – which is part of a much broader move to 'Serbianize' the movement since the 1990s.

52 The third edition of the 'EXPRMNTL' was held in 1963 at the casino in Knokke-le-Zoute (as well as the ones in 1967 and 1974) (Bardon 2002).

53 For instance, in Brussels 1958 the Austrian film-maker Peter Kubelka met US avant-garde colleagues such as Kenneth Anger, Stan Brakhage and Gregory Markopoulos, which marked his entrance into the circle of the soon-to-be founded New American Cinema group and the New York Film Makers' Cooperative (Kubelka in Jutz and Tscherkassky 1995: 35).

54 See the various reports on the festival in the journal *Film*, no. 2 (February) 1968.

55 The first feature film from the Soviet Union was shown at the Berlinale in 1974, and the first film from the German Democratic Republic in 1975 (Fehrenbach 1995: 326).

56 This, for example, is described by activists involved in the Bambi cinema in Cologne (Prinzler and Schwarz 1972: 140).

57 The Filmforum Duisburg, for example, made the 'experiment of screening films in the original language' an issue for discussion. Some films were shown in their original language and in synchronized form. Activists also expressed concerns that the use of the original language had the unwanted side effect of making the programme 'elitist' (Prinzler and Schwarz 1972: 92).

58 Thomas Elsaesser (1989: 44) mentions this in respect to the New German Cinema.

59 At the Yugoslav Amateur Film Festival in Ljublana in 1953, for example, Dušan Makavejev remembers having seen an early kino club film by Slovenian filmmaker Boštjan Hladnik, who in 1961 became internationally recognized with his film *Ples v dezju/Dance in the Rain* and started to act as a major figure in Yugoslav cinematography (I DM).

60 On the variety of these invitations, see the festival listings of artists such as Valie Export, Kurt Kren, Ernst Schmidt jr., or Peter Weibel (Lexikon zum Avantgardefilm. Österreich 1950 bis heute 1995; Elsaesser 1989: 301).

61 An example of the documentation of own initiatives is Prinzler and Schwarz (1972). See, for instance, also the bibliographies in Prinzler and Rentschler 2001: 515f. and Schlemmer 1993: 117f.

62 On such tradition-building processes of Expanded Cinema activists, see Schober 2009b: 253f.

63 On the relationship between the spread of TV and transformations in cinema-cultures in Yugoslavia, see Goulding 2002: 64ff.

64 In this way Alexander Kluge and his works became the 'bad other' of Expanded Cinema (I BH).

65 The programme of the cinema was later on extended beyond explicit politically engaged film and continued since 1981 in the Viennese communal cinema, the Stadtkino, which still exists today.

66 On the use of space by official authorities as well as grassroots groups or individuals in various state-socialist countries, see Crowley and Reid 2002.

67 Westerns were also shown and discussed at the leftist Freies Kino (free cinema) in Vienna in the early 1970s (I DS).

68　Later on it became publicly known that he was arrested not only because of making the film *Plastični Isus/Plastic Jesus* (1971) which was accused of 'antisocialist tendencies', but because he was serving in the army at the same time, and in connection to his film-making this was seen as a particular provocation (I ZZ).

69　On the history of the Student Cultural Centre Belgrade, see Veselinović 1996.

70　On such a reading of a history of perception oriented on the works of Walter Benjamin, see, for example, Hansen 1999; on the further transformation of (cinematic) spectatorship in the period of post-modernity, see Friedberg 1994: 109f.

71　This becomes particularly visible with the emergence of 'new media' in the 1960s, with which media lost their material specificity and could, for example, as digital media, be framed in various ways – which brings to the foreground the function of the body in selecting and producing images (Hansen 2006: 10f.).

72　For example, in the film *Ljubavni slučaj ili tragedija službenice P.T.T./Love Affair, or the Tragedy of the Switchboard Operator* (1967).

73　On this double-edged role cinema plays in the constitution of vernacular versions of modern regimes of perception, see Hansen 1999.

74　On this 'common man' and 'common woman' which at the same time are 'everybody' and 'nobody', see de Certeau 2002: 2f; cf. Schober 2001: 233ff.

75　See the various editions of the magazine *Kritischer Film*, 1972–1975.

76　In this respect, cinema activists are again linked to other 1968 movements: for example, the Black Panther solidarity movement but also to the in the early 1970s in the BRD strengthening terrorist fractions such as the RAF (*Rote Armee Fraktion*, Red Army Fraction) and *Bewegung 2. Juli* (2nd July Movement) which related to Black Panther activism, adopted theories coined by Third-World thinkers such as Frantz Fanon or Che Guevara, transferred them into their local context (which was seen in unbroken continuity of fascism and racism) and in doing so created a strict division of 'we' and 'them' groups (Klimke 2010: 127f.).

77　Dieter Schrage mentions in particular such an experience of 'political sensibility' as decisive if the Freies Kino chooses to project a film or not. Art-house cinema, films from behind the Iron Curtain and Third World countries, in particular Latin America, but also western films and especially the Italo-Western were shown. A documentary about a Jimi Hendrix concert in Berkeley, California, which also presented scenes of a struggle between the police and student protesters, caused some discussions but was, in the end, shown as well as some Hollywood films with a critical, political sensibility such as *They Shoot Horses, Don't They* (Sydney Pollack, 1969) (I DS).

78　She noted: '[M]ud never disappears from our streets.' According to Drakulić, mud as a sign of the enduring dependence of the city on the village and rural life persisted in post-communist times because – through a subsistence economy – it provided people with food in times of shortages of all kinds (Drakulić 1996b: 199f.).

79　On such ways of an 'appropriation' of the other for an exploration of the self, see Morrison 1992: 52f.

80　The *Außerparlamentarische Opposition* (APO, extra-parliamentary opposition) in particular saw this law as an indication that the German constitution again went in the direction of fascism. Especially during the period before the law passed, there were protests and heated discussions all over the country. Also, other artists made interventions that referred to this law – for instance, members of the action theatre in Munich, of which Rainer Werner Fassbinder was part, made a collective production choosing the *Notstandsgesetze* as a frame of reference (Rainer Werner Fassbinder in Brocher 2004a [1973]: 70f.).

81 See, for example, the orientation of the Kommunales Kino in Frankfurt/Main (Prinzler and Schwarz 1972: 101f.).

82 On a critique of the notion of 'counter-public', see Schober 2009b: 355f.

83 Ivan Martinac was also active in the kino club Split.

84 On this, see the OHO chronology in Moderna galerija 1994: 145f.

85 Also Zygmunt Bauman's (1991: 8) analysis of how modernization in both democratic and totalitarian societies goes along with efforts to produce order, to install organization, and to fight a disorder and an ambivalence it at the same time presupposes and produces questions any essential division of democratic and totalitarian societies. By showing that democracy never exists in a 'pure' way but always remains haunted by imaginary figures bound to a fantasy of unity and a cult of identity, Lefort (1986: 272) himself however offers some indication to question such a strict division he otherwise advocates.

86 The notion of an 'informal public sphere' to designate the politically relevant diversity of state-independent activities and interactions in totalitarian societies was formulated first by Oleg Yanitskii (1993).

87 On these trips to London in the 1970s see Habich 1985: 35ff.

88 In the action *Tapp und Tastkino* (Touch-Cinema) Valie Export wore a small box fitted with a curtain over her otherwise naked breasts. She called it a 'cinema' and asked people on the street to 'visit' this small box. In a manifesto linked to this action she claimed: 'The senses will be freed and this process can in no way be integrated into official rules because it leads to a direct liberation of sexuality' (m. t. Export n. d.: 1; Schober 2002: 241 f.).

89 The, in the 1990s, newly 'nationalized' research institutions such as film archives in particular tended to redefine the movement in a nationally univocal way. During my research on this book, I worked with a list of films I wanted to see in respect to the movement of the 1960s – and some of the reactions I got from some colleagues in Belgrade was that my choice of films was 'interesting'. When I went there to see some of the films, I was told that the Crni Talas is a 'Serbian' movement and all the films by authors with a different background I had on my research list were very disputable. This is in itself part of a regaining of sense and a re-directing of memory after the recent wars and expresses a desire for clear-cut divisions and a certain 'purity' of belonging.

Chapter 3

Films and urban interventions: the rediscovery of difference since the 1960s

3.1. The migrant guest worker: Fassbinder's interventions in the projection spaces of the imagination

In this chapter I mainly focus on the early films by Rainer Werner Fassbinder. What Fassbinder shares with the cinema movements I have examined in previous chapters is an understanding of film as action. Especially in the beginning he moved back and forth between film-making and action theatre: between the *action studio* cinema[1] as well as its offshoot the Action Theatre, the anti-theatre of the late 1960s in Munich and the *kalkulierte Filme* (calculated films) (Fassbinder in Brocher 2004b [1972]: 254) soon to be followed by feature films, which, dovetailing with his theatre work, he also made from the late 1960s on.

Fassbinder's actions were characterized by a search for a way of intervening critically in the present. This initially grew out of collective entities that were also involved in constituting the student movement. But soon Fassbinder started to orient his critical interventions on these circumstances themselves. In addition to these references, however, Fassbinder's filmic approach differs in several key aspects from that of other contemporary cinema activists, which makes his oeuvre especially insightful in the context of this investigation. This applies both to his relation to the audience and to what was at the time referred to as the 'culture of the spectacle'.

Cinema activists who regarded themselves explicitly as 'political' or 'avant-garde' often had a very sceptical or even dismissive attitude towards the mass-media dimension of film and cinema as well as to mass culture in general. Especially the latter is interpreted (Schober 2009b: 283f.) above all as being in continuity with fascism. Accordingly, they perceived film and cinema mainly as a machinery of manipulation and indoctrination, and focused their actions on shattering this machinery and awakening or teaching the audience. By contrast, Fassbinder maintains a sympathizing relationship with his audiences, treating them as equals. Soon his film-making was oriented to reach a large or at least larger audience – although he used varying aesthetic idioms to interact with various audience subgroups. In relation to film history, Fassbinder found guiding examples in individual Hollywood films[2] rather than in the avant-garde between the two World Wars, which had been so crucial for the tradition-inventing processes of Expanded Cinema. Another difference between him and Expanded Cinema was that for the latter 'attacking the audience' in the style of the avant-garde but also of the US company *The Living Theatre* was a key aspect. In contrast, in interviews conducted in the early 1970s Fassbinder was already talking about how important audience 'contact' was (Brocher 2004a [1973]: 19) to his theatre work and how films that focused on entertaining the audience through suspense were, in his opinion, politically fascinating. (Braad Thomsen 2004b [1972]: 234). In this respect he was also influenced by his visual experience in the film capital Munich – in particular by the 'Leopold' cinema (Fassbinder in Brocher 2004b [1972]: 249), whose programming demonstrated a similarly enthusiastic approach to selected Hollywood productions (Prinzler and Schwarz 1972, 189f.). Nevertheless, Fassbinder and Expanded Cinema or 'underground' film-makers did also share some points of reference. For example, both Fassbinder and the Expanded Cinema activist Wilhelm Hein mention films by Luis Buñuel as especially significant experiences and as a motivation for their own film-making practice (I WH; Fassbinder in Wiegand 2004 [1974]: 278).

Moreover, it can be said that Fassbinder's films also relate to questions posed in this book because he regards them as interventions in the sense of a 'setting in motion', a pushing forward and working through of processes within social spaces charged with emotions, dynamics and projections – whereby the effects produced by these interventions are explicitly kept open and conceived in manifold ways. Consequently, as a film-maker Fassbinder does not assume an outside perspective vis-à-vis the subject of his work, and at the same time his action is not driven by or associated with a means-of-reaching-an-end mentality as is often the case with other forms of contemporary cinema activism or theoretical work on films – for instance, when aesthetic means such as forced montage are described as more or less straightforward tactics used to produce subversion and a politico-oppositional effect (Schober 2009b: 34f.). Instead, through the calculated representation of the characters and their social roles in the eyes and actions of the other characters, Fassbinder urges the audience to 'examine its own very private feelings. [...] I find that more political and politically more aggressive than showing the police in the role of the great oppressor' (m. t. Fassbinder in von Mengershausen 2004 [1969]: 188). Accordingly, the interfaces between private, public and the imagination are what interest him most.

Perhaps, however, the most important reason for choosing to focus on Fassbinder's early films in this chapter is that at their core they also deal with the very imaginations and projections vis-à-vis the other (Bovenschen 1979: 12; Pechriggl 2000: 164ff.; Schober 2011: 394) which unite us as groups. To this effect, he also refers to his films as 'studies of contemporary Germany: guest workers, the oppression of the middle-class white-collar worker, our own political situation as film-makers' (m. t. Fassbinder in Rayns 2004 [1969]: 332).

In doing so, Fassbinder rejects an attitude that is often practised against outsiders of classic socialization scenarios, which consists of presenting them as 'victims' or reinforcing the 'one' versus 'the other' dichotomy and presenting them as homogeneous groups. Moreover, looking at Fassbinder's entire oeuvre, the following transition in terms of the 'other' becomes evident: while his early films often made reference to the living situations of workers or women in order, as he puts it, to 'lay bare the meaning of reality' (m. t. Fassbinder in Grant 2004 [1974]: 318), very soon his films are also peopled by homosexuals, guest workers, Jews or transvestites. At the same time he applies aesthetic means in order to lure the viewer of the films into a dialogue with him- or herself as the other. Thus with his films he intervenes into contemporary debates that shift from issues of class to questions of gender and sexual identity or ethnic differences. In this way Fassbinder seeks to bring people, relationships and projections both on the screen and between the screen and the audience into processes of mirroring and comparison, of calling into question and shifting.

The inner workings of the street

In an interview conducted in 1971 Fassbinder states: 'To me it was always important to make films about people and the relationships between them, about their dependence on each other and their dependence on society. My films are about dependency and that, actually, is quite social' (m. t. Braad Thomsen 2004c [1971]: 224). Thus unlike with Wim Wenders, places and spaces (Wenders 2004) are not what inspire his images in the first place but rather people and their destinies. The characters that especially seem to stimulate his imagination are the ones who can be described in one form or another as outsiders, which – it must be added – he defines in a very broad sense. Among these, for example, are women who are so inspiring to him because their roles are not as clear cut as those of most men (Fassbinder in Limmer and Rumler 2004 [1980]: 531). Often, however, the outsider is also portrayed as a prostitute, alcoholic, guest worker, transvestite or a character who appears to live a completely normal petty-bourgeois life but who comes out – or is outed – as the other in respect to a group or even to a couple or an individual. Thus in Fassbinder's films potentially anyone can become the outsider.

Although places may not be the main source of image inspiration in his films, they still play an important role. In a text about his literary adaptation of Alfred Döblin's novel *Berlin Alexanderplatz* he sketches the role the city can play in creative work, referring to a 'very specific alertness to everything that living in the city means. [...] Life in a big city: that means constant shifts in one's attention to sounds, images, movement. And so the means used for narrating the chosen elements shift, as the interest of an alert big-city resident may shift without losing himself as focal point, as is also the case with the story' (Fassbinder 1992 [1980]: 167).

Since Fassbinder's films are mainly concerned with the interface between the private and the public, they tend to take place indoors rather than in public places. Despite this fact, the public element is always involved via the diverse protagonists or the media – radio, newspaper and television – as recurring themes. Nevertheless, urban spaces such as the street or other semi-public situations, in particular the back courtyard, the stairwell, the bar and the tavern, are also important to his films. Especially in connection with the figure of the guest worker and the images others have of him, the street, parks, sidewalks and semi-public spaces like stairwells, bars and taverns play an important role in films like *Katzelmacher* (1969) and *Angst Essen Seele Auf/Ali: Fear Eats the Soul* (1973–1974).

These places are presented as sites where the theme is the relationships between the characters involved, the perspectives others have on them and the resulting dynamics of projection, transfer and identification (Elsaesser 2001: 49). Here people from very different contexts converge within a small area and – putting aside internal conflicts and relations of desire – constitute themselves as groups vis-à-vis others (and by excluding some as belonging to the group of the other), including the larger groups of 'native' versus 'foreigner'. At the same time these places are presented as the guest worker's habitat, so to speak: in Fassbinder's films the guest worker does not have the option of withdrawing to a private space, to his own living space; instead he is obliged to sleep in crowded or provisional sublet rooms or here one night, there the next, or he wanders through the streets, parks and bars.

Like the interior spaces, Fassbinder finds the urban or semi-public space interesting in all its labyrinthine complexity. That is why back courtyards, stairwells, or windows, doors and other passageways between various spaces appear frequently: places where watchful eyes might suddenly appear, walls or mirrors that partially hide the secret observer, or places where people run into each other by chance like the stairwell or the sidewalk, where social monitoring and defamation as well as peace offerings and deals can occur.

Relationships and characters in films like *Katzelmacher* (1969) or *Ali: Fear Eats the Soul* (1973–1974, Figure 30) are often shown as ones 'produced' through the glances and comments of others including our glances as viewers as well. Especially in *Ali: Fear Eats the Soul* the guest worker Ali (El Hedi ben Salem) and his girlfriend and later wife, Emmi (Brigitte Mira),

Figure 30: Commenting glances, *Angst Essen Seele Auf/Ali: Fear Eats the Soul*, Rainer Werner Fassbinder, 1973–1974 © Peter Gauhe, courtesy German Filminstitut, Frankfurt.

who is more than twenty years his senior and works as a cleaning woman, are practically the only ones who physically touch each other – otherwise the relationships consist mainly of the glances cast by individuals and groups at the couple and sometimes of Emmi's or Ali's glances back at the onlookers. Hence, seeing as a split operation is always part of the main theme. It is presented as an operation where what the characters or what we see is different from what 'is looking at' them or us, that is, what concerns them or us (Didi-Huberman 1999: 11f.).

In this way we are also drawn into the action as viewers caught watching from the sidelines. After Emmi and Ali get married they go to a restaurant where, as Emmi explains, 'Hitler always ate', and we are caught in the role of observers watching Emmi order from a menu of what are, to her, exotic dishes. Just as Emmi tries to explain the correlation between caviar and sexual desire, we see the blasé expression of the waiter standing in the doorway in reverse shot who like us has also been watching the couple unnoticed for quite a while. Through the gaze of the waiter we are 'exposed' as voyeurs of the scene – something that happens repeatedly throughout the film. In another scene in which we witness the two of them going up the steps to Emmi's flat for the first time, a cut to a neighbour shows us that she too has been watching the scene, and she immediately runs to another neighbour to tell her what she saw. In these cases Fassbinder also provides the characters with ample opportunity to give us a picture of their projections about guest workers and women who get involved with them.

This makes reference to the second function that streets and semi-public spaces like stairwells or restaurants/bars serve for Fassbinder: they are spaces where gossip and rumours spread and where groups bond by exchanging their depictions of enemy images and of their personal moral beliefs – which usually gives rise to the further production of projections and concomitant acts of socialization. This is described in particular detail in *Katzelmacher* in which we as the audience watch a long procession of group members come towards us two by two. We see them walking down the street arm in arm and listen to their shallow conversations. The empty phrases are full of talk of themselves and suspicions and assessments about others, especially about their relation to the guest worker, who in this film is played by Fassbinder himself. As part of this 'flood of gossip' we are also shown how this sets off other vortexes of action, which are to some extent marked by violence.

The cinema space is treated by Fassbinder as one belonging to the street and consequently has to do with a possible encounter between strangers. He juxtaposes this with the living room, which is for him interlinked with the television – for which he is also soon to start making movies. In a certain sense TV corresponds more accurately to Fassbinder's wish to use the media of film as a kind of psychoanalytical intervention into the private sphere of the audience (Fassbinder in Braad Thomsen 2004a [1977]: 402).

At the same time, however, he repeatedly emphasizes the autonomy of the audience and the significance of distance, which he also tries to provide to his viewers through his films. Even if this holds true for all of his films, including those he made for TV, gaining distance is, for Fassbinder, in a certain sense mainly tied to the cinema because he sees the cinema as a situation where one can 'refuse obedience more easily because one is in a strange space among strangers' (m. t. Fassbinder in Braad Thomsen 2004a [1977]: 402).

Fassbinder seeks to gain such a distance – starting with the film *Händler der vier Jahreszeiten/The Merchant of the Four Seasons* (1971–1972) – primarily by arousing the imagination. In an interview conducted in 1974 he comments: 'Far more than in a theory I am interested in the possibilities at my disposal of overcoming all the things that beset me, fears and whatnot. [...] As a television or movie viewer it is simply more important to me that that which is activated in me is what is also capable of being activated by dreams' (m. t. Wiegand 2004: 295).

The imagery of his films is therefore conceived in such a way that it attempts to activate the audience to confront all the charged atmospheres, feelings, and relationships present in its surroundings. At the same time Fassbinder tries to promote imagination and the ability to envision utopias. The aim of these interventions is also in his case change and emancipation. In 1977 he states: 'By emancipation I mean that the hero learns in place of the audience that a utopia is necessary. You need it' (m. t. Sparrow 2004: 407). Consequently, 'Freud was more important [...] than Marx' (m. t. Fassbinder in Hughes and McCormick 2004: 379), particularly during this work phase of the 1970s.

A filmic 'painting' of relationships and projection spaces

Fassbinder is, as he often reiterates, not interested in making 'realistic' films; rather, he wants to portray the prevailing relations in such a way that they become as transparent as possible to the audience. Consequently, he does not situate his work at a point outside these relations but within, and he rejects the taking of a single 'correct' perspective and the denunciation of others as 'false' (Wiegand 2004: 290f.). He strives for an almost psychoanalytical working through of projections, perceptions and feelings that should also be entertaining; in other words it should allow fun and pleasure in one's own reality. In 1974 he stated: 'I can imagine that the unrealistic aspect in these films might bring people closer to their reality and beyond that even to a utopia because it lets them compare and doesn't beat it into their heads over and over. [...] People don't want to see the same thing again, they want to experience it again [...] which happens if what they see lets them experience it again and doesn't keep them from having fun with their own reality' (m. t. Wiegand 2004: 294).

This 'working through' that Fassbinder repeatedly addresses includes a confrontation with images and projections circulating in one's own surroundings, whereby for him this primarily also includes images and projections that relate to the 'stranger' or 'outcast' and which have to do with hate. As he contends in 1981, the mass of the population is not involved primarily 'in positive things but in its hostility towards minorities. Everything that happens to foreigners [...] – the attitude towards them conveys the impression that people demand a strong state, and if the state doesn't sufficiently meet these expectations, this fosters hate' (m. t. Bensoussan 2004: 565). In some of his films Fassbinder magnifies these projections about the other and 'paints' – portrays – them in a very specific way, which he does, among other reasons, to allow the viewer to imagine other figurations and relationships.

Fassbinder calculates his films to demonstrate mechanisms of how the other comes to be and at the same time to carry the given system of limitations – through imagination – to the point of absurdity (Fassbinder in Steinborn and von Naso 2004 [1982]: 599; Elsaesser 2001: 302f.). To this end he believes 'that one has to paint with the camera. Just as texts, whether poetry or prose, must be written, one cannot leave images to their own devices: one has to fashion them' (m. t. Fassbinder in Steinborn, von Naso 2004 [1982]: 608).

As part of such a filmic painting of relationships and the projections involved in them he magnifies certain individual elements and at several places introduces a kind of filmic accessory. Moreover, he edits the films in such a way as to show not only the gap between the characters and the projective figurations engulfing them like clouds of imagination but also the various connections emerging between them. This painting with the camera can sometimes be executed to a more or less elaborate extent or at other times merely sketched. Fassbinder made films that, from his perspective, have something timeless, potentially enduring about them, and others that he himself refers to as 'throw-away films' (m. t. Wiegand 2004 [1974]: 285). He himself regards the latter as sketches addressing situations and themes that needed to be construed by him so that the public could see them, but which could be 'forgotten' again immediately afterwards. At the same time such sketched, painterly elements have also been smuggled into some of his very straightforward, enduring films such as *Die Ehe Der Marie Braun/The Marriage of Maria Braun* (1978–1979) – for instance in the form of views of ruined houses destroyed by bombs where the protagonist (Hanna Schygulla) sometimes still sojourns long after the end of the war, the rat-tat-tat of machine-gun fire that runs through the film like a soundtrack, or the close-ups of the beads of sweat covering the naked bodies of the protagonist and her black lover.

Some of the devices of painting and sketching with the camera used by Fassbinder are, for example, blocking or obfuscating rather than giving the audience an unrestricted view, as is common in typical Hollywood movies, by means of various objects such as curtains, dividing walls, wooden boards, flowers or branches, window gratings and ledges or bottles standing on a windowsill; the enhanced framing of the shot using doorways, picture frames or fantastic paintings and mirrors in which through the characters we are confronted with ourselves and our desires and fears; seemingly non-motivated camera movements, decisively tableau-like frontal shots of the characters (*Katzelmacher*); or the camera's multiple 'revealing' of someone in the movie who seems to observe us watching the film (*Ali: Fear Eats the Soul*).

Whereas in the typical Hollywood movie the camera angle usually corresponds with the point of view of the characters, this is often not the case with Fassbinder. Through all these devices and obstacles it becomes impossible for us as viewers of the film to acquire imaginary control over the action, our view is called into question and misled in associations that slip away in various directions. Thomas Elsaesser (2001: 135) refers to this as, in a classic sense, an inadequate 'sewing up' of images by which a gap between heroes and their social and sexual roles is made evident and the viewers are incorporated into the action.

In addition to the already mentioned mirrors, another example of such elements is the large, dark and at the same time bright fiery picture on the wall in *Ali: Fear Eats the Soul*. It is in front of this picture that Ali, near the end of the film, again asks Emmi to dance with him to the song 'Black Gypsy'. A similar function, however, can also be achieved by a demonstrative repetition of scenes – when Emmi is first left sitting alone in the stairwell, physically and spatially excluded from the group, so to speak 'cut' out of the picture, after the other cleaning ladies find out she is married to a foreigner, and then a few weeks later after Emmi has been accepted back into the group, the same mobbing procedure is repeated in the same stairwell in the same way, only this time the odd man out is the new Yugoslavian cleaning lady, Yolanda (Helga Ballhaus).

Nevertheless, these films do not just stir up insecurity, as Elsaesser contends. The sketched and painterly nature of some of the scenes also serves to encourage our imagination to turn that which is represented into something else. For this it is important that the various devices be applied unsystematically and more or less based on feelings.[3] The sketched, random and associative nature of many of the films as well as the fact that they elude the audience at times and yet remain fundamentally open make reference to the processual nature of vision. They maintain the presence of an active aspect of the imagination in a 'raw' form. In this way these elements embody a potential to become something else – something that we as the audience can, to a certain extent, 'produce' through our imagination.

Here, Fassbinder envisions something similar to what Cornelius Castoriadis dubbed 'radical imagination' (2007 [1997]: 73), which he interprets as *creatio ex nihilo* involving representations, wishes and affects and bringing forth new forms of being, able to produce a crisis for institutionalized society and its crystallized and fossilized imaginations. Thus to Castoriadis, radical imagination is ontological creation. Applying almost the same reasoning, Fassbinder too assumes that the painterly and more or less sketch-like nature of his films can activate the imagination, that is, allow the shown to continue to develop in an unexpected direction and in this way challenge the existing, institutionalized world.

If viewers are well acquainted with Fassbinder's filmic work, their imagination is further fuelled by the fact that a number of his films converge to give a large cohesive picture in which some issues are addressed repeatedly, some ideas or characters are broached on a small scale at first but are later dealt with in more detail, or the same actors and actresses appear in different figurations but often with a similar climax. This, too, can encourage the viewer to pick up the loose ends and invent his or her own, different connections between the stories and characters or imagine independent solutions (Elsaesser 2001: 387).

In addition to this, Fassbinder foregrounds the sensualities of surfaces and certain bodies (Figure 31) and connects these with an eroticization of the view in order to intervene in the spaces of the audience's imagination and to activate something here. One example of this is the disproportionate representation of the nineteenth-century 'woman' as the (private,

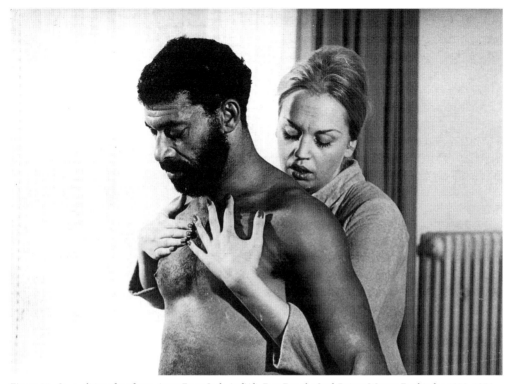

Figure 31: Sensualities of surfaces, *Angst Essen Seele Auf/Ali: Fear Eats the Soul,* Rainer Werner Fassbinder, 1973–1974
© Peter Gauhe, courtesy German Filminstitut, Frankfurt.

sensuous, unstable, sexually erotic) other vis-à-vis the public, career-oriented and socially upwardly mobile world of man through the enormous use of white lace curtains, etched-glass doors and dainty wooden lattices in *Fontane Effi Briest* (1972–1974). These elements both stage, hide and reveal the protagonist and turn our gaze into a peering or reaching into the scene.

Especially in connection with the guest worker Ali in *Ali: Fear Eats the Soul,* Fassbinder repeatedly addresses the theme of the sexually arousing body, in this case in connection with the fascination that comes from the ethnic other. An example of this occurs when we watch Ali taking a shower through the mirror and a pan suddenly shows that we are not the only ones gazing at his dark physical presence, Emmi is too, and she even comments on the events by saying: 'You are very handsome, Ali.' In subsequent films Fassbinder intensifies this sensuous presence and sexual fascination stimulated by the ethnic other – in the extreme, almost abstract close-ups of the naked body of the protagonist's African American lover (George Byrd) in *The Marriage of Maria Braun* (Figure 32). Contemporary artists such as Isaac Julien pick up where Fassbinder left off, again adopting this way of

Figure 32: Lovers, *Die Ehe Der Marie Braun/The Marriage of Maria Braun,* Rainer Werner Fassbinder, 1978–1979 © German Filminstitut, Frankfurt.

dealing with the imagination and fantasies of the other, but taking them further out of context and representing them as rather autonomous elements or by tracing potential effects.

Ali: Fear Eats the Soul addresses the theme of the simultaneity and ambivalence of sexual fascination and rebuffing discrimination when Emmi presents Ali as a kind of real gem in his tight white T-shirt and snug jeans to the other cleaning ladies and us as the audience, and the other ladies exclaim: 'He looks good, and so clean!'. To which Emmi invites them to feel Ali's muscles and skin. Furthermore, this scene makes reference to the fact that at certain points in his films Fassbinder gives the gaze a corporeal dimension: he 'teases' it out by showing certain bodies or relationship constellations, and the viewer is encouraged to touch or explore, whereby this is also able to shift into an act of violence, which is also tactilely experienced. This can be seen when Emmi, who is sitting at a table in an outdoor restaurant holding hands with Ali, is abruptly overcome by the hostile glares of the others and bursts into tears.

At the same time, by focusing on the subject of the gaze in an enhanced way, Fassbinder also makes a statement about the milieus represented in his films – in *Fontane Effi Briest* about the hostile attitude to the body and the prudery of nineteenth-century bourgeois society in which women are presented in public packaged like pralines, but touching is not allowed; or in *Ali: Fear Eats the Soul* about Emmi's bodily loneliness as a cleaning lady living in a tenement in West Germany in the 1970s. As viewers, however, we can also be stimulated on a physical level by these sensual elements, that is, we can be encouraged to address the meaning of being-in-the-world and to confront our relation to the other as well as our own corporeality.

From this angle, Fassbinder's filmic interventions differ most emphatically from those of other politically motivated cinema activists of his day, such as Expanded Cinema proponents. As discussed in previous chapters, a number of protagonists of this movement aimed at disrupting or attacking relationships that engender societal power or sought to bring about a 'liberation' or 'abolition' of societal institutions – for example the 'nuclear family' – a liberation and abolition that they, at the same time, claim to have achieved through their actions. Interventions were staged with the intent of shocking, provoking, working and in some cases even physically attacking the audience – hurling barbed wire at it or setting off fireworks (Schober 2009b: 157; Schober 2007). The rhetoric of this movement is thus characterized by dichotomy, by a splitting into 'them' and 'us': 'non-affirmative art' versus 'affirmative art', 'subversion' juxtaposed with 'control' – although the practised clarity of this rhetoric contrasts sharply with the fact that in public these actions or interventions were often interpreted as highly contradictory and double-edged (Schober 2002: 256).

With his films, Fassbinder also seeks to achieve an emancipation of the audience, and his filmic as well as theatre work is initially fuelled by protest frameworks linked-up with the student movement and inspired by the same anti-family ideologies and utopias of the collective. Very soon, however, he moves away from this romantic glorification of the collective and also starts to direct his critical investigations at the power mechanisms involved in these kinds of contexts.

By the late 1960s he has already begun relying more on seduction and less on provocation. He then sees emancipation rather as a potential of his films. This means that it mainly depends on how the audience receives and processes what is shown or (seen the other way around) to what extent he will succeed in activating the imaginations of the viewers. Correspondingly, he does not position himself and the audience in a hierarchical relation to each other in which one (the film-maker) might manipulate the other (audience), but considers himself and the audience to be on the same level. In 1974 he stated that he was 'trying [...] through language to retain certain mannerisms of the characters, but on the other hand didn't want to let this block access but to expand the possibilities of the viewers to what they get as images and dreams' (m. t. Wiegand 2004: 296).

In this way he does not engage in making ambivalences univocal but wants instead to encourage us in the audience to confront the ambivalences that we are involved in on a physical and emotional level so that we can go somewhere else and invent an altered way of being-in-the-world. Thus to him film-making (like film reception) is an activity not primarily determined and guided by language. In 1981 he stated: 'I would rather do something than talk about it. If you can talk about something, it is no longer necessary to make a film about it, it's as simple as that' (m. t. Bensoussan 2004: 558).

The other and (semi-)honesty as a utopia

In respect to his filmic work Fassbinder repeatedly talks about utopias, which he refers to as necessary for survival: one recurrent utopia is that of (semi-)honesty in respect to what is being portrayed. In 1982 he summarizes his main concerns as follows: 'I want to make films that are as beautiful and wonderful as Hollywood movies but not as phoney. In other words, films which please and don't try to conform' (m. t. Steinborn and von Naso 2004: 612f.). In his vision there are not merely the two poles of honesty and lie but also many nuances of (semi-)honesty (Fassbinder in Jansen 2004 [1978]: 434) which furthermore can never be expressed and depicted directly but are only fleetingly palpable between the perspectives, images, imaginations, relationships, dependencies and projections. To him, this ties in with the utopia of love purged of all societal exploitations and a utopia of the body.[4]

To Fassbinder these utopias are linked closely to figurations of societal outsiders and to how they are dealt with. About his last film, *Querelle* (1982), he says: 'The subject is the individual's identity and how he attains it. As Genet says, this has to do with the fact that one requires oneself in a doubled way in order to be complete. And I absolutely agree with Genet on that' (m. t. Schidor 2004 [1982]: 621). In his films Fassbinder often presents these alter egos – to the characters and to us in the audience – as social outcasts in order to peel off what he regards as phoney.

Here, again, Fassbinder adopts practices infused with myths that consist in the self being reflected in the other, identifying with him or her and assimilating certain traits possessed by the other in order to position the self and to perceive the self as, for example, non-conventionally acting or even as one that is able to experience a truth or authenticity of the self (Morrison 1992). The staging of the underdog as an expression of a longing to position oneself in society has been an important tendency in the arts (in literature as well as the fine arts, soon also in cinema) especially since the people's revolution of the eighteenth and nineteenth centuries. This longing has led to various figurations of the other (as a mirror of the self or as somebody living on the border of humanity (Schober 2001: 250)) – as a member of the working class or lumpenproletariat, as a prostitute, small-time crook, poacher, or as an ethnic minority, or a 'racial' other, as it was referred to at the time.

In this aspect – among others that I will not be able to discuss in detail here – Fassbinder's work seems to share aspects with that of Pier Paolo Pasolini, who also repeatedly allies himself with the lumpenproletariat in his early literary and filmic work and later with people in the Third World in order to attain a 'certain realism' of narration (Schober 2012). At the same time, however, Fassbinder's approach differs from Pasolini's because the latter expresses his identification with the societally other in a more open and candid way, even celebrates the other body consistently as a more or less 'holy' body. By contrast, Fassbinder employs the bodies of the other in order to also expose the jumble of preconceived notions about them and the dynamics of socialization that arise from this – and he does so in a plural and reciprocal often also challenging way. Thus his films reflect both the fascination emanating from the other and the actions of the 'victim' as circumstances characterized strongly by ambivalence.

In the film *Ali: Fear Eats the Soul*, the fascination as well as the sexual dimension tied to the other become apparent right from the start. It is the seductive, foreign music that lures Emmi into a bar she has walked past almost every day until now, the place where she will meet Ali. At the same time, in the first scene that shows Ali in close-up he is immediately introduced as a sex object. A woman at the bar comes on to him and he turns her down with a brusque: 'cock broken'. Finally, it is the dynamics of rejection and Ali's defiance towards the group at the bar that bring him and Emmi together – whereby these dynamics will also shift at times, directing themselves against Emmi and in favour of the group.

Fassbinder shows quite a broad spectrum of fantasies and emotions in respect to Ali: enjoyment, admiration, pride and human understanding or a live-and-let-live attitude (on the part of the building owner's son or the bar owner). Above all, however, the viewer is confronted with images and words of hostility, envy and shame and accompanying this also a disdaining or even demonization of the other.

By bringing these attitudes, fantasies, images, rumours and the related dynamics of socialization together in a film, Fassbinder wants to activate the audience to take a 'semi-honest' or 'less phoney' view of the prevailing world. Hence even in respect to our relation to the other he does not position himself and his actions as being situated outside – rather he assimilates the myth-infused practice of positioning oneself through the other and at the same time tries to make individual elements and figurations of these myths and their functions understandable. Through the previously described sketching approach and an amplification of the sensual, affective dimension of our relation to the other, he focuses on the level of the radical imagination and aims at what I have in previous chapters called 'events towards the other'. Such events, however, always occur in a contingent way and thus cannot be made into a concept (Schober 2009b: 344f.).[5]

Nevertheless, his films in which guest workers are used to achieve a '(semi-)honest' view of the world did not cause a scandal, as opposed to some of his other productions – instead they were highly acclaimed and awarded prizes.[6] This is in itself insightful in respect to the historic contexts his films were made in. For his films then stirred up discussions and attacks by the audience if they challenged the contemporary self-image of left-wing activists or of exponents of the homosexual scene[7], and conflicts with those who had commissioned the films arose or planned projects were cancelled if they showed labour disputes and other social clashes (Elsaesser 2001: 51). Primarily however, it was the addressing of the figure of the Jew and of notions of the Jew beyond the role of the victim and the depiction of how anti-Semitism arises that caused the biggest scandals. This came to a head particularly in the debates about Fassbinder's play *Der Müll, die Stadt und der Tod/Garbage, the City and Death* (1975) (see Markovits et al. 1986), which led to the cancellation or dropping of related projects (Fassbinder in Braad Thomsen 2004a [1977]: 394f.).

These scandals over the figure of the Jew beyond the role of the victim and the success his 'guest-worker films' attained can be explained in much the same way: all these films are about what happened in Fassbinder's environment – West Germany from the 1950s to 1982[8] and they show glimpses of hidden or otherwise often hard to grasp charges and tensions. In this respect it is also important to note that the following changes, which have already been mentioned elsewhere in this book, can be witnessed parallel to the making of these films. If modernism was characterized by an exclusion, suppression and controlling of difference beyond a handful of privileged differences such as the nation (or the proletariat in socialism) and by a dominance of the institution of the bourgeois, patriarchal family, this was being supplanted –among other driving forces also through the student movement – by a new politics of difference that was also inextricably tied to a market of differences. Fassbinder's films can be found in this transition zone and are at the same time involved in it. They are themselves characterized by a hunger for the other, and yet they also put it up for discussion. They document a longing to become somebody else (and in this way to find oneself or to receive love) or to differentiate oneself through the other. By contrast, the images he creates of the Jew beyond the role of the victim address a taboo, they refer to something that in West Germany had been shrouded in silence for decades because it had been repressed. For that reason when it resurfaced it often did so accompanied by strong conflicts (Fassbinder in Bensoussan 2004 [1981]: 568; Koch et al. 1986: 37).

The fascination of the other and the practice of distinguishing oneself by a mirroring of oneself in the other became enacted in a new way in West Germany during the post-1968 era: the fascinated appropriation of different lifestyles, for example, became increasingly tied to always new fantasies of 'dropping out' of society. The film *Katzelmacher* (Figure 33) addresses

Figure 33: Dreaming of becoming someone else, *Katzelmacher,* Rainer Werner Fassbinder, 1969 © Fassbinder Foundation, courtesy German Filminstitut, Frankfurt.

this theme when Marie (Hanna Schygulla), the guest worker's temporary girlfriend, dreams of moving to a Greek island with him – to a place where, as she says, 'everything is different.'

This becoming different through a relationship with the other is a (sometimes painful) phenomenon that Fassbinder addresses in other films too; for example in *In einem Jahr mit 13 Monden/In a Year of 13 Moons* (1978, produced for the WDR, *Westdeutscher Rundfunk*) where the protagonist Erwin (Volker Sprengler) has a sex-change operation for love and becomes Elivra (Figure 34). Similar fantasies of self-transformation are explored by his contemporaries, for example by Peter Weibel in the collage *Selbstportrait als Frau/Self-portrait as a Woman* (Figure 35, 1967). And connecting lines also exist to the figure of the Jew in Fassbinder's films. So Sheila Benhabib (Markovits et al. 1986: 19), for example, says of Fassbinder's most contested play, *Garbage, the City and Death*, that it stands for a process of 'becoming different'; for many Germans the play was about the possibility of being able to speak of oneself and the others, the Jews, in a new way, not censored by guilt; and for the Jews in Germany it was about being able to become actively involved in the way people talk about them here and now, rather than to simply accept the role of the victim.

Figure 34: Self-Transformation, *In einem Jahr mit 13 Monden/In a Year of 13 Moons,* Rainer Werner Fassbinder, 1978, produced for the WDR, *Westdeutscher Rundfunk* © WDR. Westdeutscher Rundfunk.

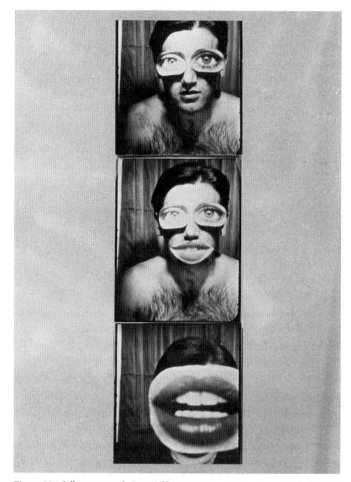

Figure 35: *Selbstportrait als Frau/Self-Portrait as a Woman,* Peter Weibel, 1967
© Peter Weibel.

Fassbinder's films are in this way a part of an already described new orientation of post-1968 cinema towards a stronger presence of the other, and yet they try to express a further difference. These films are not merely ambivalent in the way they become involved in processes that use the figuration of the other for the sake of self-discovery and try to make these experienceable and changeable in their complexity or to enable events towards the other. The double-edgedness of these films also stems from the fact that they also affirm a tendency towards the internalization of ambivalence and conflict-resolution. This tendency consists, as Zygmunt Bauman (1991: 96f.) has shown and I have mentioned in previous chapters, in the fact that conflicts and tensions resulting from the most diverse social demands and acts of differentiation must now find their balance within each individual.

Fassbinder's films correspond to this in that they also shift the subjectivity of the individual beyond the family and the traditional patriarchal structures into the foreground. The individual is in this way presented as an authority that to some extent assumes quite contradictory identifications and at the same time becomes the main entity that takes responsibility for solving conflicts and tensions and indeed must take this responsibility. In Fassbinder's later films this exposure of the subjectivity of the individual stands in stark contrast to the utopias of the collective and of solidarity which he has articulated with particular vehemence in his very early work. Thus his films also document a fading of this utopia – it is replaced by a utopia of love, (semi-)honesty and the (tortured, mortal) body.

3.2. The figuration of difference as aesthetic, sexual and ethnic difference in Yugoslav cinema since the 1960s

Dušan Makavejev's approach to cinema, like that of other cinema activists presented in this book, is nourished by cinema itself. He did not learn film-making at an academy but through numerous cinema visits – in particular by frequenting the Belgrade Kinoteka – as well as by engaging first in the Novi Sad cinema club but then mainly in the kino club Beograd (I D M). Moreover, he too sees his films as actions in social and above all psychically lived spaces and has maintained a pronouncedly positive relationship vis-à-vis mass culture. Nevertheless, this closeness to other contemporary cinema and film activists is not the main reason why the following remarks take their point of departure from the films Makavejev made in Yugoslavia, between 1958 and 1973.

The reason for this is rather that his career is at the same time paradigmatic and extraordinary for Yugoslav cinema of the decades since the Second World War. As he himself stated in an interview conducted in 1977: 'The films I made (as well as films made by people in similar cultural situations in the 50s and 60s) were the first justification of socialism after many years of sterile, Stalinist production – pure desert. People were quite deprived of anything meaningful, unless, of course, you were heavily romantic, and liked films full of glassy-eyed people looking into the future. The critical films (mostly from Eastern Europe) which came out of the 50s and 60s represented complicated inter-relationships between people and society, between power and society and between different levels of power and the kinds of myths which had been guiding people's lives' (Makavejev 1977: 50). Such films made him a representative of 'new Yugoslav culture', but besides being that, Makavejev was also considered to be *the* enfant terrible of the novi film movement.[9] His films repeatedly became the subject of more or less heated conflicts with official representatives of Titoist politics.

Another reason why I start this chapter with a reading of Makavejev's early feature films is that he responded to official aesthetics and its celebration of the partisan and the proletarian as representatives of the 'people as one' (Lefort 1986: 297f.) with a pronounced rediscovery of difference – which he mainly figured as an aesthetic and sexual difference, with the latter sometimes being strongly merged with ethnic features. This chapter investigates how this staging of difference in Makavejev's films was dealt with in the (informal) public sphere emerging in former Yugoslavia in the 1960s and early 1970s and the ways in which what is stated in these films diverges from as well as corresponds to the official 'world in stories' (Geertz 2000: 254) promoted by the one-party system.

Another way of putting the main question is: How does what is stated in these films show features of collective ways of inhabiting social and political space which were excluded or repressed in official visual culture in Titoist Yugoslavia, but which, with the breakdown of the one-party system, gained an enormous politically explosive force in the wars of the 1990s? In this respect Makavejev's films are related to the works of a film-maker of the next generation, Srđan Karanović, who shortly before these wars picked up on what Makavejev had posed, also staged a story of a rediscovery of sexual difference, and was (again) involuntarily involved in 'national' articulations and re-negotiations of difference, which were now however staged in a very explicit way.

Film as action, bodily self-confrontation and collage

For Dušan Makavejev movies are closely linked to questions of sense and to life practice. In an interview in 2000 he stated: 'Movies always follow us as reference material or as some kind of dreamlike material for dealing with things we don't understand in our lives. Movies give us solutions, or provide a whispering commentary on what is happening around us' (Privett 2000: 3). As a consequence of this, he calculated his films in order to 'trigger a chain reaction in the spectator, so that the film could be not just a film but a sort of *action*' (Makavejev in Durgnat 1999: 55).

In the beginning of his film-making activity, from 1958 until 1967–68, his vision of film was strongly inspired by Praxis philosophy – a version of Marxist humanism that was formulated by a group of intellectuals around the journal *Praxis* (1965–1975) as a reaction to Stalinist dogmatism and bureaucratism.[10] In accordance with this strand of discourse, which was an important pillar of the 'Yugoslav way' of socialism, he understood film, similar to other film-makers of the novi film movement such as Živojin Pavlović, as taking part in an ideology-critical programme.

This means that during this period Makavejev adhered to a Marxist notion of 'false consciousness'. He maintained that there are distorted illusions, false ideas and idealistic representations circulating in social space, from which one has to liberate oneself. At the same time he put the emphasis on the irrational where he saw such ideas and image worlds as rooted (Makavejev in Ciment 1968: 17). An example of this is the figure of the hypnotist who appears at the beginning of *Čovek nije tica. Ljubavni film/Man is not a Bird: A Film Romance* (1965) and several other times in the course of the film. He first shot these scenes depicting a hypnotist's speech as a kind of separate documentary during the preparation of the film. While developing *Čovek nije tica* however, this figure became increasingly important and was finally not only included but also made into a formula for the whole film – the hypnotist indicates that people's gestures, opinions, habits and ideas are 'impregnated with ideology' (m. t. Makavejev in Ciment 1968: 17). Even if in this period of life, in the mid-1960s, he still used to act occasionally as a kind of UNESCO 'film deputy' for Yugoslavia (I DM), he retrospectively claimed that in contrast to his strong political activism as a student, he then saw himself as being less politically involved, 'less linked to society. I found that it had taken a not very interesting path' (m. t. Ciment and Cohn 1971: 51).

Some years later, around the time he made *WR: Misterije organizma/WR: Mysteries of the Organism* (1971) and somehow culminating in his next film *Sweet Movie* (1974) his approach had in part changed. On the one hand there is an explicitly expressed re-politization. He saw the cinema now as a kind of guerrilla operation, using 'everything that comes to hand, fiction, documents, actualities, titles. "Style" is not important. You must use surprise as a psychological weapon' (Makavejev in Robinson 1971: 177). Simultaneously, he started to describe film as a 'therapeutic' initiation to fight (sexual) repression (Robinson 1971: 180). In an interview with Jonas Mekas about *WR* he stated that he had conceptualized the film as 'an active dream, as a healing dream […] a sort of machine for self-confrontation' (Mekas 1972: 65). Consequently the main theoretical references were now no longer Karl Marx or Praxis Philosophy, but Wilhelm Reich and anti-psychiatric discourse, for instance Ron Laing (Codelli 1975: n. p.).

In between these two positions stood the student movement of 1968, a profound reading of the writings of Wilhelm Reich and several research trips in connection with a documentary about his life, which forms part of *WR*. Besides, and perhaps even more influential, were the troubles *WR: Misterije organizma* had in Yugoslavia after it first had passed censorship – something that led to Makavejev being 'advised' to leave the country in 1973. About the latter he retrospectively stated in 2001: 'The horse's head appeared in my bed in January of 1973 in the form of three screws from the right front wheel of my VW bug, unbolted and pedantically left under the wheel's hubcap, producing a strange farewell noise' (Makavejev 2001: 8).

With this transformation of his position also the demarcations, the 'bad others' had changed. His first films were made as a reaction against partisan movies and mainstream amateur films as well as against conventional forms of narrative. He presented himself as being inspired by author's cinema and claimed to make films that demonstrate a social consciousness and were integrated into national culture (Makavejev in Bontemps and Fieschi 1966: 55). After 1968, by contrast, he rejected author's cinema as 'intellectual perversion' (Makavejev in Cozarinsky and Clarens 1975: 48f.) as well as films made for a 'public of cadres' (m. t. Kramer and Makavejev 1975: 21f.). He now criticized in particular – what he had been aiming at before – the fact that film authors from 'marginal countries' were 'supposed to express national cultures. And being interesting', he added, 'becomes part of a secondary duty' (Makavejev in Cozarinsky and Clarens 1975: 49).

This change in Makavejev's film-making shows a different and to some extent antidromic tendency one is able to witness in the oeuvre of other film-makers usually associated with '1968' – for instance that of Rainer Werner Fassbinder. The latter started his film-making activity, as shown in the previous chapter, inside collective frameworks of the student movement, but soon developed an increasingly critical relationship vis-à-vis the dynamics working in them and turned more and more towards entertaining films for various and sometimes also broader circles of the public. Makavejev, by contrast, became first known to a wider public through ideology-critical and at the same time entertaining movies, but oriented himself with the making of *WR: Misterije organizma* ('WR' means 'Wilhelm Reich' but also 'World Revolution') more pronouncedly towards the student movement – although he did not become a member or leader of a particular group but rather acted as a kind of sympathetic observer. Besides, he again started to define his films increasingly in a politically activist ('guerrilla'-like) way and to challenge linear narratives even further than before – even if he continued to adhere to an approach directed towards entertainment and returned to more linear forms of narration for the production of certain films.

A feature both directors shared, however, was that Makavejev like Fassbinder maintained a continuously positive relationship towards US movies. For his early films – besides other inspirations such as the French *Nouvelle Vague*, Italian neo-realism and 'black' Polish or Czech films (I DM) – Makavejev acknowledged a strong influence of the New American Cinema: 'They make a lot of things that are completely nothing. But they have a strong sense of equality which consists in showing everything without selection. And this equality between something that counts as something and something that does not count at all touches me a lot. I love *Guns of the Trees* and *Hallelujah the Hills* and the films of Bruce Conner, Stan Vanderbeek and Emshwiller and Shirley Clarke, on the other hand. I find that the films from Eastern Europe, especially Czech and Yugoslav, are the proof of importance and the vitality of the New American Cinema' (m. t. Ciment 1968: 26). Some years later, around 1975, he seemed, however, to be less close to the underground than to 'classical' US films: 'The great quality American movies had in their best days', he stated, 'was to be made under market dictatorship. They were not afraid to please the market, and just had to be interesting all the time' (Makavejev in Cozarinsky and Clarens 1975: 48f.).

But there is also a whole range of further characteristics which are rather continuously present in Makavejev's films. Already the early films such as *Parada* (1962), *Čovek nije tica* (1965), *Ljubavni slučaj ili tragedija službenice P.T.T.* (1967) and *WR* (1971) show central features of what can be described as his aesthetic approach: an enhanced 'montage' or rather 'collage' of images and even of image genres (photography, scientific films, cartoons, musical, diagrams, typography, etc.) that usually are not brought together and that somehow echo aspects of each other; the re-sampling of found stories and things; strong contrasts of surfaces of various kinds (hard and soft, sticky and smooth, small and big); the pronounced use of humour, irony and parody which, however, are not made into a programme; female characters as leading figures who keep the stories in motion; and the staging of what in mainstream visual culture in Titoist Yugoslavia was usually treated as a taboo or as marginal.

Another feature that has an enduring presence in all of his films is a strong relation to the popular. In *Čovek nije tica* for instance he portrays a whole range of popular spectacles such as a circus, the already mentioned hypnotist or a *kafana* singer. In *Ljubavni Slučaj*

Figure 36: Moments, *Ljubavni slučaj ili tragedija službenice P.T.T./Love Affair, or the Tragedy of the Switchboard Operator*, Dušan Makavejev, 1967 © Dušan Makavejev, courtesy Jugoslovenska Kinoteka, Belgrade.

he works with bits of pop-culture which in this case are rather of an urban type: records, TV and radio or advertisement. In these pieces of everyday life and of what happened in the entertainment arenas of broad circles of the population he found 'more affective and intellectual meanings than in the classic forms of art: museums, concerts, theatre', which he saw as 'incredibly empty places' (m. t. Makavejev 1967: 41).

Here it is particularly important to him to depict the co-presence of various realities and how they converge or enter into conflict with each other. The aesthetic tactics of montage and collage allow him to both show the gaps between official life and the private and intimate experiences as well as to demolish boundaries between fixed entities and establish correlations (Makavejev 1975: 8). In this respect his aesthetic approach is coextensive with what happens in modern city space. Referring to his editing of some street scenes in *Ljubavni Slučaj* he explains that he wanted to work with the fact that urban life is constantly marked by the unexpected. He compares this to what he does with montage: 'I show a thing, then I cut to another one. They walk through the streets and suddenly an event or an idea gets them to embark in a different direction. I always felt that this simultaneity of direction and counter-direction is working in us and I always wanted to show that' (m. t. Makavejev 1967: 39).

Such collisions between fragments of the everyday and of public, political life tend to 'equalize' various phenomena, that is, to destroy existing hierarchies between facts and values (Makavejev 1967: 38), or to introduce a mysterious, almost surreal quality into his films. This 'equalizing' and 'surreal-making' function of Makavejev's use of montage was particularly provocative in socialist Yugoslavia where it was able to challenge the officially attributed meaning and importance of certain official symbols.

This can for instance be seen in the case of a few images that appeared in several of his films and became a controversial subject of discussion. For *Parada* (1962), a film that, as already mentioned in a previous chapter, was first banned but after some modifications passed censorship, Makavejev filmed not the pompous event itself but the various actions, efforts and objects involved in the preparation of an official parade held by the Communist Party in Belgrade on 1 May, international workers' day. Part of the imagery produced were shots of some enormous plates with worker's hands painted on them – the official symbol of the proletariat that represented the socialist state. Makavejev recalls: 'I took various shots because I love these plates. I had seven or eight of them, very good ones, and I needed (for *Parada*, A. S.) only one or two' (m. t. Ciment 1968: 15). Later he decided to introduce them as well as other leftovers from *Parada* into subsequent films he made – for instance into *Čovek nije tica*, so that, when the technician from the north arrives in the city of the copper mine, a procession of panels started to cross his path. In *Ljubavni Slučaj* some exposures of this parade depicting gigantic banners of Lenin, posters of Mao Tse Tung, enormous tubes of toothpaste and boxes of soap powder – together with cinema posters or advertising placards showing pretty young, smiling women – line the city streets the female protagonists are passing through.

Makavejev says about such harsh collages: 'I found that I had the right to destroy the normal course of time for the sake of gaining something that for me is more important than time. If time is quite logical in the rest of the film, one can destroy it in order to gain an effect of something mysterious. [...] I have the [...] strange feeling that the spectator sees here that things are not organized according to a normal order' (m. t. Ciment 1968: 15).

This mix of propaganda images and everyday actions exposed a gap between the official discourse conveyed by the party and the experience people gained in respect to their everyday lives. Consequently it was exactly this unusual, almost surreal adoption of a socialist symbol that a few years later, after Makavejev had left the country and the party had reorganized and re-centralized itself by eliminating so-called 'anarcho-liberal' forces, was used as evidence against the author himself. In an article published in 1975 that critically re-examines the representation of the working class in Yugoslav cinema, the use of these plates in *Čovek nije tica* is described as follows: 'The [...] sequence of the rough hands of workers is [...] in reality a kind of demagogic trick of manipulating the argument in order to become able to use this "workers' emblem" as a kind of crutch for a critical reflection about society as a whole' (m. t. Boglić 1975: 46). Makavejev's films were now discussed as being part of a 'protest cinema' that is 'asocial', 'directed against all' and 'relating solely to itself' (m. t. Boglić 1975: 43). In this way the feeling of confusion and ambiguity Makavejev was able to produce through tactics of montage and collage was again unambiguously condemned.

Nevertheless, through using montage and collage to create a variety of contact points between things, people, persons and surfaces Makavejev was able to bring minute attention to the material, spatial, sensuous, bodily and sexual qualities of the everyday and to the gaps between the various ways of handling them. In this way, he focused on those features of public and private life which official film production lacked – with the representation of the sensuous, bodily and sexual in connection with official (party) symbols especially making some of his films the subject of even more outraged discussions. This will be elaborated upon in the next section.

Tactile contrasts and the figuration of difference as (mainly) aesthetic and sexual difference

In several of his films, Dušan Makavejev operates with sensuous, tactile materials of contrasting qualities. He produces 'haptic' (Marks 2000: 162) images that dwell on the detailed textures of bodies and things and have the capacity of 'pulling' the viewer into what is represented. In *Čovek nije tica* for instance the camera repeatedly lingers on various 'hairy' surfaces and makes the unusual correspondences between them almost tangible. In several sequences one sees close-ups of the female protagonist Raika (Milena Dravić) and her soft, blonde, wavy hair, which she sometimes brushes or shakes in front of the camera. In the love scene it contrasts with the unusual, dark, hairy bedcover, under which the lovers lie naked. In another sequence the 'hair' theme is accentuated through the figure of an old, peregrine hair-collector, who at a certain point enters the hairdresser's saloon where Raika works, takes some hair out of the bin and, in passing, reaches deep into her blonde hair. Together with the light, showing sometimes extreme contrasts of darkness and luminosity, these tactile details bestow an enhanced erotic dimension on the film.

Other examples can be found in *Ljubavni Slučaj*. In one sequence the fingers of Izabela, the female protagonist, operate – zoomed in close-up – with flour and eggs, producing a paste which she then playfully stretches out and 'blows up' in various directions in order to get an extremely thin, almost skin-like plane. On this she puts blueberries and sugar, covers them and rolls everything into strudels, which she butters before putting them into the oven, while a black cat wanders around the legs of the table.

The dark and soft fur of this cat is presented in an 'enlarged' way also in another scene in which it is contrasted to the smooth skin of Izabela stretched out naked on her bed (Figure 37). The cat can first be seen slinking alongside her legs, but then settles down close to the soft mounds of her buttocks. And an egg yolk, hands and fingers are also featured in his next film *WR*, which already opens with such haptic images, turning them

Figure 37: Fur and skin, *Ljubavni slučaj ili tragedija službenice P.T.T./Love Affair, or the Tragedy of the Switchboard Operator,* Dušan Makavejev, 1967 © Dušan Makavejev, courtesy Jugoslovenska Kinoteka, Belgrade.

into a kind of motto for the whole film. While the opening credits are running, one sees close-ups of pairs of hands playing with a delicate, slippery egg yolk and passing it from one to another.

These examples already show that Makavejev is particularly interested in visually representing senses such as touch (hairy, smooth and slippery surfaces), smell (the strudel) and taste (the strudel, the egg). He manages to deliver such sensuous evocations by giving actors 'something to do' during the shooting and so encourages them to act in a more casual way before the camera (Makavejev 1967: 40).

These sequences blur the boundaries between the factual and the documentary and – through a minute registering and a playful and often unusual handling of things – bring the materiality of everything involved into the foreground. They are calculated in order to reach forms of experience that go beyond what can be expressed verbally. In an interview published in 1985 Makavejev summarizes the effects he thus tries to achieve: 'It is in the nature of really good movies that they create this bridge between the spectator and the screen and you have this glue – that's really good linking [...] they relate to our dreamworld and our understanding of ourselves on a gut level' (Makavejev in Oumano 1985: 167).

With such sensuous evocations he opposes the 'over-verbalization' he finds so typical in socialist countries. 'The so-called socialist places', he states, 'are that verbal, the people live in such a verbal routine so that really nobody speaks to anybody else' (m. t. Kramer and Makavejev 1975: 27).

In particular in his two early feature films, *Čovek nije tica* and *Ljubavni Slučaj*, but to some extent also in *WR*, Makavejev links such a sensuous spectacle of surfaces and textures closely and mainly to the female protagonists of his films. Collages of haptic surfaces, accentuated by contrasts, unusual correspondences and particular lightening underscore the erotic vibrancy of the female characters, which usually keep the stories in his films in motion. And the bodily presence of these female leading figures makes the various substances, fabrics, textures and materials depicted even more palpable and 'taste-able'. In this way, aesthetic and sexual differences come to the fore and mutually reinforce each other. Simultaneously, indications of a belonging to groups conceived in ethnic, religious or national terms, which are also shown in these films, are rather used to accentuate sexual difference or difference vis-à-vis official party politics but do not become main issues around which the stories unfold – also because, as already pointed out, national or ethnic difference was one of the most closely controlled features of Yugoslav political life.

Before going into a more detailed analysis of some films in this respect, a general note regarding figurations of difference may seem appropriate: In our everyday lives we constantly encounter 'cultural differences' which might cause incompatibility with others. Difference here never arises in a pure form, but various (aesthetic, sexual, ethnic, national) aspects are indistinguishably mingled. As Naoki Sakai (2005: 5 and 18) has shown, in order to figure out difference (aesthetic, sexual, ethnic, national) as something specific, for instance between two cultures, we require the mobilization of a particular schema already circulating in society – officially expressed or rather latent – which in this way can become enforced or even re-invented. Hence the figuration of difference in particular terms always needs mediating discourses that link to us as subjects – such as discourses on national culture or sexual identity – which make 'us feel as if events that are distant in social space and historical time are in fact "our events"' (Sakai 2005: 18).

In Yugoslavia between the 1960s and the 1980s, the core notions of official mediating discourses shifted from 'self-management' to the 'nation' (Shigeno 2004: 236). But also oppositional discourses such as the one articulated by Makavejev were organized around core notions that were in themselves changing – with 'sexual difference', 'sexual liberation' as well as 'the individual' assuming an increasingly prominent role after '1968' and sometimes entering into unexpected, strange linkages with pieces of other discourse that started to figure 'the ethnic' or 'the nation' more prominently.

Figurations of difference in the form of the representation of particularities of ethnic groups or nationalities are present in most of the films Makavejev made in Yugoslavia and – as already mentioned – are usually not made into the main, explicit subject of the stories told but somehow linger 'in between' all the details and conjunctions they offer. This, however, also means that ethnic difference is always already part of the rediscovery of difference through which Makavejev (as well as other novi film authors) challenged official world-views, which tended to make the existence of such kinds of difference taboo. Such a presence of ethnic difference is in particular graspable in his early feature films.

Makavejev filmed *Čovek nije tica* in Bor, an industrial city close to a copper mine in eastern Serbia. Inspired by Italian neo-realism, he decided to make a film composed solely of stories 'found' on location by talking to various kinds of people and combing through local newspapers. He was especially intrigued by discovering parallel realities and double standards of life practice – for instance, technicians from other regions living beside rural people and peasants, those opposing religion besides those practising traditional religions and people who officially 'pass' as Serbs while privately speaking Romanian (Makavejev in Bontemps and Fieschi 1966: 56f.). In the course of the film he tried to represent these parallel worlds and these double standards. An example of this is the figure of the *kafana* singer called Fatima, which is considered to be a Muslim name but could also have been adopted by an artist with a different background,[11] whose body movement we can follow so closely at the beginning of the film and who, before being killed, in the midst of a crowd of workers sings a folk song first in a local south-Serbian dialect[12] but then switches to more or less standard Serbian.

In *Ljubavni Slučaj* ethnic features are represented in a slightly more pronounced manner. In a non-linear way – interrupted by various bits of discourse circulating in society (such as sexology, criminology, sanitary science, pornography) – the film tells the story of Izabela (Eva Ras), a young switchboard operator and Ahmed (Slobodan Aligrudić), a somewhat older sanitary inspector and party member. The two meet casually in the streets of Belgrade and soon enter into a lasting and happy relationship. While Ahmed is away for work for a few weeks, Izabela betrays him with her young colleague at the post office, Mića (Miodrag Andrić). After Ahmed returns, Izabela discovers she is pregnant, with it being left open which of the two men is the father of the child. Izabela enters a state of crisis and brusquely turns down Ahmed's offer to marry her. During one of the ensuing fights, while trying to keep Ahmed from committing suicide, Izabela accidentally falls into a well and drowns. Ahmed is the main suspect and is arrested and charged with murder.

This basic story about love and betrayal is animated by strong contrasts between the two main characters, Izabela and Ahmed. Whereas Izabela is playful, sensuous, modern, open minded and sexually very active, even promiscuous, Ahmed is portrayed as being tense, anxious about his reputation, bound to his job and the party, he abstains from alcohol and is not very experienced erotically – he confesses that Izabela is his 'first modern woman'.

These opposites are linked to ethnic belongings. Izabela is presented as a member of the Hungarian minority which is associated with a more modern life style, whereas Ahmed is a member of the Muslim Slav group of citizens, which was seen – as the film shows – as being the more conservative, traditional and male-dominated strata of society. These differences sometimes enter into conflict that at first is portrayed as rather light and playful (even if, of course, in the end it turns out to be serious and even violent). So for instance after their first night together Izabela remarks that she had not had a man for two months and coquettishly adds 'and that is long for a Hungarian girl', after which Ahmed jokes about what his colleagues say about such modern Hungarian women. In another scene he calls her 'Eve' and she refers to him as 'Suleiman the Turk'. Other times they are shown as being set apart by a cultural gap – for instance when Isabel sings a Hungarian song for him and Ahmed remarks 'I do not understand a word'; or when she tap dances naked through his apartment, past windows with the curtains open and he anxiously asks her to put on some clothes.

But even if such indications are represented, they are constantly linked to sexual difference. Makavejev rarely makes ethnic differences between various men or between groups of women an issue, but rather accentuates sexual difference through the figuration of ethnic difference (and vice versa) – whereas such a difference usually appears at the same time as one that also distinguishes a more playful, free and open approach towards the world, and in particular towards the party and communism, from a rather closed, inhibited and rigid one. This can, for example, be seen in a scene in which Ahmed is enthusiastically absorbed in some revolutionary German communist songs by Hanns Eisler, a record of which he has brought home and which he plays on the balcony for the whole building complex, with Izabela being depicted as an amused bystander.

Through Izabela, as Daniel J. Goulding (1994: 224) stated, Makavejev celebrates 'sensual liberation, joy, humor, spontaneity, and creativity as the anti-death mechanisms of counter-repression'. In this function Izabela resembles Raika, the female protagonist in *Čovek nije tica* (Figure 38) who is represented in a similar contrasting way in relation to her lover Jan Rudinski (Janez Vrhovec). This celebration is carried out through a multitude of small scenes, showing Izabela voluptuously sucking on milk cartons or unconventionally brewing coffee on an upside down iron. Ahmed's (as well as Jan's) behaviour mainly serves as the foil of rigidness and conventionalism against which Izabela's (and Raika's) freer and spontaneous approach becomes more luminous.

Izabela and Raika are examples of the strong female characters that are typical of Makavejev's films – which is why he is sometimes called a 'feminist' (Durgnat 1999: 87). But what he shows in these two films is not a political self-representation of women, as this attribution would suggest. Makavejev is rather linking up with another tradition – one

Figure 38: Raika, *Čovek nije tica. Ljubavni film/Man is not a Bird. A Film Romance*, Dušan Makavejev, 1965 © Dušan Makavejev, courtesy Jugoslovenska Kinoteka, Belgrade.

that connects figurations of femininity with everything the male-dominated world of official, bureaucratic, economic life excludes as 'other', for instance sensuousness, sexuality, beauty, unconventionality, etc. In this tradition, which is strongly present in the arts (literature, painting, political allegory) in the eighteenth and nineteenth centuries, representations of femininity serve as a projection space that allows those, who create them, the artists, writers or more or less revolutionary politicians, to position themselves opposite the status quo they were living in (Pechriggl 2000: 164ff.; Schober 2011: 394). Similar to the figure of the bare-breasted Marianne of the French Revolution, who accommodates anything 'new', utopian and 'other' against which male patriots were able to socialize as 'equal', Raika and Izabela stand for a new, joyful, and less repressed approach to life that Makavejev and some of his colleagues were missing in an environment, they viewed as characterized by corruption and 'social schizophrenia.'[13] Hence the author projects his utopian view of society onto the female figures of his films – and even employs ethnic features in order to enhance their 'difference' vis-à-vis the existing world.

The representations of Izabela and Raika fit into this tradition, but do not expose or alienate it. The female protagonist of his next feature film *WR*, Milena (Milena Dravić), differs from this. She also adopts this tradition, but overplays it at the same time and – again in a form of a collage with fragments of various examples of political representation and adoration – exposes it and makes its functioning graspable for us as spectators.

Despite the already mentioned opening scene of *WR* showing the egg yolk and various pairs of hands playing with it, the film is more abstract then the earlier two. It is composed of two sections which are continuously inter-cut. The first is a documentary about the life, persecution and death of Wilhelm Reich in the United States as well as how his theories are used in contemporary bio-energetic and primal-scream therapeutic practice. The second is a fictional story set in Yugoslavia in the late 1960s, which is kept in motion by Milena, a young revolutionary woman inspired by Reichian ideas about sexual freedom. Milena meets Vladimir Ilyich (Ivica Vidović), named after Lenin, a handsome young ice skater with political mainstream communist ideas, falls in love with him and tries to seduce him. She succeeds, but pays the price, for after they have made love and as a kind of punishment for the fact that she was able to expose his weak side, he decapitates her with his ice skates. In the final scenes one sees the decapitated head of Milena in the autopsy room speaking about Vladimir Ilyich as a 'red fascist' and the latter with blood on his hands in a wasteland where gypsies are warming themselves around fire pits, appealing to an unknown God – in the words and tunes of a song of the Russian underground poet Bulat Okudjava.

The film can be described as being more abstract than his earlier feature films because Milena's and Vladimir Ilyich's actions are not represented on an everyday 'street level' but are rather allegories for the different forms of socialism created in Yugoslavia and the Soviet Union. The film brings Milena's naive, energetic and rhetoric presentation of Reichian sexual politics frequently in connection with items representing Yugoslavia. In one scene she gives a passionate speech on the balconies of her tenement building about socialism and sexuality, dressed in a short nightie, army jacket, army cap and combat boots on her feet. As part of a *kozara* snake dance that is spontaneously organized by some of the inhabitants, a partisan song is sung, altered by a new text celebrating love and free sexuality. Vladimir Ilyich, by contrast, stands for a sexuality that is inhibited and directed towards power politics – something that the film brings into association with various images depicting totalitarian leaders and their followers – be it Hitler, Stalin or Lenin – as well as with militarism in the United States in the context of the Vietnam War. Hence their love affair can be interpreted as mirroring the relationship between Yugoslavia and the USSR, after the invasion of Czechoslovakia and in the midst of 1968 and the sexual revolution.

In *WR* Makavejev does not celebrate Milena the same way as he celebrated his female protagonists in his previous films. The film deals with her in an always ironic (Figure 39) – and thus to some extent controlling (Schober 2009b: 197) – way. She is depicted as a kind of

Figure 39: Ironic representation, *WR: Misterije organizma/WR: Mysteries of the Organism*, Dušan Makavejev, 1971 © Dušan Makavejev, courtesy Jugoslovenska Kinoteka, Belgrade.

macho type with metal-rimmed glasses on her nose, feet on the table, smoking a cigar and reading the journal *Communist* – before going into her Orgone Box. In sharp contrast to this Jagoda (Jagoda Kaloper), Milena's room-mate, whose name means 'strawberry', appears similarly to Raika and Izabela in the first two films, as a candid incorporation of freely lived sexuality and refreshing unconventionality. Next to Jagoda, Milena reads Marxist literature or gives passionate speeches, whereas the former is seen making love with Ljuba 'The Cock' (Miodrag Andrić) – partially covered by a carpet.

Standing out from this pattern of femininity that Jagoda incorporates, Milena assumes a rather didactic function. In one scene, she explains the personality cult and erotic attraction of totalitarian leaders to Vladimir Ilyich and to us as spectators. When he discovers a photograph on her wall depicting Hitler surrounded by women who stare at him adoringly and asks 'why do you keep this hideous photograph?' Milena explains to him that it is the depicted women on the photograph who 'endow authority with the primordial power of sex' and it is through them that this 'inhuman, bestial force' can be 'made to seem human'. By simultaneously assuming an enhanced erotic pose and tone of voice, she also questions her own role as a projection figure.

This is made even more explicit in a later scene. When she tries to seduce Vladimir Ilyich by kissing him and finally touching his private parts, he reacts by slapping her face, whereupon she formulates a strong plea: 'You love all mankind, yet you are incapable of loving one individual. […] You said I was as lovely as the revolution. But you couldn't bear the 'Revolution' touching you! […] You place your body at the service of art. […] A bunch of lies is what you're serving the people and the party! A toy balloon is what it is – not a revolution!'

Hence *WR* is much more ambivalent in respect to femininity as a projection space for otherness than the earlier two films. Milena exposes the ways in which she is made into a 'picture' from which the creative artists gets his inspiration for serving his art (and his country). But at the same time the film also playfully repeats such mechanisms of projection in the figure of Jagoda, 'the strawberry'.

WR shows the globally connected, transnational character of events and happenings – in politics as well as in the sexual field. In contrast to the earlier two feature films and in tune with the wider student movement of 1968, difference is here almost solely figured as a sexual and aesthetic difference or as a difference in the ways in which sexuality is lived. This has become the main mediating discourse that Makavejev links up to. Details indicating ethnic or national belonging and tension are less present than in *Čovek nije tica* or *Ljubavni Slučaj*. In this respect the sharpest opposition *WR* establishes is the (political) one between Yugoslav and Soviet socialism.

The main strands of internal criticism present in Yugoslavia in those years, the one formulated by the Praxis group, excluded Lenin from their re-examination of totalitarianism (Goulding 1994: 236). In *WR* Makavejev by contrast implicates him in the figure of Vladimir Ilyich, who also quotes some famous Lenin phrases and even links him to questions of the body and sexuality. This turned out to be one of the main reasons why the film became such a bone of contention in socialist countries.[14]

The strongest attack on *WR* came from the Soviet Union. Western critics who had written positively about the film were not invited to the following Moscow Film Festival (Robinson 1971: 180). In Yugoslavia the film first passed censorship, but then, Makavejev remembers, 'a screening was organized by people hostile to the film – they got about 400 people, mainly older people, [...] people who are taking care of monuments and graveyards and museums, plus old revolutionaries, so-called hard-liners [...] and they were mad [...] because Stalin was connected with sexuality! Stalin was connected with the phallus. And they are just completely unable to see *any* connection between political power and sexuality [...] They were sweating, trembling, a lot of physical signs: they were just showing complete physiological distress. But these reactions were expressed in very political terms: "politically unacceptable", "ideologically wrong", "attitude of the enemy", this kind of political cliché were all activated against the film' (Makavejev in Sitton et al. 1971–1972: 6). As a consequence the film was eliminated from the official register of produced films and a decision was attached to it that stated 'the film is not finished and will never be finished' and was signed by the president of the film-makers union of the Vojvodina region of Serbia and the secretary of the party cell of the Film-Maker's Union (Makavejev 2001: 8).

Author cinema, the authentic and the 'ethnic' or 'national' question

As *Čovek nije tica* and *Ljubavni Slučaj* show, in Yugoslavia in the mid 1960s details that indicated a belonging to an ethnic group could be represented if this did not amount to explicit conflict-ridden stories in respect to national unity.[15] Nevertheless, directors were used to treating this issue with extreme caution. So Dušan Makavejev recalls the story of a detail in *Čovek nije tica* that was not planned in advance. The role of Božko, the young truck driver the female protagonist Raika is betraying her true love Jan Rudinski with, is played by the Croatian actor Boris Dvornik, who came from the costal area around Split. In order to get rid of the strong and for him 'fantastic' and 'funny' sounding intonation typical of this region – something he did not want to have in the film at first, also because it was in danger of clashing with the way he was supposed to deal with such particularities – Makavejev had his voice dubbed by a Serbian speaker. But after hearing the result, he found that the character and the new voice did not fit at all – which was why he stuck to the first version and 'restored' Božko's original voice (I DM). In this way the particularity of his regional belonging remains present in the film, and turned out to remain un-contested.

In *Ljubavni Slučaj* such details are present in a much franker way. The erotic tension between Izabela and Ahmed are even staged by inserting sensuous memory fossils (Marks 2000: 110f.). One of these is the strudel, which is able to evoke olfactory memories of the Austro-Hungarian past, another the German songs by Hanns Eisler, which were mistaken for Nazi chants by contemporary audiences and therefore caused some irritation (Makavejev 1967: 40). These details created a kind of anthropological comment in respect to the everyday surroundings of the cinema audience, but also staged affiliation to attributable groups in ethnic or national terms or caused confusion, though sometimes also interest.

Around the time *WR* was made, the tensions between various ethnic groups in Yugoslavia began to emerge in a sharper way than before – most notable with the 'Croatian Spring' (1967–1971). Symptomatically for this period in which real existing ethnic conflicts started to rise, the portrayal of difference as an 'ethnic' (or 'national') one was controlled more and more – something which is reflected in *WR*. In a scene in which Vladimir Ilyich is presented in person to Jagoda for the first time, the latter asks him: 'Are you a real Russian? Or maybe a Jew? Or a Lithuanian or something else?' Upon which Vladimir Ilyich answers: 'To us nationality means nothing […] Only work and achievement count' – an answer that closely resembled official propaganda language in Yugoslavia and in the context of the Croatian uprising could only be understood ironically.

But besides such remarks and the Gypsies shown sitting around the fireplaces at the end of the film, the main difference in respect to ethnic or national unities staged in *WR* was simultaneously a political one – between different regimes of sexuality and their connection to power mirrored in the relationship of a Yugoslavia influenced by Reichian ideas and the Soviet Union.

In one of the interviews he gave, Makavejev quoted an old saying, stating 'We have five regions, four languages, three religions, two economies, and one Tito' (Makavejev in Arthur 2001: 13). The events around *WR* demonstrate that around 1971 the emphasis of what one could legitimately express in public had again shifted away from the various regions, religions, languages (and economies) towards Tito and the 'people as one' (Lefort 1986: 297f.) he (Tito) was seen as representing – which made the connection between sexuality and the totalitarian leaders portrayed in the film so troublesome for official politics in Yugoslavia.

Makavejev was well aware that the author cinema he himself first took part in and later tried to differentiate himself from had a double-edged role in respect to everything 'national'. It was created and disseminated as a kind of transnational movement using inspirations from films made in both Western and Eastern Bloc countries, but at the same time contributed to new kinds of nationalizations. However, he refers to this double role most explicitly not in connection to Yugoslav, but to Czechoslovak cinema: 'In Czechoslovakia in the 1960s the cinema was at the beginning of social change, of the Prague Spring. The cinema, a non-verbal means, was the first to shatter this verbal armour forged by the regime. Nobody had been able to invent new words. […] The Czech films – visual, poetic, playful, oneiric and fantastic – had revitalized a national sensibility. The Czech people by tradition love to convene and all that had been stalled by self-named socialism, by the violence of the Soviet occupation, by the "stranglehold of brotherhood". The films have to guide people back to their existential problems, to life, death, to questions of freedom and slavery which they don't have in mind and for which they have to seek solutions in the course of their everyday lives' (m. t. Kramer and Makavejev 1975: 27).

Around 1970 the new visual language Makavejev himself was working on had – as a consequence of his enthusiasm for '1968' – resulted in focusing mainly on figurations of sexual difference, of aesthetic difference and of non-repressive forms of sexuality. In respect to this, the representation of national or ethnic difference almost disappeared – he dealt with it only in an ironic way. Nevertheless, he was then also viewed as an author – by people from outside at festivals and in reviews, as well as by people inside the country – who was linked to something like 'Yugoslav culture'.

According to Dušan Makavejev, film-making has the potential to enable the spectators to gain a new, unexpected, more authentic relationship vis-à-vis their lives. 'Because our everyday life', he explains, 'is not our real life. Sometimes we have more authentic relationships with ourselves when we view a film' (m. t. Kramer and Makavejev 1975: 21).

Although he never subscribed to an essential, fixed notion of authenticity, similarly to other authors of his generation he did identify certain phenomena as more 'authentic' than others. In the mid 1960s he connected authenticity not only, as already mentioned, to the female figures of his films but also to various kinds of rural people (with all their religious, regional, social, national or ethnic particularities) as opposed to urban ones (Makavejev 1967: 41). Around 1970 this had shifted – he now linked authenticity mainly to non-repressive, more liberated forms of sexuality that also go beyond the realm of the sexual in the close sense towards an enhanced creativity of life practice.

Consequently, he also judged the Croatian uprising in 1971 and the official dealing with it under these premises: 'We have this conflict between the Croats and the others, and now we have changed the constitution, but in fact it was the conflict that had started everything. It's about conserving what one has, not about organizing it differently. The conflict takes place first, and we repair it afterwards. There is no creative change without spontaneous or creatively provoked conflict. I respect the Croats who made the conflict visible because it is useful. On the other hand I didn't see this creative activity in the Reichian sense' (m. t. Ciment and Cohn 1971: 51f.). Hence in the early 1970s he even described the rising tensions between various nationalities in sexual terms – which also means that 'the national' or 'the ethnic'[16] as a political problem in its own right can be seen as being a blind spot in his then world-view. It was not part of the mediating discourses he was mainly drawing on.

Simultaneously, and connected to depictions of the rural or sexually liberated other as mirror-figures for the authenticity of the spectator (and himself), Makavejev, like other authors from the 1960s and 1970s such as Rainer Werner Fassbinder, brought the individual – in the form of Milena, Izabela, Ahmed or Raika – into the foreground and empowered it, but also burdened it with resolving questions and demands that formerly in his context had been strictly dealt with as 'social' by official procedures. Even around 1968 he was already paying special attention to 'individual action' and opposed this to the control of everything personal in socialist societies. He stated: 'The whole world is participating in social movements, but one is not forced to be in a group all the time. Individualism is love, it is the right to be lunatic, it is the right to have personal conflicts. In Russia you have the impression that it is shameful to have personal problems' (m. t. Ciment 1968: 19). Such foregrounding of the individual became even stronger in *WR* and was, a few years later, also adopted by a younger generation of film-makers such as Srđan Karanović or Emir Kusturica.

As the developments in former Yugoslavia in the 1980s and 1990s showed, authenticity soon became represented in other figurations of difference – mainly as 'national' ones, which now turned into the dominant mediating discourses – and was simultaneously linked to ever more far-reaching roots into the past. In this process, the individual, so much foregrounded at the end of the 1960s, was confronted with new offers to become part of associations conceived as 'one': in the form of the nation, for which again a plurality of differences was erased and a singular, stable identity imposed. Related to this, the figuration of difference as sexual and aesthetic that is so present in Makavejev's films then often again, and much more explicitly and vividly than before, became perceived and re-configured in national terms – as I will now show by presenting the production and reception history of a film, *Virdžina/ Virgina* (1991), made by Srđan Karanović.

Karanović is more than a decade younger than Makavejev. Nevertheless, he also made his first moves as a film-maker in the kino club Beograd and claimed to be strongly inspired by the work of his older colleague (Centar Film Beograd et al. 2000: 189). Besides, he was part of the 'Czech school' of Yugoslav cinema since he attended the famous FAMU (film academy) in Prague – he was thus part of the next generation of film-makers who learned film-making not only as amateurs but also engaged in specialist and professionalized training. Karanović started to project *Virdžina* in 1979, but realized it – after two other films made in between – only in 1990/1991.

The production history of the film is heavily marked by the offshoots of the Tito era: Around 1979 Srđan Karanović came across a newspaper article describing an Albanian girl, who lived as a boy and later as a young man, but came – through a love story – to rediscover her original sexual identity and to go on to live as a woman. Her story was closely connected to Yugoslav history and identity, since she even joined the group of partisans in her village, went with them across Yugoslavia to Trieste and so became one of the soldiers 'liberating' the city (I SK).

In speaking to ethnologists and consulting ethnographic literature it was immediately clear to Karanović that this was far from being an isolated case. In some parts of Montenegro and present-day Albania and Kosovo, families and clans who failed to produce a male heir could decide to raise a girl as a boy, who this way became a fully socially accepted male member of society (including the right to carry arms and to become the head of the household). Whereas these former women as well as people from their surrounding referred to themselves as respectable men, the name others also used for them was *virdžineža* in Montenegro, *burrneshë* in Albanian, *muškobanja* in Serbian or *tobelija* in Bosnian – coming from the word *tobyé*, meaning 'a vow' (Young 2001: 62). This already indicates that the right to live as a man was connected to a vow to maintain life-long virginity, taken either by the father of the girl or by herself. There were both secretly sworn virgins, whose original sex was only known to their parents and themselves, and others 'made' by public declaration, according to Srđan Karanović (I SK).[17]

Srđan Karanović was not attracted by the sworn virgins as a social phenomenon so much as he was by the problem of a person who wants to be what she or he really is, while society wants her or him to be something else (I SK). Besides, he was interested in those elements of life practised during recent Yugoslav history that were hardly talked about officially – such as partisans engaging in religious or superstition-driven acts (Karanović 1998: 12f.). He decided to turn the 'found' story into a film, but for a long time encountered huge problems.

For national producers the issue was 'too hot'. For what was planned was a war partisan movie, a film that dealt with the main representative figure of socialist Yugoslavia, but at the same time the story threatened to tarnish the myth of the partisan, since it again (similar to Makavejev's *WR*) raised issues of sexuality, but also of religion and superstition. Because of this, Karanović soon decided to change the script and to focus entirely on the childhood and coming of age of the girl. He now positioned the story at the end of the nineteenth century, when migration from the mountainous regions of Montenegro, and present-day Kosovo and Albania was high. But things remained the same. He even ordered translations of the various versions of the scripts into English and French, but international co-productions did not materialize for a long time – first because the story seemed to be located in a too remote region, later because of the looming war (Karanović 1998: 65).

Finally, around 1990, a French-Croatian-Serbian co-production was mounted and it was decided to shoot the film in locations around Knin, a town in Croatia (but predominantly Serb populated), mainly because the co-production required that the money granted by Croatian authorities was spent in Croatia.

Karanović's plan was to 'create the impression, that the whole story takes place on the moon' (I SK). This meant that a setting of stone houses was constructed high up in the mountainous, rocky, dry and bleak landscape and greenery was avoided as much as possible during shooting (I SK). At the same time he intended to avoid ethnic references completely. 'I simply thought that the story is not about that', Karanović stated in a retrospective interview (I SK). Besides, he had already dealt with the rising ethnic tensions in another film, where he also portrayed how the media were involved in enlarging and dramatizing these tensions: *Za sada bez dobrog naslova/A film with no name* (1988).[18]

The rocky landscape dominating the set for *Virdžina* was accompanied by 'an alternation of extreme long shots with extreme close-ups and details. I wanted the relatively long shots to appear massive. Just like […] stone sculptures' (Centar Film Beograd et al. 2000: 189). To this he added darkened colours and a special laboratory process that reduced colour film and approximated it as much as possible to a black-and-white gamma (Centar Film Beograd et al. 2000: 188).

The result should be a film 'set in stone', strong enough to make a stand against the historical political circumstances and to redirect the view again towards the individual and its desire for self-discovery. The context however continued to interfere strongly with the fate of this film. Because as a kind of irony of history the location chosen for the shooting of the film was accidentally situated on the border between a Croatian and Serbian village in an area that in 1991 would become the 'Republic of Serbian Krajina', a self-proclaimed Serbian entity in Croatia which claimed independence (I SK).

When shooting started on 3 October 1990 in the city of Knin, barricades were already established and it was difficult to pass between the Croatian and Serbian side. Spurred on by this and by rumours about the rising tensions, some members of the team, which was mostly composed of Croatians, left (Karanović 1998: 79ff.). Srđan Karanović and his friend Rajko Grlić, who had helped to secure the Croatian funding and was himself a resident in Croatia, were accused of making the film solely for nationalist reasons. Thereby Raiko Grlić was even called a *Chetnik* – a name that was being used for Serb nationalists or royalists at the time (I SK). Because of these events, as well as some technical problems, shooting had to be interrupted several times – and then winter came. The film was finished in the course of a few days shooting in March 1991, shortly before the war 'started in earnest' (I SK).

But even then the troubles were not over. Because of the war and the dissolution of Yugoslavia, the film was never publicly shown in Croatia, Slovenia or Bosnia-Hercegovina, except privately on DVD. At the same time the film was a huge success in Serbia and a 'decent success' internationally (I SK). In parallel, also the French co-production company fell apart – so that today no print of the film is available, it exists solely on DVD.

The story itself is staged in an almost paradigmatic way as a step by step resolution of an identity crisis. At the beginning, the film pictures the difficulties of a peasant clan, caused by aridity and famine which are superstitiously and collectively attributed to the lack of a son in a family with several daughters. When yet another daughter is born, the father first wants

Figure 40: 'Stevan', *Virdžina/Virgina*, Srđan Karanović, 1991–1992 © Srđan Karanović, courtesy Jugoslovenska Kinoteka, Belgrade.

to shoot her, but then decides to raise her as a boy, as Stevan (Figure 40). Most of the film shows Stevan growing up, the conflicts and inner turmoil produced by the situation, and an awaking love relationship with one of the boys in the neighbourhood. After the death of the mother in childbirth to another child, this love experience leads to a strong conflict with the father, which culminates in a gunfight during which the father dies. Stevan, her young lover and the newborn baby, again a girl, form a kind of 'family' and join a group of peasants, who are leaving for the United States. Stevan thus changes from a crisis-ridden sexual identity into a stable one, characterized by a maternal caring for the newborn baby.

The film includes us as viewers from the beginning through a narrative 'view behind'. As opposed to the various characters in the film, we as an audience know (because the film has shown it to us, but part of the story is the fact that it is not revealed to them also) that Stevan was born a girl. In addition, strong gales, rituals prayers for rain and the clan members' constant conversation with God through their Orthodox 'house-saint' Saint George remind us that the sexual coercion practised by the clan also has a strong religious-magic dimension. These religious references also make evident that the film is set in an Orthodox milieu.

Like Makavejev's films, *Virdžina* is also inter-cut by shots bringing various sensuous materials tangibly close to us. Close-ups of food – milk, corn and bread – as well as the bandages around Stevan's breasts or of the firm soil the peasants have to work interrupt the long and massive narrative shots. Similarly important is the detailed depiction of bodily conduct and bodily sensation: when Stevan watches her older sister taking a bath at night, we also to some extent see what she observes: a half-naked female body, breasts and wet skin – before she is invited to touch her, and the sister enthusiastically talks about how beautiful it is to be a woman. In this way, 'memory-fossils' in respect to femininity are brought into the film.

This depiction of a rediscovery of sexual identity corresponds to some findings writers and anthropologists such as Slavenka Drakulić or Ivan Čolović report for the period of the downfall of socialism in former Yugoslavia and the war following it. They too describe a strong rediscovery of sexual difference, which usually, however, was also a process of pronounced re-invention, often closely connected to consumer culture – in the form of the emergence of hyper-feminine or -masculine appearances and of the alteration of ordinary womanhood into enhanced erotic and extravagant beings. Slavenka Drakulić expounds in detail how women – among them herself, a friend and her mother – started to buy fur coats, because of their 'desire to be a woman, not just the sexless human being propaganda was teaching [us A. S.] to become' (Drakulić 1993: 141). And some photographs of Dragan Petrović (Figure 41) show that around 1990 ordinary young women had started to dress up in hot pants and net stockings and so appeared in the hypersexual way that in other environments is usually associated with prostitutes.

Ivan Čolović highlights another aspect of this by demonstrating how closely the rediscovery of sexual and ethnic or even national difference was often interlinked. The 'battle for the nation' he explains 'is not only something patriotic but something very masculine' (Čolović 2000: 48). He quotes an article published in *Javnost* (12 November 1994) that reports about a part of Sarajevo, considered dangerous to Serbian fighters

Figure 41: Hypersexual public appearance, Saturday night outfit, Dragan Petrović, 1990s © Dragan Petrović.

and only approachable by those 'who knew what they had between their legs' (Čolović 2000: 48).

Hence particular clothes but also some forms of behaviour, and in some cases even violence, could be employed to make oneself unambiguously feminine or masculine (and simultaneously Serbian, Croatian, or Bosnian), so that they could help reduce the confusing and multiple stories circulating in this crisis-ridden environment to some that are suitable for easy reading and identity-securing.[19] The above quotation from Slavenka Drakulić mentioning that official Titoist propaganda reduced everyone to a status of 'sexlessness' again highlights that this strong rediscovery of (sexual, ethnic, national) difference happening in the 1980s and 1990s had to do with the denial of difference in the fetish-like handling of the 'people as one' and the strong control of difference that characterized official language in the socialist one-party state.

In the context of the early 1990s even the subtle depiction of a re-formation of sexual identity as it is present in *Virdžina* was open to the emergence of non-intended correlations and articulations with the phenomenon of newly invented nationalism. As the production and reception history of the film shows (Karanović 1998: 85f.), despite Srđan Karanović's intention to keep the film as free as possible of clear ethnic and national attributes, the depicted story could be perceived in such a way. Hence the film could be read – and was read – as a 'Serbian film'. Such associations and correlations were also supported by the fact that the core of the Serbian political myth of the 1990s consisted, as Ivan Čolović (2000: 64) has shown, in the assumption of a stable, unchanging national identity that constantly has to be asserted and can be summarized as 'Let us be what we are!' The 'becoming what she always was' and the radical re-affirmation of Stevan's (gender) identity in *Virdžina* could be integrated into this.

The fact that the film depicted the re-assertion of a woman was not an obstacle – on the contrary. Like Izabela, Raika, Jagoda or Milena in Makavejev's films Stevan can also be read as incarnation of an involvement in processes of emancipation juxtaposed with an everyday life viewed as characterized by constraints and insufficiencies. For with the breaking away of Tito as the uniting body and figure of power that 'what one always was but was denied to be by society' was strongly opened up to new interpretations and life practices. And the individuals were increasingly thrown back onto themselves in coping with this and in positioning themselves vis-à-vis the newly emerging national, ethnic, religious and hypersexual offers.

Hence in a similar way to those in central Europe, film-makers in Yugoslavia who were associated with '1968' also participated in a sometimes emphatically staged rediscovery of difference. Like Makavejev's films show, they emphasized the sensuous, haptic, sexual and erotic dimension of film, linked it to stories that featured rural people, women and characters associated with particular social and regional milieus and used unconventional forms of representation involving collage, enhanced montage, parody and humour. In this way they opposed a modern political order characterized by the privileging of certain differences such as 'the nation' or 'the proletariat' and a suppression or at least strong control of all other appearances of difference. And again, in a similar way to film-makers in the FRG or Austria, in Yugoslavia too this went together with an emphasis on the individual outside traditional familial and patriarchal structures and turned this individual into the main social conflict-resolution entity.

Nevertheless, the case of Yugoslavia around 1990 reveals more clearly that this rediscovery of difference potentially also has an – often hidden – side linked to a violent policing of the borders between 'we' and 'them' groups. An experience of authenticity by way of hypermasculine (or -feminine) appearance and warfare in ethnic terms exist side by side. At the same time it becomes graspable that the various figurations of difference can be 'converted' into each other: gender difference can be used to articulate national difference and the latter can be expressed in gender terms. In the process, cinema plays a double-edged role: it acts as a projection space for entrenching the self and the other, but it can also serve as an event space, where prevailing figurations of self and other can be called into question.

Notes

1   The *action studio* is a cinema in Munich that was frequented by Fassbinder in 1960s. It was run by Ursula Strätz and her husband, who together later organized the Action Theater in Munich. See the interview with Ursula Strätz in the film *Für mich gab's nur noch Fassbinder. Die glücklichen Opfer des Rainer Werner Fassbinder* (2000) by Rosa von Praunheim.

2   In particular Raoul Walsh, Douglas Sirk and Howard Hawks, in addition to European film-makers like Jean-Luc Godard or Luis Buñuel (Bensoussan 2004 [1981]: 575).

3   On the relation between sketchiness and imagination, see Bippus 2009.

4   Fassbinder speaks of 'a love unbound by constraints, one that cannot be exploited.' (m. t. Limmer and Rumler 2004 [1980]: 524f.). On the relation between physical suffering and salvation in Fassbinder's work as addressed, for example, in the film *In a Year of 13 Moons* (1982), see Koch et al. 1986; see also Elsaesser 2001: 338.

5   The attempt to turn *Eventmentalisation* into an aesthetic concept and position it in the filmic work itself – rather than in the confrontation of work and audience reception – can, for example, be found in various contributions in Ezli 2010. In this way, however, the concept of the event becomes politically 'defused'.

6   *Katzelmacher* won the top prize in five categories (German Film Prize/*goldenes Filmband*) and a film prize awarded by the Federal Republic of Germany. As an example for the critics' positive response, see Baer 1970. *Ali: Fear Eats the Soul* won the Prize of the Ecumenical Jury in 1974 at the Cannes Film Festival and the German Film Award in Gold for the leading actress Brigitte Mira. The critics called it a 'sensation'. See Schütte 1974.

7   Because of the depiction of two communists as an elegant and wealthy couple living in a bourgeois period flat, several viewers left the cinema in protest at the 1975 Berlin Film Festival during the screening of *Mutter Küsters Fahrt zum Himmel/Mother Küsters Goes to*

Heaven (1975) (Sparrow 2004 [1977]: 411). Some homosexuals felt they were portrayed negatively in *Faustrecht der Freiheit/Fox and His Friends* (1974–1975) and criticized Fassbinder (see Fassbinder in Sparrow 2004 [1977]: 411).

8   On this, Fassbinder stated: 'At this point I can only give exact information about the Federal Republic of Germany. If I wanted to talk about anything else, I would have to resort to things I have read and the experiences or news I have personally gleaned from that. That would be wrong' (m. t. Jansen 2004 [1978]: 441).

9   In this he was joined for instance by Želimir Žilnik, who was 'advised' to leave the country at about the same time (I ZZ).

10   The philosophers of the Praxis group called 'classical' Marxist concepts such as economic determinism, class, base/superstructure and society/state into question. They brought the concepts of 'consciousness' and 'false consciousness' as well as 'alienation' and 'subjectivity' into the foreground and discussed these often using the notion of 'human nature'. Erich Fromm's 'Socialist Humanism' (1965) was influential for Praxis philosophy (Shigeno 2004). Erich Fromm was also important for the development of Makavejev's approach. In an interview published in 1984, the latter stated: 'At that time [around 1967, A. S.] I knew Erich Fromm better [than Wilhelm Reich, A. S.] and was influenced by his ideas of escape from freedom, of de-repression and social organization that has to involve personal happiness' (Makavejev 1984: 84). From the mid-1980s the national question appeared increasingly as part of the discourse circulated by Praxis Marxists from Serbia. The 'nation' started to occupy the central place in their discourse and to replace 'self-management' which previously was at the core of Praxis negotiations (Shigeno 2004: 236ff.).

11   Ana Hofman (2010: 145) has pointed out that in the rural society in Serbia, professional *kafana* singers like Fatima were identified with the Roma, regardless of their ethnic background, since for women singing in public was seen as an immoral and stigmatizing activity.

12   I would like to thank Ana Hofman who helped to locate the dialect.

13   In respect to Yugoslav socialism, Makavejev stated: 'We have an extraordinarily good constitution, […] perfect laws, an excellent programme, democratic and liberal human principles. The praxis has nothing to do with that. […] In our case everything is more visible. One knows that the same functionary who makes a democratic and humanitarian discourse is at the same time misusing his power' (m. t. Ciment 1968: 19).

14   In the United States, some Reichians also criticized *WR*, which caused the insertion of some modifications. But especially in Europe, the film mostly received positive reviews and even won the prestigious Luis Buñuel prize at the Cannes Film Festival (Goulding 1994: 237).

15   In a previous chapter I referred to a short film made by Marko Babac in 1964 which he attempted to call *Kain i Avelj/Cain and Abel* but was explicitly asked to re-name it *Braća/Brothers* (I MB).

16   Marilyn Halter (2006: 172) has pointed out that a wider use of the term 'ethnic' for the self-description of both white and black people emerged only with 1960 counterculture in the United States. With '1968' the activist free of all particularities was replaced by the enhanced colorful non-conformist activist whose individuality was now usually staged using ethnic

terms. As some examples negotiated in the previous two chapters of this book show, through the transnational student movement, individuality expressed in ethnic terms became adopted also in Europe. In Yugoslavia 'ethnic' particularities appeared in films by novi film-makers since the 1960s, but a wider use of the term 'ethnic' can only be witnessed in the course of the 1980s, prior to that terms related to 'nation' like 'narodni' or 'narodnost' were in use. On traditions of 'ethnic' and/or 'national' belonging in Yugoslavia see: Fischer 2013.

17 Most examples have been documented over the last 160 years, mainly in cases when male family members were reduced by blood feuds, but also by migration. Nevertheless, the custom is already mentioned in the famous *Kanun*, the orally delivered Albanian code of common law, collected by Lekë Dukagjini in the fifteenth century (Young 2001: xxi and 56).

18 Contrary to the rising national discourse in Serbia that portrayed Albanians as a threat (Shigeno 2004: 252), the film depicted a gentle love story between an Albanian girl and a Serbian man that was turned by anonymous nationalists and chauvinists into a tragedy that was widely exploited (and this way enhanced) by various strands of the media system.

19 On violence as a symbolic activity linked to experiences of authenticity and to an unambiguous feeling of belonging to a (Serbian, Croatian or Bosnian) nation, see van de Port 1998: 219f.

Chapter 4

Follow-up initiatives

4.1. Violence and humour: cinema activism in times of war

Between 1997 and 2003, in cities such as Belgrade and Subotica a particular form of cinema activism emerged. Under the name 'Low-Fi Video' activists organized regular screenings, the 'Low-Fi Video convention', and film festivals such as the 'Trash Parade', the 'Trash Marathon' or 'Mikrokino' in Belgrade (Figure 42) or the 'Cheap Film Festival' (also 'Yugoslav Festival of Cheap Film') in Subotica, a city in the Autonomous Province of Vojvodina. In these venues they promoted short films and audio-visual works by amateurs as well as more professional film-makers and artists from local as well as international scenes who all shared one main distinguishing quality: humour. Hence this kind of cinema activism that emerged in a situation characterized by war, mass migration and poverty strongly re-animated the humorous tradition of Yugoslav cinema.

Even if at first glance the combination of humour and the difficult, violent and painful period of war in former Yugoslavia seem strange and incongruous, a second closer look shows that the use of humour in a situation marked by these circumstances is far from accidental. According to Sigmund Freud, of all forms of the comic, humour is the only one that is linked in a particular way to disturbing and painful experiences. Humour thus appears as a tactic that can be used in order to gain pleasure out of situations marked by anger, pain, sorrow, compassion, emotion, contempt, indignation, atrocity or disgust. As Freud analyses, humorous pleasure results from a saving in expenditure of affect; it emerges out of saved affect-efforts whereby the affects are re-directed onto other and often incidental or secondary things – a displacement that remains unconscious or preconscious. The humorist takes the model for this from childhood: she laughs about her present painful affects like adults used to laugh about painful affects in her childhood (Freud 1992a: 240ff.). This chapter explores the use of humour in Yugoslav and post-Yugoslav cinema since the 1990s.

Low-Fi Video, Trash Parade and the Cheap Film Festival in Subotica

Despite its name, Low-Fi Video was bound to cinema-like situations the activists used to organize themselves. For the distinguishing feature of the group was that activists were not only making films themselves but were collecting short films through public and internationally distributed calls which were then shown to a wider audience in local public screenings. The main criterion for selection was that films were shorter than 10 minutes.

Figure 42: Mikrokino, Low-Fi Video, Fest 2002 in Belgrade © Low-Fi Video.

Besides, 'Low-Fi' film-makers, the organizers and the audience were united by a certain aesthetics. Miloš Kukurić[1] an initiator of Low-Fi Video described it as follows: 'You couldn't see very many politically engaged films at Low-Fi Video, but you could have seen some comments on our [...] everyday life [...] Love more than anything else [and ...] the big cult films at Low-Fi Video were very funny. [...] Even to talk about serious stuff with some funny elements' (I MK).

At the venues in Belgrade and Subotica the films were shown on VHS regardless of their technical quality. On this, Miloš Kukurić stated: 'That's why [we chose] the name 'Low-Fi'. [With this] we were saying that we were showing good ideas no matter what [...] their technical quality. That was important to us' (I MK). In addition, he mentions that this focus on video-quality also had to do with the environment: 'People were not so rich, maybe they had small "chickens", like VHS cameras at the beginning [...] so we wanted to see those films [... made with a] very small or low [...] budget. Because for some films the only expenses we had were the cost of the tapes, or maybe some of us reused old tapes [...] and the costs were completely zero.' (I MK)

All the films collected were shown during the regular screenings, the 'Low-Fi –Video conventions', in the first years once a month and after 1999 every other month. Only for the various festivals were special selections made according to the taste of the selectors. In this respect Miloš Kukurić especially highlights 'some flow' that had to emerge between the viewer and the film. As part of this 'flow' he mentions in the first place: 'comedy, humour, then idea, if it is something original or very bizarre or something very personal. […] But no art films in this very intellectual and very serious [style]. […] We were interested in emotions. I think art films, most of them, are without any emotions, only beautiful pictures with some greater idea' (I MK).

He then also describes a certain 'evolution' in film-making: 'At the beginning they [the films] were like, very different, and then there was the evolution of digital media and then they started to get some form […] nice films […] but they kept the idea. That was important. So we had some very funny and very witty films but now they were made on the computer and shot with a digital camera but still very crazy and very individual and very different from the institutional documentaries and fiction and experimental films. Very modern and very fast. I think that Low-Fi-authors were much more aware of the DVD, of the media and of what is happening around them, than the "educated" film-makers […] The motivation is different' (I MK).

The Low-Fi aesthetic also extended to how the screenings were themselves staged. They showed films at various already well-known cultural places in Belgrade like 'Cinema Rex' (which, as already mentioned in a previous chapter, was never a real cinema but a cultural centre that was 'dressed up' as a cinema for a film shoot in the 1980s), in the Cinematheque or in the Dom Omladine (House of Youth), but also in some cafes, some cultural centres or even a museum space in a city near Belgrade. Usually there were wooden seats, a screen arranged in the style of a 'real cinema' and a very low, 'only symbolic' entrance fee. Invitations came by e-mail, small posters were photocopied and distributed personally and only a few brochures printed for certain special events (such as Mikrokino). Some of these places had a bar and sold beer, wine or coffee. 'The only things we sold', Miloš Kukurić remembers, 'were drinks, schnapps and bad cigarettes for the "Trash Parade", because it was trash, so we were saying, we are selling very bad cigarettes and one bottle of really bad vodka, it was just for fun not for money' (I MK).

The authors of films shown at Low-Fi-events were young, between 17 and 25, but some also around 13 or 14 and a few 30 or 40 years old, mostly male. Only about a quarter of the film-makers were women, who, however, otherwise participated as actresses or co-workers in the making of films and formed about half of the audience. Some of the film-makers were still at high school or in the first years at the university and their background was quite diverse: they studied electrical engineering, literature or film. For some, film-making was a kind of passing activity, others saw themselves also being professional film-makers in the future; some combined film-making with playing music in bands or with drawing comic-strips and for others it was their sole and overriding passion.

A further characteristic of Low-Fi events was that authors and audience mingled. The film-makers whose works were screened constituted part of the audience and brought their friends and colleagues. So the events sometimes attracted a huge audience: the screenings at Cinema Rex were crowded, with between 250 and 400 people and some of the bigger events such as the Cheap Film Festival in Dom Omladine attracted more than 600 spectators (I MK).

An example of the aesthetic style featured at these screenings is the short film *Nineteen ili kineske baterije/Nineteen … or Chinese Batteries* by Aleksandar Vasiljević (2001, Figure 43) that simultaneously adopts the aesthetics of a video game and that of a documentary. It shows a green field where, among other elements, figures of soldiers emerge, which, as one slowly understands, can be 'shot down' like other targets with the remote control of a TV set. In parallel and rhythmically interrupted by quick tunes and the sounds of shooting there is a male off-voice, similar to those in solemn TV documentaries, saying 'In World War II the average age of a soldier was 26; in Vietnam it was 19'. Suddenly, after another explosion and another unsuccessful attempt at operating the remote control, another voice can be heard saying in a casual tone 'Damn! Chinese batteries' – a sentence that also concludes the film.

This short film operates with condensation and displacement: the presumably neutral voice informing about the age of the average soldier in various wars overlaps and merges with the flow of a video game and both are interrupted by a sentence that seems to come

Figure 43: *Nineteen ili kineske baterije/Nineteen … or Chinese Batteries,* Aleksandar Vasiljević, 2001 © Aleksandar Vasiljević.

from backstage, commenting on it and linking it to seemingly secondary things such as non-functioning Chinese batteries. In these Chinese batteries, however, the present economic globalized condition of the spectators crystallizes – for this condition was characterized by the trade embargo and sanctions imposed by the United Nations on Serbia and Montenegro in 1992 and the subsequent dependence on goods from China, as well as by increased poverty and the consequent backlog of very cheap goods, which often did not work. In this way, a difficult, painful situation characterized by an over-presence of the facts of war, poverty and dependence on cheap, imported goods is on the one hand represented in a seemingly 'neutral way'. On the other hand, this reality is co-opted by a kind of joke, re-directing the omitted effects towards something as incidental as Chinese batteries.

Political-aesthetic dispute

Low-Fi films were directed against a prevailing media representation depicting the ongoing war in former Yugoslavia, but simultaneously also against quite a prominent, explicitly politically involved aesthetics in Belgrade and an activism that was strongly supported by the Soros Foundation, fighting openly against the Milošević regime (on this Schober 2009b: 313ff.). Miloš Kukurić describes this double delineation of Low-Fi Video as follows: 'Maybe we had enough war on TV and in our everyday lives. […] We had been watching it for years, five to six years, on TV, every day, every day. There was fighting here, dead people there, information like that. It was really stressful. […] I didn't feel well listening to those successful battles and conquests. I think we got tired [… at the same time] for me much of those activist things like, you know, fighting explicitly against Milošević was pretty fake. Like for me, the student protest was completely fake. […] If you want to change something, then go and change it, don't make a party in the centre of Belgrade and get beaten by the police or something like that. For me that was always pretty fake, so, those films looked much more sincere to me, because they were from some personal angle. […] Not so direct and so open, like "I think this about that", no, they were coming from some other side […] maybe like […] some rebel teenage […] statement, but still for me very important. Because those people seem like they do think for themselves, not about some important national […] point of view. […] That's why I really enjoyed and liked [these films] and why we worked for six years' (I MK).

The emphasis on 'the cheap', 'the low' and on 'trash' too is directed against other cultural offers that were perceived by the activists as dominant and as showing off wealth, abundance and lavishness. Miloš Kukurić again notes: 'When I heard about those big Serbian films, feature films, which were shown around the world at festivals and everything and when I heard the budget of one of those films [I found it] impossible, like one million euros in a country which is very poor and where everyday life really sucks and they are making such very big films. And I know that in Europe they can shoot a film for less money than [here].

That's why it was really important for us [...] that we were showing films that are made for no money or for very little money' (I MK).

Hence everyday life and the observation of other film and cinema practices that were seen by the activists as dominant led to special experiences of lack and of inadequacy that triggered practices and the articulation of an aesthetic language suited to fill this lack and to confront this inadequacy. Humour thereby appears as an emphatically adopted way of dealing with a present situation marked by war, violence and other options of political activism – a way the activists themselves see as being closely bound to notions of 'truth' and 'directness' and because of this suited to confront a world full of 'fake' representation and public 'passivity'. In this function humour is combined with other elements that are also seen as incarnations of 'truth' and 'directness' such as an emphatic exposition of the body and of bodily fluids such as blood, spit, urine or sperm or obscene or pornographic gestures which are also featured prominently in some of the films screened.

So even if the activists themselves describe the films presented at Low-Fi Video events as being 'not so politically engaged', the aesthetics they coined and the way activists publicly exhibited these films can be judged as taking part in a 'political' struggle in the sense that a loose group constituted itself united by the desire for 'truth', 'authenticity' or 'directness' (as opposed to 'fake') and by using a specific aesthetics in order to call ways of being and the qualities of those present at a common stage into question (Rancière 1999: 36f; Laclau 1990: 68f.).

By stimulating video production, by collecting films and by screening them in the form of open and public events Low-Fi Video participated in creating a local, but globally connected public sphere in post-socialist Yugoslavia. Thereby Low-Fi events show again that the emergence of such a public sphere is bound up with a regaining of difference in the sense of an exhibition of a pronouncedly 'different' aesthetics and the circulation of 'other' meanings and values contesting the reigning ones. But at the same time this kind of activism also testifies that the public sphere now had been transformed into one in which political manifestations and figurations of difference emerge predominantly in cultural spaces, in which entertainment and political engagement mingles and in which the aesthetic level and individual psychic involvement and identification processes come to the fore and give rise to quickly changing communities.

The ambivalence of humour

The huge audiences that films like Aleksandar Vasiljević's attracted show that such humorous films assume an important social and psychic function: they strengthen the morality of the viewers – as Antonin J. Obrdlik (1942: 715ff.) had already maintained in respect to jokes used by Czechs during the German-NS occupation in the 1930s. This function of humour becomes especially evident when Miloš Kukurić describes the difference between the motivation they experienced in the years of their video activism, between 1997 and 2003, and the one of the period after the end of these activities: 'We had all that energy, I don't know how and why, but probably we were expecting something better in the future and we were younger, a little bit younger. […] [But] now, people are really, really tired […] my friends, my family […] now they […] are really, really depressed. No, nothing is happening and we do not see each other for weeks and months' (I MK).

Hence the experience of humour comes together with a certain triumph. This can be seen especially when the Cheap Film Festival in Subotica is remembered as a zone where a certain grandeur could be experienced: 'I will always remember […] that festival in Subotica, which was amazing, because it didn't happen in Belgrade, that was really important […] in 1998, 1999, 2000, 2001 it was really becoming something […] I will always remember some of those moments […] from that feeling of that festival, very relaxed, and very, very […] I don't know […] very simple, but so cool, different energy, so cool, good vibrations and so. […] You know unknown people were coming to Subotica, we were sleeping in some school dormitory […] some of them were being paid by the organizers […] people could pay some really small amount of money to sleep there, to be there for five days, to enjoy, to see those films, to go to concerts […] to get involved' (I MK).

In these statements humour appears as an attempt to cope with a current situation strongly marked by violence, emotion, indignation and disgust. In such contexts, as Freud too found out in relation to the examples he investigated, humour tesifies to the triumph of the ego and of the pleasure principle as well as a rejection of a demand of reality – which also implies that through humour reality is repelled and illusion sustained (Freud 1992b: 254). Perhaps because of these latter regressive tendencies to reject the demands of reality, my interview partner from Low-Fi Video refuses to retrospectively review or re-evaluate the history of their own actions, for instance to re-read the interview he made with me, to read any text about it or to go through any of the material he had collected during his years of video and cinema activism.

In this function of restoring triumph to the ego and the pleasure principle, a variety of short but also of humorous feature films produced in ex-Yugoslavia in the 1990s correlate. This means that besides Low-Fi Video productions also several other films were produced which employ humour in a particular way. Some of these films even explicitly addressed the Titoist past. So Želimir Žilnik's film *Tito po drugi put među Srbima/Tito's second time among the Serbs* (Serbia, 1993, Figure 44) and Vinko Brešan's *Maršal/Marshal Tito's Spirit* (Croatia, 1999) show the re-appearance of Tito in erstwhile Yugoslavia: In *Tito po drugi put među Srbima* an actor dressed up as Tito strolls through the streets of Belgrade and enters into conversation with various passers-by about past and present. In *Maršal* Tito re-appears as a 'ghost' on a small island in Croatia – who at some point is discovered to be a patient from a nearby mental hospital – causing a series of misunderstandings and even the revitalization of the fantasy 'Tito lives'.

In both films the fake Tito is treated by some of those entering into contact with him with the same ritualized respect the real one was celebrated with during socialist times – in the case of Vinko Brešan's film even after his real identity is revealed. This is even more

Figure 44: *Tito po drugi put među Srbima/Tito's second time among the Serbs*, Želimir Žilnik, 1993 © Želimir Žilnik.

puzzling in Želimir Žilnik's film where those coming in contact with 'Tito' were mostly chance encounters without previous training. The conversations and actions the 'second' Tito is involved in thereby often also make continuities between the past one-party and contemporary national ideologies graspable, but also discrepancies came up. For instance one woman in *Tito po drugi put među Srbima* tells 'Tito' that when he died, she cried, but now regretted it. A man in the crowd remarks: 'We used to have one Tito, now we have 55 of them', whereas another one accused him of not having been forward-looking enough: 'You should have promoted Milošević as your substitute and Yugoslavia would not have fallen apart'. In this way, both films get their viewers, especially those from former Yugoslavia, to confront their past and to detach themselves to some extent from previous judgements and idealizations, but at the same time the humour so extensively employed in these films puts them in a triumphing position towards this past and allows them to sustain illusion in respect to it.[2]

Tradition-building and the affective life of the nation

Like other modern states, Titoist Yugoslavia was a designing power engaged in 'social engineering' (Bauman 1991) and in doing so it promoted assimilation and linguistic, cultural and ideological unification around the worker/partisan, the party and its leader Tito rather than cross-cultural exchanges and a heterogeneity of political and aesthetic positions. Yet at the same time this struggle for the 'one-ness' and 'non-ambiguity' of the people and the party was always already contaminated by modern consumer (and cinema) culture which operate through diversification. In the 1960s the novi film movement described in previous chapters brought public attention to productions that did not reduce but strongly augmented ambivalence and even caused the confusion of officially set up parameters – which led to heated discussions and the introduction of new measures to secure socialist order. Low-Fi Video activists in the 1990s related to this movement of the 1960s, which is also known as Crni Talas (black wave). These young video and cinema activists highlight the continuities that exist: especially in their 'amateurism', the style of public gathering adopted, as well as in the film languages coined both by the movement of the 1960s and by themselves (I MK). And similar to those of their 'forefathers', the films made by them in the 1990s also emphasized love, humour and bodily experiences and staged difference by programmatically exposing an experimental aesthetic style.

Simultaneously, however, and despite engaging in such a tradition-building process, activists also distanced themselves from the older movement. Miloš Kukurić recalls: 'We were students of Dunav school, a semi-private school; […] so we went to Rex [the cultural centre in Belgrade]. They [the members of the novi film movement, A. S.] were interested in doing some regular screenings […] we were interested in […] non-professional production, especially at that time digital cameras and computer editing were just starting, so we saw some big future in this, and we were right. […] That was how we started. […] Because the old Yugoslavia used to have that big amateur production in the last 30 years, before the war in the Balkans. So it was not a rootless idea. [… But] I think, they were much better organized and they were supported by the state or by the city or some institutions. […] We started with no support except Rex with their space and their logistics, computers […] and everything […] that is the big difference between them and us. […] And probably in some creative way […] we were […] continuing that idea of do-it-yourself cinema or something like that […] but in some more liberal way' (I MK).

With their screenings and festivals the Low-Fi Video activists, however, participated in a much broader new cultural politics that opposed the older 'modernist' universalism and its attempt to obliterate ambivalence. They emphatically encouraged a re-reading of history and the present in a context where a 'rediscovery' and exhibition of various forms of difference occurred[3] and where the 'nation' had become the central locus for the invention of narrations and counter-narration.[4]

The above-mentioned festival organized in Subotica, for instance, was called the 'First Yugoslav Festival of Cheap Film' – which also means that this activism participated in the passing on of something as a 'Yugoslav nation'. The collective subject taking part in this kind of video and cinema activism is thus trying to gain mastery not only through humour but also through taking part in such a nation-maintaining process. In doing so, this particular way of staging and celebrating the nation enters into struggle with other ones that proclaim a 'Slovenian', 'Croatian' or 'Serbian' nation, usually employing other issues and another aesthetic style. Here, such a relating to the nation was even more complicated by the fact that parts of the Serbian political and cultural elite emerging in the 1980s also adhered to a vision of a Yugoslav nation, but saw it under Serbian leadership (Shigeno 2004: 241f.). Hence in Yugoslavia in the late 1990s there were various motivations and offers to get involved in a nation-constituting process present in public space. These offers were competing with each other; but at the same time correlations also emerged between political and ethical positions which were often quite far apart from each other. The Low-Fi Video aesthetic, which highlights humour and ambivalence, personal views, emotional investment and significant encounters and a mix of international viewpoints, had to confront forms of rediscovering and re-figuring difference that were rather bound to univocal attributions of identity, the extermination of ambivalence as well as to fantasies of purity and clear-cut divisions of friends and enemies.

Humour, irony and the purity of clear-cut divisions

In former Yugoslavia humoristic interventions such as those by Low-Fi Video were joined by a variety of artistic and filmic statements that also employed humour and other forms of the comic in an enhanced way – with jokes and irony being particularly frequent. The above-mentioned films by Želimir Žilnik and Vinko Brešan are part of this. The various forms of the comic are thereby used with such a frequency and empathy that Andrew Horton (2002: 24) speaks about a tradition in films from (former) Yugoslavia that has existed since the 1960s to 'mix social satire, embracing or bordering on surrealism, with playful imaginative tales of individuals attempting to find personal happiness against all odds' (Horton 2002: 24). In the process, older films such as *Ko to tamo peva/Who is singing over there* by Slobodan Sijan (1980) – which through repetition in TV, Internet presence and the spin-off of certain songs featured in them were already firmly anchored in cultural memory – once again became a strong focus of attention in the 1990s. The film for instance played several times on TV when Belgrade was being bombed by Nato in 1999 (Horton 2002: 24). Besides humorous films there were also artists such as Raša Todosijević (Belgrade) or artists groups such as Škart (Belgrade) but also TV programmes such as 'The Top List of The Surrealists' (Sarajevo), which emphatically adopted humour, but also parody and irony.

Simultaneously however, the ambivalent reactions that such films and artworks were able to trigger again were seen as something threatening. As a result, certain films, artworks, or even whole cinema movements were redefined in a (nationally or aesthetically) univocal way – a process in which cultural criticism, film archives and cultural studies investigations also participate to some extent. This can clearly be seen in the case of the novi film movement, which today is more commonly known as Crni Talas, and which was the subject of previous chapters of this book. As already mentioned in chapter two, from the 1990s the Crni Talas was often redefined as a 'Serbian' movement and all Bosnian, Croatian or Slovenian traces tended to be removed from it.

Sometimes the nationally 'pure' divisions are replaced and merged with aesthetic divisions. Then some films employing humour, parody or irony together with a pronounced surrealistic style are regarded as 'resistant' or 'subversive'[5] and hence 'anti-nationalist', whereas others that also use humour and parody, but employ a rather naturalistic style (combined however with surrealistic elements) are considered to support a nationalistic position. An example of this tendency to obliterate ambivalence again and to sustain a dichotomous division of the aesthetic-political world is Pavle Levi's assessment of Emir Kusturica's later work, in particular *Underground* (1995), as being pro-Serbian, 'ethno-expansionist' and 'ethnocentrically motivated' through a 'quasi-transgressive aestheticisation of collectivist enjoyment' (Levi 2007: 101 and 105).[6] In contrast and in the wake of such a binary division of aesthetic procedures and their supposed political effects, the author simultaneously considers the Bosnian youth movement 'New Primitivism' – to which Kusturica had strong connections at some early point in his career – and in particular the TV series 'The Top List of the Surrealists' (TLS) to present 'a distinctly anti-nationalist and multiculturalist perspective' achieved through the emphatic use of humour and irony (Levi 2007: 77).

In judgements like this we encounter an approach that focuses mainly on single artworks and ascribes a quasi-essential political statement to certain aesthetic tactics employed in them, regardless of how they are read and what public reactions and subsequent further treatment these works trigger. Pavle Levi's readings are thereby characterized by a tendency to split the effects of humour into two dichotomous parts. He, for example, describes only one aspect of the effects of TLS's humorous approach to the world and drops the other one when he describes the 'sharp' and 'dark' humour of their sketches as well as the 'resistant orientation' of TLS and New Primitivism as leading to a 'deeper subversion of the elementary discursive coherence, without which ideologies cannot be generated in the first place' (Levi 2007: 70) and equates this with an anti-nationalist and multiculturalist perspective.

As stated above in reference to the writings of Sigmund Freud and the examples given by Antonin J. Obrdlik, there is an ambivalence in using humour to deal with a situation. Humour strengthens the morality and the spirit of struggling with a certain status quo and enables one to feel superior vis-à-vis a certain situation, but at the same time it rejects reality and sustains illusion. And it is exactly this regressive aspect of the effects humour has – the one rejecting reality and sustaining illusion – that Pavle Levi does not take into consideration in his analysis of TLS sketches.

But even if one gives more weight to the ironic and parodic components of these sketches they remain ambivalent. Because irony, which is mixed strongly into the humour produced by TLS, goes together with ambivalence too: contrary to humour, which can also emerge and be completed in one single person and because of that is, according to Freud, the 'most undemanding among the various forms of the comic',[7] irony happens as part of a communicative process. Irony lies in the eye or the ear of those who form the audience of an ironic statement – hence the presence of others is constitutive for the event of 'irony'. When irony 'happens', however, this goes together with surprise. Then stated meanings are undermined, security is removed and customary viewpoints are shaken and distracted. Exactly because of this, irony cannot be made into a concept but is precisely what defies definition and leads comprehensive speech and ways of showing into difficulties (Schober 2009b: 112f. and 188f.). This means that irony has a 'trans-ideological duality' (Hutcheon 1994: 30ff.): despite repeated efforts to make it part of certain (leftist or anarchic) 'resistant tactics' – which has occurred especially since the 1960s – it cannot be bound to a particular political position, but can be used by various political sides also to ridicule innovations or to police the boundaries of what is allowed to be said in a certain situation.

Similar to humour, irony can thus serve to achieve a certain distance from a present situation and the ways it is signified. Whereas in the case of humour this goes together with an experience of grandeur and with a triumph of the self, irony goes together with surprise, with a removing of security and with a shaking up of assigned meanings, which can have uplifting effects for those involved in an ironic event too. Such a diverting of sense and shaking of meaning, however, can also be used to sustain a nationalist view – for instance, by using irony in relation to actions that oppose a militarist, nationalist view and support a pacifist or feminist view. Ambivalence and double-edgedness thus go together with both humour and irony – and because of this, neither can be bound to certain defined political positions but are rather tactics that link our perceptions in an unforeseeable and for ourselves often surprising way to those of others.

In the same way as Pavle Levi describes only the unsettling and distancing aspect of irony in relation to TLS sketches and not its controlling and policing effects, and drops the reality-rejecting and illusion-sustaining effects of humour, so he analyses Kusturica's late works, especially *Underground* (1995), using a similarly one-sided reading, as exhibiting an aesthetic that univocally supports a pro-Serbian nationalistic position. He thus describes these films as lacking any form of humour or irony; he depicts Kusturica as being somehow outside the above-mentioned humouristic tradition, which contradicts most contemporary observers who see Kusturica as a kind of incarnation of this tradition. Beyond that, Levi highlights what he calls the 'principle of excessive, antirational expenditure' (Levi 2007: 104) of these films and exclusively emphasizes their uplifting, self-indulgent aspects (Levi 2007: 87). In doing so he almost solely focuses on the self-triumphing and reality-rejecting aspect, which he has omitted in his readings of the humour in TLS sketches. Levi thus attributes an 'ideologically produced form of relief' to Kusturica's *Underground*, and even goes as far as to speak about 'the promotion of the self-gratifying tendencies of a centripetally oriented, closed community' (Levi 2007: 104 and 105). He thus describes the 'excess' that Kusturica's films show univocally as supporting a 'Yugo-nostalgic view', which acts as a 'façade' for Serbian 'ethnoexpansionist aspirations' (Levi 2007: 101).[8]

Hence Levi splits the effects of humour and irony up into self-triumphing aspects and destabilizing or subversive elements and links them to certain political – 'nationalist' and 'subversive' or 'anti-nationalist' – positions. In this way his reading of Kusturica's films engages in dissociations that support dichotomous divisions between 'we' and 'them' groups.

Contrary to such clear-cut distinctions, I would insist that both the TLS sketches and Kusturica's late films allow for reception processes that are not only plural but can be seen as producing a kind of ambivalent 'doubling' (Bhabha 1990: 298f.): even if the reception histories of these films and sketches – through enjoyment, fascination, identification, involvement and projection – constitute certain 'dominant' chains of readings, such as that of Emir Kusturica as being 'pro-Serbian',[9] there is simultaneously an excess of meaning involving humour and irony at work that also allows for other, non-nationalist or anti-nationalist readings.

Hence what is omitted in such clear-cut divisions of aesthetic tactics, the artworks employing them and the political effects they achieve are the various and sometimes significant encounters that the audience is able to have with these films and TV programmes. Such encounters can have a 'violent' or 'deconstructive' aspect about them in the sense that they are able to involve us as viewers without refuge into the viewing process, to change the course in which we read the world and to trigger processes of re-articulation – and so have a potential for developing a transformative force (Schober 2009b: 142f. and 188f.). Such encounters have to do, in a more obvious way, with irony than with humour, since irony needs to happen between producer and receiver. However, as the frequent adoption of certain humorous films (such as *Ko to tamo peva* by Slobodan Sijan) in recent decades in former Yugoslavia shows, to produce such significant and ambivalent encounters is a potentiality of a public life of such films too.

Events of reception bind various representations of 'the nation' together and constitute the plural and 'double' (Bhabha 1990: 298f.) affective life of groups in certain historical situations. Because of this such events should not be kept out of our descriptions of the present by ascribing univocal political effects and 'pure' belongings to certain films, artworks or film-makers and artists. They should rather guide us in tracking down the various struggles that are fought in certain historical situations in respect to meaning and sense – which are sometimes also hidden in seemingly secondary or not obviously political things such as Chinese batteries or funny movies.

4.2. Enthusiasm and critique: cinema between flash mob, new urban transition spaces and art

Since the 1990s, novel adaptations of cinema have also appeared in cities such as Hamburg, Vienna, Zurich or Paris – sometimes linked to a new visibility of political claims of women, the queer scene or ethnic groups. And here too in connection to such interventions in urban spaces it is now often highlighted that mobile equipment, accessible spaces and 'trashy' materials have lowered the threshold when it comes to public involvement. In the process, city spaces have, on the one hand, become the backdrops for mobile projectors and the temporary screenings of films on city surfaces linked to a bundling of streams of people.

These cinema initiatives are part of a wider phenomenon that also became known as flash mobs. On the other hand one is able to witness a revival of the idea of the 'cinema pub' of the 1960s – cinema adaptations have been created that do not survive on an economic level primarily from collecting admission but from the business generated by an affiliated bar or restaurant and which are also directed towards providing temporary hospitality for a variety of other initiatives. Moreover, some of the urban interventions that deal with the cinema setting now simultaneously claim to be 'art'. These phenomena again demonstrate that cinema has not been superseded by new communication media such as video, Internet and digital image production techniques but that, in interaction with these, it has re-emerged in an altered form – with the persistancy with which cinema appeared at the turn of the millennium once again being bound to its potential for producing a public, political sphere.

At the same time these forms of cinema activism reveal an elementary characteristic trait of cinema movements in general: the linkage of enthusiasm and critique. As a kind of irrational aberrance, enthusiasm is often set in contrast to the political – even if it is unlike its counterpart, fanaticism, which is usually judged in a negative way, thoroughly seen as a positive affection and agitation. In the following, I will show that contrary to such assumptions it is exactly in this conjunction of enthusiasm and critique that the political dimension of cinema initiatives lies.

Empty city centres and the fascination of imagined transgression

In Hamburg in May 2003 an event was carried out for the first time under the title 'A Wall Is A Screen' during which a stream of people was guided through urban space by short films projected onto the walls of buildings and other urban surfaces using a beamer, a computer and a portable generator. Since then, this kind of intervention has been repeatedly performed in various European cities and has gained international reputation and even triggered follow-up initiatives – such as the group Mauerstreifen (Wall Strips) in Leipzig.

The first of these live art performances in 2003 originated as part of the International Short Film Festival in Hamburg and in cooperation with the lecture series 'gocreateresistance' (Matthias von Hartz) held at the Schauspielhaus Hamburg. During these lectures representatives of the visual arts, sciences and film and performance arts commented on current political issues. At that time the three initiators of 'A Wall Is A Screen' Antje Haubenreisser, Kerstin Budde and Peter Stein – besides having experience in the realms of stage design or experimental movies – were active as the technical directors of the Short Film Festival.

However, they no longer wanted to just work backstage but to also become involved in a more artistic way (I KB). In addition, they were eager 'to catch more from the festival and from short films in general' (I AH). A further motivation for creating a new kind of cinema event was to appropriate the 'no-go areas of the city', the downtown shopping streets, which in the evenings tend to be deserted. The group thus decided 'to take over space' and to play with the difference between reality and cinematic *mise-en-scène* – for instance by projecting a film of a screaming woman onto a shopping centre (I AH).

The basic dramaturgy of the 'A Wall Is A Screen' events has only changed slightly over the years. In the beginning long distances were covered by various projection stations, which eventually led to a loss of the public 'in-between', but these intervals gradually became shorter. In addition, the cortege of the intervention is now held alternately in busier and quieter city areas, which results in a 'picking-up' of spectators during the course of an event. The core element of the intervention continues to be the combination of urban places and short, at most ten-minute films, with the group aspiring to create new combinations for each event. In most cases these 'collages' depart from individual urban situations but sometimes also from the films (I KB).

For some of the activists it is an important aspect to stage the performances in the city centre. Kerstin Budde explains: 'It is like it was before with protest demonstrations. If the city did not really want to permit a demonstration but had to permit it, you were sent into the suburbs. There you marched between yards and shouted rallying cries, but that doesn't do any good because one has to reach the heart of the city. […] I think that a history-charged environment influences a film differently' (I KB).

This reference already points to the political connectivity in which the activists[10] position themselves. Before starting the initiative, two of them were involved in autonomous groups and the squatter scene, among other places in Hamburg (I KB and I AH). Today, however, the members prefer to emphasize the artistic traits of their activities and put humour, irony or the detection of social foci into the foreground.

The performances by A Wall Is A Screen (Figure 45) dissolve and rearrange the classical cinema situation and splice it into urban space. They maintain a tradition of brusque

Figure 45: *A Wall Is A Screen, International Short Film Festival*, Hamburg, 2005 © Schweizer, courtesy *A Wall Is A Screen*.

assemblages of cinema and city – a tradition the activists were not familiar with in the beginning. Part of this tradition is, for instance, the 'street film' *Notstandsbordstein/Emergency Curbstone* (1969) by Wolf Vostell, which has been described in a previous chapter. Besides, these urban interventions show an affinity to forms of rearranging the cinema setting such as the *film discos* which emerged in Vienna in the 1990s, organized by a group of musicians, film-makers and artists.[11] These were multimedia spectacles and dance events held in various urban locations such as art spaces, squatted abattoirs and factories, film studios, museums or bars and discotheques. They were composed of various screens, a huge number of noisy, crackling super-8 projectors, slide projectors, 16mm film projectors and video projectors, as well as a sound system and numerous lights. The organizers and the public both participated through ad-hoc selections of the visual material used during the events, by transforming their bodies into temporary 'screens' for the films, and by simultaneously trying to find dancing movements that resonated the various images and sounds (I FF). These *film discos* relate further back to the famous *Exploding Plastic Inevitable* (1966) by Andy Warhol, for which he was already combining film shows with disco events.

In contrast to these latter examples, however, A Wall Is A Screen is based less on a dissolution and re-assemblage of the hierarchical cinema setting than on utilizing the space-creating function of cinema for a bundling of flows of people and of attention and on the collage-like – sometimes ironic or humorous, sometimes alienating – combination of films and city fragments. Today, traditions of related forms of art dealing with urban space are actively reconstructed by members of the group themselves. They, for instance, compare the choreography of streams of people through the city to the practice of the French Situationists (1957–1972) or to contemporary art groups such as the Ligna Radio Ballett Hamburg[12] (I KB) who link flash mob-like urban gatherings to the radio programmes broadcast by the Freies Sender Kombinat (FSK), a public non-profit radio station in Hamburg.

These recent self-categorizations of the group underscore the fact that the actual star of A Wall Is A Screen is the public, which from the beginning has responded enthusiastically to the events. If the first walk brought together about 200, mostly young, that is, between 20- and 45-year-old, participants coming mainly from middle-class or student environments, the second was already attended by 400 and the one in 2008 by 1,000 people – which pushed the intervention to the threshold of feasibility (I KB und I AH).

Even if bottles of strong alcohol were found after some of the events, the organizers do not remember any conflicts involving the audience. They usually participated in a quiet and disciplined way – which again demonstrates the socializing and attention-bundling force of the, in this case, quite mobile cinema setting. Yet sometimes there have been conflicts between audiences and the people living in the neighbourhood of some projection stations. This is particularly the case in central or south-eastern European cities such as Debrecen (Hungary) and Prizren (Kosovo), where water balloons or stones had sometimes been thrown – even if most of the other tours there also proceeded in a peaceful way.

The sharpest conflicts, however, occurred as a result of intervention by public and private security services and the police in German and Swiss cities, who often assume that such public and informal gatherings are probably not allowed and who interfered, blocking access to some buildings chosen for projection, requested permits or even recorded the organizers' personal data. These confrontations already indicate that the urban environment in which A Wall Is A Screen operates is a highly controlled, monitored and segregated area where any activity that goes slightly beyond the usual seems suspicious and can provoke interventions.

Since there has been an enormous influx of participants from the very beginning, the group has been requested and booked by a number of other, sometimes official, other times rather informal initiatives since around 2005. These include film or other cultural festivals that want to take their programmes 'onto the streets', NGOs such as Attac Germany or the Peace Brigades International (PBI), public cultural institutions such as the Robert Bosch Institute which is mainly active in Eastern Europe, as well as the monument preservation service or the PR department of the federal government – with the latter, for instance, there was a collaboration on the issue of *Zwanzig Jahre Mauerfall/Twenty Years after the Fall of the Wall* in November 2009 in Berlin. Sometimes even marketing agents of big enterprises show an interest – but in these cases the group mostly declines the offers. Cooperation is only accepted if the issue also seems interesting from an artistic point of view and if the group is free to choose locations and films (I KB).

This involvement of A Wall Is A Screen by dint of various contracting entities is in sharp contrast with the myth of it being a kind of urban guerrilla group, an image that has adhered to them since they started. This myth is passed on by word of mouth, but is also reflected in posts on various Internet platforms where participants discuss the events afterwards. In this respect, Kerstin Budde maintains that, besides the event and party character and that it is for free, what is particularly appealing to audiences is mainly the transgressive qualities that are ascribed to the group's activities. She says: 'I believe two thirds [of the participants A. S.] think that we are doing it illegally. They don't understand the enormous organizational effort that goes into these events […] and then it is a little bit like being in a theatre and one realizes that the actor forgets his lines. […] It differs from TV, you are suddenly in a singular situation. With us it is always like that' (I KB). Also some of the potential host institutions spread this myth, by saying things like 'we don't want to have an illegal situation' (I KB).

Yet, contrary to such beliefs, every event carried out by A Wall Is A Screen is secured by advance authorizations – in the beginning a permit for every building, but in the meanwhile only for special constructions. In some cities, the group falls into the category of 'street musicians' and is granted a corresponding permit (I AH). The impression of spontaneity and low organizational effort that helps to sustain the myth of being a guerrilla-like group is mainly produced by the mobility of the equipment, the presenters appearing in an accentuated informal way, the choices of locations and films and their often provocative collage, but also due to the fact that the public usually bring their own drinks as well as camping mats to sit on and that the screenings lead to an experience of momentous, 'clandestine' collectiveness.

It is, however, this very persistence of the myth of A Wall Is A Screen as a guerrilla-like group that indicates a central feature of the current condition of our public sphere. It demonstrates that on the part of the audience there seems to be a strong desire to interrupt the flow of the everyday and to transgress the usual. The transformed urban rituals emerging as part of the events choreographed by the Hamburg group – like the older ones from which they derive, such as going to movies or participating in demonstrations – again provide the opportunity to gain pleasure and to position oneself in the world by acting out one's own aesthetic self (Flusser 1994: 172f.). Yet the particular fascination of the clandestine and the transgressive aspect linked to A Wall Is A Screen contributes to enhancing this ritual, almost religious dimension of these performances of the self. While stepping temporarily beyond the usual and the everyday, the difference and individuality of the self as well as its capacity of acting is demonstrated. And simultaneously, this acting out of one's own aesthetic self constitutes a temporary collective body composed not only of friends and colleagues but also of strangers – the self is thus momentarily able to submerge into and also become part of an accumulation of bodies which mutually activate and entrain each other.

Besides A Wall Is A Screen, other urban initiatives that in a similar way combined the use of the Internet and mobile phones with live events using set pieces of cinema also emerged in various European cities at the beginning of the new millennium. For instance, in September 2004 the police in Paris unexpectedly discovered a cinema situation in Les Catacombes, the miles of tunnels and caves under the city. A journalist described what was found as follows: 'After entering the network [...] the officers came across a tarpaulin marked: "Building site, No access." Behind that, a tunnel held a desk and a closed-circuit TV camera set to automatically record images of anyone passing. The mechanism also triggered a tape of dogs barking, "clearly designed to frighten people off," the spokesman [for the police. A. S.] said. Further along the tunnel opened into a vast 400 square-metre cave some 18 metres underground, "like an underground amphitheatre with terraces cut into the rock and chairs." There the police found a full-sized cinema screen, projection equipment, and tapes of a wide variety of films. [...] A smaller cave next door had been turned into an informal restaurant and bar. [...] "The whole thing ran off a professionally installed electricity system and there were at least three phone lines down there." Three days later, when the police returned accompanied by experts from the French electricity board to see where the power was coming from, the phone and electricity lines had been cut and a note was lying in the middle of the floor: "Do not", it said, "try to find us"' (Henley, 8 September 2004). Some days later it became known that the group of squatters calling themselves 'The Perforating Mexicans' and 'urban explorers' had gathered beneath the surface of the city in order to 'reclaim and transform disused city spaces for the creation of zones of expression for free and independent art' (Henley, 11 September 2004).

The Paris urban explorers base themselves even more strongly than A Wall Is A Screen on the socializing force of the secret and the clandestine (Simmel 1992: 406f.), which works to enhance the border between those who are inside the group, sharing the knowledge of its existence, and those who are outside. This is indicated clearly by the use of the tape with the barking dogs – only those 'in the know' will pass this barrier and will be able to participate in the screenings of the hidden cinema. In this case the secret of the cinema's existence offers the possibility of a second world besides the obvious one. By contrast, the events of the Hamburg group are inclusive, they address 'all of us', but still give their participants the opportunity to experience themselves in an enhanced differentiated and individualized way by transgressing the usual and participating in something cloaked in an aura of the clandestine.

These cinema initiatives are linked to practices of contemporary protest movements such as the Global Justice Movement or the Occupy Wall Street Movement who also constitute themselves around notions of 'direct action' and by the use of the Internet and mobile phones. Retrospectively, campaigners of these movements sometimes critically remark that participating in urban actions is able to provide a kind of euphoria that can lead to addiction (Häntzschel 2011). Others speak of the 'glamour of direct action' (Häntzschel 2011) that can dazzle and prevent a clear sight of things. But at the same time participating in protest action is never solely action but also a means of staging new issues and perspectives as facts that can be judged and are able to challenge reigning allocations.

In contrast to these forms of political activism, however, in the case of cinema initiatives such as A Wall Is A Screen or the Paris squatters, the role of spectatorship and – connected to it – of witnessing, imagining and judging sometimes even geographically or historically very distant events is much stronger. And it is in this potential to involve us as spectators, to imagine different worlds, to encourage us to judge facts in which we are not directly involved and to challenge the existing order of things where the political aspect of such initiatives can be found.

The cinema as a harbourage

Around 1996 in Vienna a new type of cinema came into being, though this was not even obvious to the initiators themselves at first. At this time the former film projectionist Johannes Wegenstein and a business partner decided to take over the Schikaneder cinema, where Wegenstein used to work. The cinema is located in the entertainment and café district near a famous market, the Naschmarkt. In the beginning there was not really a concept for operating the cinema – other than the decision not to follow a concept, but to work 'with' the public rather than programming for them. Nevertheless, there was a role model and a flop (I JW). The role model was a cinema in Zurich, the Xenix, which is described by Wegenstein as 'an enormous bar, a garden and a small cinema' (I JW) and gave him the idea of financing the cinema not through admission tickets but by a connected bar business. The flop was that nobody attended the first screening programmed by the new team. But soon young artists and art students from the nearby Academy of Fine Arts started to take the Schikaneder over for projections, parties and exhibitions, and the programmers began to learn what kind of films could work in this new context (I JW).

In this way a form of cinema emerged that was no longer seen as the one-dimensional screening of films but as a meeting point: walls were offered for projections, rooms emptied for parties and installations and even the display window was made available for temporary artworks. In 1998–1999 the first Turkish film festival was hosted and turned out to be a success. 'It was cross-fertilization', Johannes Wegenstein said, 'there were inquiries and we asked others' (I JW).

Afterwards, the Schikaneder team decided to play this card even more strongly and to become a kind of harbourage for other initiatives. The key idea was to give initiatives the freedom to do whatever they wanted and to offer a 'dense atmosphere' composed of bar, music, cinema and art. The various initiatives always brought their 'own' audiences along, which, at least in part, mingled with the more steady one attracted by the location itself – they came mainly via word of mouth and were again composed of young people between 18 and 40, often from a student or middle-class milieu (I JW).

As a result, the Schikaneder became an important urban transit space, where people would meet, whether or not they came to see a film; it became somewhat famous for its reputation of being a trashy place where it was easy to meet or flirt with someone new. At the same time the cinema-bar unit is described by the organizers as a kind of 'anarchic space' that is repeatedly 'discovered' by new generations of young artists (I JW). Because of this, another cinema only a few blocks away, the Topkino, opened in 2003 as a more 'conservative' space, at least from a cineaste's perspective. Here the cinema is seen in a rather classic sense as a venue for the projection of films, but is again joined by a bar in conjunction with a restaurant and a small front garden which, also in this case, can again be run independently from the cinema. Linked to this, the Schikaneder was also reorganized: it is still made available for various initiatives, but in addition it also functions as an internal second-run cinema (I JW).

Since the first host festival in 1998–1999 a variety of other initiatives have taken place, but after 2003 have mainly been held at the Topkino: among the regularly hosted festivals are, for instance, tricky women, the Identities Queer Film Festival, the VIS Vienna Independent Shorts and the Anilogue – Budapest Animation Film Festival. Furthermore, sixpack film, a non-profit organization involved in PR and distribution of Austrian film and video art, holds its public screenings at the Topkino and a variety of ethnic initiatives also use the cinema: festivals hosted here include Croatian, Tibetan, Korean, Iranian, Czech and Polish film days, the festival 'Women Film-Makers from Turkey', and for a while special screenings of Bollywood films. Since 2008 the team has been co-organizing a festival on human rights called 'This Human World'.[13] Unlike A Wall Is A Screen, where the political aspect is no longer seen as the main focus, for the Schikaneder-Topkino unit it is maintained that 'the political claim was less important in the beginning, but has grown with time' (I JW).

While the cinema operators strongly emphasize their role as harbourers of others, those who brought their initiatives into these spaces mainly mention the low threshold for getting into contact, which for them is associated with the Schikaneder and Topkino in particular, but sometimes also with cinema in general. Kumru Uzunkaya for instance, who organized the Erstes Türkisches Frauenfilmfestival: Filmemacherinnen aus der Türkei (First Turkish Women's Film Festival: Women film-makers from Turkey, Figure 46) at the Topkino in April 2007, says in this respect: 'For example the National Library or public libraries in general scare me very much even if we had more books than the average migrant family at home, walls of books […] but they were not destined for me. […] In a certain way the low threshold of films, to be able to switch them on or to go to the cinema, was for me a form of gaining knowledge' (I KU). Because of this – while she travelled to San Francisco, Berkeley, Paris or Mexico – she experienced the cinema as a place, 'where I could find myself […] find a point to lodge myself in wherever I am. I do not go to the theatre or the opera [for that A. S.]' (I KU).

Kumru Uzunkaya started to think about getting in contact with the Schikaneder after she encountered the women film-makers collective Filmmor in the spring and summer of 2006 as part of her research on the women's movement in Turkey. Especially their film *Klitoris Nedir?/What is Clitoris?* (Melek Özman, 2002), in which various people passing through public space in Turkey are caught off guard by the question about the female sexual organ,

Figure 46: *First Turkish Women's Film Festival* in the Topkino in Vienna, April 2007 © Anna Schober.

called into question the parameters with which she used to judge the world. She explains: 'It made me realize to what extent we live behind the times here and that over there the women were much further' (I KU). This as well as the everyday frustration of seeing how Turkish women are represented in Austria – mainly as wearers of scarves – stirred a desire to bring this film and similar ones to Vienna. First, she wanted to show them at the Schikaneder, because she had heard 'that they give small initiatives a chance' (I KU). Then she understood that they work together with the Topkino, and 'I hovered around outside a while […] before I stepped in personally' (I KU). With other cinemas she did not experience such a low threshold.

For Barbara Reumüller, too, curator of the Identities Queer Film Festival (Figure 47), which has been held in Vienna since 1994, that is, some years longer than the founding of

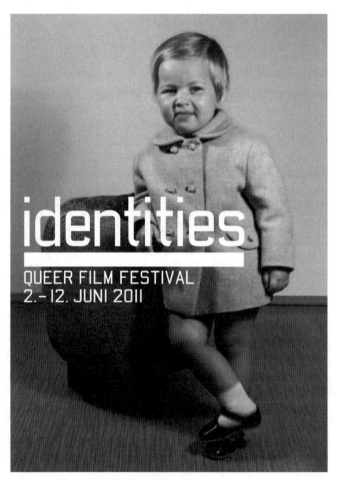

Figure 47: *Identities Queer Film Festival,* 2011 © DV8-FILM, identities 2011.

the Schikaneder or Topkino, the public, easily accessible character of this form of cinema is important. The main reason why she chose the Topkino as one of three locations for holding the festival, however, is mainly its central location in the city. The core cinema of the festival is the Filmcasino, located in a neighbouring entertainment district, but a bit further away from the city centre. The Topkino lies within walking distance of the Filmcasino, but is closer to the centre in an area where a lot of cafés, bars, shops and restaurants invite passers-by to stop in for a break. Soon also a third cinema was added: the Cinemagic, formerly known as the Opernkino, which is again a short walk from the Topkino and is right in the city centre. Hence, the three cinemas encompass an easily accessible festival space in an urban area that, when the festival started, was already recognized as a nightlife, entertainment and alternative shopping district.

This precise spatial positioning of the festival is combined with good, well-calculated timing as part of the annual festival calendar of the city. The festival is held in the first week of June, before university ends and before the big international queer film festivals, such as the one in San Francisco, take place and when it is already possible to spend time outside in the cafés. This spatial as well as seasonal positioning allows the festival to develop the 'knock-on-effect' it is famous for: bringing people together to watch films for about fourteen hours a day, and in addition take part in discussions and other social gatherings and sometimes also spontaneously organized events. In this way the festival emerges as an exceptional situation, able to trigger the impression, 'Wow, these are films that open up a new perspective on the world. And celebrating oneself as well as diversity is a very important aspect' (I BR).

Hence, both the First Turkish Women's Film Festival and the Identities Queer Film Festival strongly employed the socializing force of the cinema setting for the purpose of creating a visible presence for positions they view as otherwise missing in their environment and as holding the capacity to challenge reigning viewpoints and attributions. At the same time, the ambiance of the Topkino transforms and somehow 'softens' this force by adding a practice of sociability. In this respect, the cinema as a harbourage resembles A Wall Is A Screen, which also combines the attention-bundling power of the cinema with a sociable party-like event.

The form of cinema emerging in the Schikaneder and Topkino goes back to the *Kinokneipe* (cinema pub) of the early 1970s as it was realized for instance in the Kinokneipe Meisengeige in Nuremberg or in the Kneipenkino in the Rationaltheatre in Munich. For the former, in 1970 an old bakery was transformed into a cinema, with seats being arranged in a rather loose, pub-like way, drinks being served during the screenings and smoking allowed. As usual, the idea of the cinema as a pub is also in this case accompanied by an emphasis on sociability and a programmatic involvement of the audience: the selection of films was carried out in collaboration with 'interested people in the public' (Prinzler and Schwarz 1972: 217f.). And the Kneipenkino in Munich was initiated by the film-makers Edgar Reitz and Ula Stöckl in the bar of a cabaret theatre in 1971. In the evenings after the theatre performance had ended, they set up a 16-mm projector and a screen. On the tables in addition to the usual menu there was also a 'film menu' which offered films by the film-makers themselves (for instance, *Geschichten vom Kübelkind/ The Bucket Kid Stories*, 1970), but also a selection of other films, mainly American and French silent movies and early talkies (Prinzler and Schwarz 1972: 185f.).

These films point to another trait of cinema tradition which is revitalized by the cinema pubs of the early 1970s as well as by the cinema-harbourage of the 1990s and the new millennium: the combination of silent films and informal public gatherings recalls early forms of film exhibitions that emerged in US cities between 1903 and 1911. During these events, films or sometimes only single reels of film were shown as part of vaudeville and variety shows, dime museums and penny arcades, summer parks, fair grounds and travelling shows, or since 1905 also in early specialized places for screening films known as 'nickelodeons'. In several of these locations, film was also mixed with live events, music and other art forms and was used by various initiatives, often immigrant groups, in order to stage, negotiate, contest and challenge the new public, private and commercial order they found themselves thrown into (Hansen 1991: 45f. and 91f.).

This demonstrates that there are continuities in the way cinema is used to constitute a public sphere where an expression of diversity – in terms of groups using the socializing force of cinema, but also in terms of media and art forms – could take place. But notwithstanding such connective lines, cinema initiatives such as the Schikaneder and the Topkino are also differentiated from previous ones. Most strongly they are set apart from the communal cinemas emerging in the late 1960s and early 1970s. These are seen as financed by the city on a large scale, but are judged, for example, by Johannes Wegenstein, as 'built on sand because they don't work any longer […] in terms of visitor frequency as well as in terms of atmosphere' (I JW). Even if he immediately adds that 'the Topkino and the Schikaneder are not in accordance with the severe cineaste gaze. But that is an old hat' (I JW).

At the same time, the fact of being a harbourage for other initiatives not only variegates the social and political space constituting itself around these urban nodal points, but also causes conflicts. Sometimes such conflicts have to do with who is responsible for the clean-up efforts. Other times, however, they are staged as a clash of ethnic cultures or religious convictions. So, for instance, the organizers of the Iranian film festival were bothered by the fact that the bar in the Topkino also serves alcoholic drinks and wanted to close the cinema off from the pub facilities. The solution they found was to cover the bar behind a curtain for the duration of the festival (I JW) – which once more shows that the cinema is able to work as a kind of ambivalent space, where impure and provisional actions can take place that escape any clear-cut (self-)attribution.

Enthusiasm and spectatorship

Kumru Uzunkaya points out that linked to the festival she organized, her own enthusiasm and that of the women film-makers from Turkey, especially from the Filmmor Women's Cooperative, joined and mutually vivified each other (I KU). Barbara Reumüller, by contrast, mainly mentions the enthusiasm the public of the Identities Queer Film Festival in Vienna expresses, for instance, in the form of fan e-mails in which they call the festival their 'highlight week of the year'. At the same time, she sees the essence of cinema anchored in 'making journeys around the world through the eyes without leaving the city'. Like other journeys, they too 'have the capacity to open a new perspective in the world' (I BR).

In these statements the enthusiasm emerging around cinema situations appears as a strong affect, linked to desire. Simultaneously, it goes together with spectatorship, that is with being a witness to events and facts that are sometimes located far away in environments different from those where the watching takes place – something that comes into the foreground all the more since a big part of the movies shown at these screenings are documentaries (I JW).

Also in scholarly and philosophical negotiations these two aspects – a strong linkage to affect and the fact of being bound to spectatorship – are mentioned as the main characteristic traits of enthusiasm. For Jean-François Lyotard, for instance, enthusiasm is a modality of the sublime, that is, an extremely painful joy and a strong affection. Simultaneously, it is 'an energetic sign, a tensor of *Wunsch* [wish; orig. in German]' (Lyotard 2009: 29ff.). Furthermore and like other authors[14] before him, he links enthusiasm closely to the political by pointing out that it 'calls upon a "consensus" […] that is an immediate and singular anticipation of a sentimental republic' (Lyotard 2009: 35).

This political dimension of enthusiasm is usually closely related to spectatorship and not so much to acting in history. The reason for this is that the enthusiasm of the spectators is, different than that of actors, not driven by one's own immediate interests and motivations. Because of this the reflection about as well as the judging of distant events bound to other kinds of public order can also enter into conflict with one's own parameters of viewing the world or can cause a crisis – which constitutes the core political trait of enthusiasm.

Consequently, the enthusiasm of spectators is an ambivalent affection, oscillating between desire and aversion, attraction and repulsion. Again, according to Jean-Jean-François Lyotard, the main difference between the modality of aesthetic judgment that can be called sublime and another one that judges something as beautiful lies in this ambivalent intersection between yes and no. The former way of judging has to do with a touching; it is a double-edged agitation, whereas the latter is, rather, experienced as an interaction between imagination and reason, which is triggered by certain forms. Both, however, are something we feel, that is, we do not arrive at it by following a rule or a doctrine but by being caught by something that triggers our imagination (Lyotard 1994: 50ff.).

This relation of enthusiasm to spectatorship and being a witness of sometimes distant events indicates that it is in a particular way characteristic of the cinema setting and also gives some hint as to where its public, political dimension lies: in the link between the affection of enthusiasm and the aesthetic-political judgement of things.[15] But the examples mentioned so far, for instance, the participators in A Wall Is A Screen or the initiatives in the Topkino, also show that it is not always possible to separate the actor and the spectator clearly. Indeed, the examples of a public sphere constituting itself around cinema initiatives presented throughout this book demonstrate that the spectator can be so deeply touched that he or she turns into an actor, and that initiators themselves occasionally pause for a moment and become spectators again. Hence these notions do not refer to two kinds of people but rather to modes of participating in public processes.

There is however also a universal dimension inherent in all these initiatives. This is indicated by the fact that they usually address their activities and offers to 'all of us'. So even if these initiatives claim to represent particularistic viewpoints and interests, as the Identities festival does, they nevertheless emphasize that their programme is directed at appealing 'to everyone' (I BR). And initiatives such as A Wall Is A Screen or the Turkish Women's Film Festival also aim at being as inclusive as possible by setting out to 'overcome inhibition thresholds related to art' (I KB) and to 'touch people on an emotional level, beyond the intellect' (I KU).

In doing so, these initiatives – similar to those of the late 1960s – often present films staging new iconic figurations that try to involve us as spectators and that simultaneously stand for truth claims in respect to what is discursively represented. Among these, two kinds of figuration stand out in particular: the (often female) migrant[16] and the hermaphrodite.[17] Both are singular figures that tend to combine formerly binary split assignations – the male and the female or the citizen and the foreigner – in one bodily being and emphasize a potential for self-transformation and flexible accommodation vis-à-vis different circumstances.[18] The repeated staging of such figures in contemporary cinema situations turns them into somehow privileged carriers of enthusiasm.

Nevertheless, the link between the experience of enthusiasm triggered by cinema initiatives and the community evoked in this way is not a linear one. As Roberto Esposito (2006: XIV) has shown, the universality that is called on by the sublime or the beautiful comprises only an idea of a community. There is no proof of it but only indirect, analogous 'as-if' representations. Hence, the feeling of enthusiasm does not bring a community into being in a direct way, but is bound to translation. In this process what is experienced in enthusiasm is figured in symbols, signs or emblems.

An example of this is the festival organized by Kumru Uzunkaya, since it can itself be read as a translation of the enthusiasm she had encountered for the productions of Filmmor, similar to the website she established to accompany the festival[19] or the photographs published in social web-networks related to it. Other traces of translations of enthusiasm are, for instance, small social events or discussions organized spontaneously in the course of the Identities festival or comments, discussions and photographs published in blogs and discussion sites. And sometimes what has been encountered vis-à-vis certain films enters the ways we present ourselves in public and the opinions and self-stylizations we express in this way. In order to show such a passage and to communicate it to others, one 'translates' it by starting to pose differently, to collect certain kinds of objects or images and to plant them into the everyday environment or to stage certain issues as novel objects for discussion. In triggering such translations, enthusiasm can create bridges, passages, between the sensuous realm of aesthetic judgment and the ethical-rational ordering of a community.

The enthusiasm of spectators emerging in cinema situations is usually linked to critique. This is highlighted by another cinema initiative, Kinoapparatom (Wolf Schmelter and Simone Schardt), which started in Zurich in 2003.[20] One of the activists, Simone Schardt, states in an interview that their motivation 'was less triggered by a light-bulb moment than by the desire to critically interrogate all sorts of things' (I SS).

Yet also to judge something critically is an activity that can be seen in analogy to politicking. Similar to aesthetic judgment and different, for instance, from legal practice or logical argument that follows rules and derivations, both have to find or even to invent symbols to represent their ideas – which relates them again strongly to the faculty of imagination (Lyotard 2009: 2; Esposito 2006: 77).

As I have shown in chapter one of this book, criticizing, but also judging things aesthetically or politically or starting a public initiative are all space-creating activities (Rancière 1999: 27; Zerilli 2004: 85f.). They constitute a public sphere in which new phenomena that can be judged are able to appear, where various viewpoints can be staged and where imagination, that is, the capacity to represent things in new, unusual ways can be aroused and further actions stimulated. In this way what is counted as being political, what is worth being judged and whoever is allowed to enter public processes can be transformed: new actors can emerge who consider themselves as belonging to this sphere and who stage issues and aesthetic solutions for public debate that – as is often the case with phenomena of mass culture – were previously regarded as 'low' or 'debased' amusements. In this process, enthusiasm acts as a capacity of passage on various levels: between what happens on-screen and inside the auditorium, but also between happenings and bodies in the auditorium itself or between the various phenomena projected.

Some cinema activists explicitly emphasize the spatial aspect of their initiatives. So Kumru Uzunkaya points out how important it was to see her initiative anchored in the exterior world of the city and to create a place where one is able to encounter others (I KU). And Barbara Reumüller sees the festival as a space where a new kind of self-confidence linked to visibility in urban space can come into being and reigning regimes of seeing and being seen can be questioned – for instance, by challenging the belief that queer issues are only bound to sexuality or by claiming some films as being 'queer' which, like *Auf der anderen Seite/ Yaşamın Kıyısında/The Edge of Heaven* (Fatih Akin, 2007), attracted great attention in the mainstream cinema world, but without this aspect being mentioned (I BR).

Forms of attachment and involvement created by positioning oneself in cinema in general or in certain cinemas in particular allow – together with the double-edgedness connected to spectatorship – forms of positive self-attribution to emerge that escape the pressure to be unambiguously either 'Turkish' or 'Austrian' or 'gay' or 'heterosexual'.[21] This often stands in a certain tension with processes of naming a festival or an initiative – which is related to the spatial dimension, since it too provides presence and a positioning vis-à-vis other alternatives. Consequently, these processes of naming sometimes cause conflict. The festival organized by Kumru Uzunkaya was, for example, entitled the 'First Turkish Women's Film Festival', which stirred some critical remarks by Kurdish initiatives. Because of this, the initiator retrospectively regards the second part of the title, 'Women Film-Makers from Turkey', as more open and inclusive (I KU). And Barbara Reumüller points out that the title 'Identities Queer Film Festival' was chosen exactly because it evokes diversity on a broad scale, but immediately adds that the notion 'queer' is not to be seen as a 'label for everything and nothing' but is directed at a self-conscious questioning of the binary, hetero-normative models that older terms such as 'gay' or 'gay-lesbian' cannot easily convey, since they stood in a tradition of campaigning for tolerance (I BR). Which again indicates that these initiatives are involved in adaptations and kinds of vivifications of universalism but no longer handle these 'as one' but as an issue staged by a particular viewpoint, thus contesting other expressions of universalism raised by different groups (Jullien 2008: 145f.).

As various examples in this book show, cinema initiatives are themselves often a kind of 'translation' of an enthusiasm that emerged vis-à-vis certain films or viewing situations. At other times, however, they are calculated in a rather planned, strategic way and become part of efforts, for instance, of political initiatives in a more narrow sense of the word, to create a new political order. The journalist Ali Can, representative of the association Presse und Literatur aus dem Orient (Press and Literature from the Orient) who is also involved in the organization of the Kurdische Film Woche (Kurdish Film Week, Figure 48) held at the Votivkino in 1999, shortly after the First Turkish Film festival was hosted at the Schikaneder, explains this kind of approach as follows: 'Because of the war, Kurdish people have become

Figure 48: *Kurdish Film Festival* in Vienna, 1999 © 3007 agentur, photo: Mehmet Emir, courtesy filmcoop WUK.

known in public through demonstrations, not necessarily rowdy ones, but they have been connected with demonstrations, war, dying, fleeing, donations, etc. [...] But there is also another, cultural side of Kurdish people: Kurdish film. That should be known too, and that was the political background to all this' (I AC). Also, in this case through cinema, culture has shifted to the centre of society and been called upon to create the attention and involvement that political events in a more narrow sense are viewed as not being able to provide. Nevertheless, the depictions of initiatives such as A Wall Is A Screen or those hosted at the Schikaneder and Topkino demonstrate once more that the political potential of cinema does not end with such explicit and self-conscious employment for the creation of a transformed political order. Rather, it lies in what happens in the cinema, during the screenings and discussions, where events are able to occur that lead to a questioning of reigning representations and assignations and initiate translations between watching, judging and acting – usually facilitated by the enthusiasm accompanying these initiatives.

The city and the form of cinema adaptation

Each of these cinema initiatives is – as a collective body – held together not so much by positive references that various people share, but rather by something that they experience as lacking in their own environments (Esposito 2006: XVI). This means that the various ways cinema is practised are related to the compulsions and desires that come up in processes of everyday life. An experience of excess and vivification that is usually attributed to a practice of cinema described as one's 'own' finds its correspondence in an experience of lack, frustration and shortcomings that are linked to the current political order, the environment of the city and the mainstream cinema or art world.

Therefore, the main motivations for calling certain cinema initiatives into being include the 'backwardness' of one's own context or the absence of certain aesthetic and political positions (I BR, I KU). Sometimes even stronger feelings such as 'dissatisfaction' and 'fury' in respect to how certain groups are represented are expressed (IKU). But 'disappointing experiences' with strands of current intellectual debate are also mentioned.[22] And in the course of the cinema walks, the audience of A Wall Is A Screen – as analysed above – finds exactly the experience of clandestine transgression linked to an affirmation of the self that the strictly controlled, segregated urban environment they are living in otherwise denies them.

This shows that how cinema is staged, inhabited and experienced is closely bound to the environment of the city and the form society is organized in, which have both undergone transformation in recent decades. In the first chapter of this book, I mentioned the following characteristics as indicators of such a change: enhanced segregation, an increase of trans-national and global processes replacing older national ones, the loss of attractiveness of classical arenas for creating a public sphere, such as parties, unions and associations and a rise of new cultural arenas such as cinemas, stadiums or concert halls as well as a stronger presence of new social movements staging various forms of difference as 'cultural' ones and focusing on 'direct action' instead of on complicated strategic procedures inside official (for instance, state or regional) institutions.

Michael Sorkin (1992) points at another dimension of this transformation process. He shows that urban life since approximately the early 1970s has been characterized by the emergence of a so-called 'ageographical city', that is, a wholly new kind of city without a place attached to it and made up of computers, the Internet, credit cards, phones or faxes, TV and video culture. According to him, this city, which overlaps with other strata of the city fabric, gives evidence of a rapid evisceration of a historical politics of propinquity, which was the characteristic of the older, traditional city.

But again, since the late 1960s and in connection with the rising student movement, certain kinds of urban space like the cinemas, which – as the slogan of the 'dying cinema' indicates – were also subject to such an evisceration, re-emerged in a strengthened form as places linked to enthuasism and political judgement. Yet this happened not despite, but exactly because of the emergence of such an 'ageographical city'. The film-maker Floran Flicker, co-organizer of the film discos, emphasizes in this respect the sensuous, bodily attraction of film and the cinema situation in times of video. He says: 'Video is again so anonymous and so ungraspable. But we went [in the course of the film discos, A. S.] from projector to projector, sweated and worked and did not merely sit behind the computer. This was analogue, palpable, mechanical, well! film' (I FF).

Besides, contemporary social spaces are also characterized by the fact that people tend to draw back into containable communities – even if they still desire and imagine happenings between the various players in public space. There is thus also a tendency towards a walls-up policy pursued by various groups constituted through strong identification as well as a trend towards heightened security efforts and a monitoring of self and others. Social exchange often appears as a culture marked by problems, avoidance and fear (Delany 1999: 61f.; Sennett 2003: 294f.).

If we consider this newly emerging context, then the transformation of the cinema into a space of excess, into something that is 'more' and 'other' and that we find lacking in everyday environments, appears to us in another light. It then becomes obvious that what is important in respect to these cinema initiatives is the tangible, the bodily and the potentiality to encounter something other and unfamiliar – for instance, the red plush seats, the sensuous experience of other people's presence, the possibility of unexpected happenings, the beer or coffee that is drunk before going into the cinema, the very presence of the place as a shared space, etc. This means that the historic politics of propinquity re-emerges in a (more or less) nostalgic way in these spaces. At the same time they act as a kind of protective covering, where we can confront the anxiety connected to transition and the loss of symbolic mastery, as well as the fact that we have a body to expose to others. Hence, in respect to the various cinema initiatives analysed in this book, we are also dealing with forms of celebrating a built, tangible and, in a bodily way, shared space to move in, located in a context where the old city spaces are increasingly overlapped by ageographical spaces and techniques of control.

Furthermore, with the emergence of media such as TV, computer and the Internet or of an enhanced event culture and the buildings and areas connected with it, such as hybrids between entertainment parks and shopping malls, our regime of perception and the ways we ourselves perform in private and in public have again changed. In the process, two forms of relating to moving pictures have become dominant: the fragmented domestic performance and the public outing (Corrigan 1991, p. 27f.). Living with cable TV, video and the Internet means that we have an enhanced, distracted and fragmented relationship to pictures. These media-combinations offer a stream of images, an ever-present 'out there', in which we, as consumers, can enter at every point, without becoming completely absorbed by them. We are still able to position these images by remote control, video and computer, but at the same time we are also increasingly positioned by them.

Simultaneously, an enhanced distracted and eventful reception, which merges images, objects, fantasies, wishes and anxieties, not only dominates our homely cocoon around the TV set or the computer but also our public outings. The latter is now increasingly characterized by the fact that we leave the house in our leisure time not above all to pursue a certain, well defined action, but because of the outing itself, that is, we are searching for an event in which we can dip into a crowd together with others and which stands out from the mundane. This now often happens in cultural arenas that lie beyond institutional structures provided from 'above' such as schools, universities, party locations or official institutions. This indicates not only a broader participation of citizens in public processes but also a drawback of offical entities from public missions and responsibility – which again highlights the ambivalence of these initiatves.

The transformed cinema situations created by A Wall Is A Screen, Topkino or the Identities festival are bound up with such transformations. And at the same time they also act as agents pushing them forward. In several of these cinema situations, the 'piloting' is different from the one practised in the classical cinema. There is no longer any compulsory scheme for inhabiting these spaces, but – at least besides the more classical cinema rituals – new forms of self-performance emerge within which people act out their own aesthetic being in the world. Besides, in the 1980s and 1990s also very direct correlations between the practice of cinema initiatives and the broader context of the city emerged. Some innovations made by these initiatives have been adopted and incorporated in a quite brusque way by rather mainstream cinema settings. So for instance in the last two decades not only do the film discos, the Schikaneder, the Topkino or A Wall Is A Screen act against a 'silent' cinema by rearranging the cinema setting and mixing pub and dance floor features with the screening of films, but the newly constructed multiplex cinemas also combine the now technically perfected classical cinema situation with a variety of pubs and bars, dance floors and restaurants. Moreover, the latter has also started to organize thematic film programmes – often explicitly addressing certain segments of the public, such as particular immigrant groups.

Nevertheless, such adaptations never go solely in one direction. Since the beginning of cinema, elements of it have been appropriated by consumers and have been incorporated into various forms of a staging of the self or certain issues in public and to position initiatives. In the course of such processes, cinema culture leaves the cinema setting itself and enters everyday life. It is thus linked to a novel kind of visibility of a creativity and expressiveness of the public that – despite enhanced control and segregation – also goes along with modern mass culture and tends to use materials that do not come from 'high culture' but from the streets, the new popular arenas of cinema and music halls or of shopping malls and entertainment parks (Suárez 2007: 5f.). In recent decades, such appropriation practices have often also been turned into an issue themselves and become objects of, for example, artistic investigation.

In a series of photographs called *The Looking-Glass Photos* (2009, Figure 49) the Swedish artist Helga Härenstam deals with the practice of picturing the self, which she adopts,

Figure 49: *The Looking-Glass Photos*, Helga Härenstam, 2009 © Helga Härenstam.

but also transforms and alienates by choosing unusual perspectives, introducing blurred or overexposed picture elements or by setting various shots into unusual and mutually commenting montages. In one installation a snapshot-like photograph depicting a woman, perhaps the artist herself, in a T-shirt covered by a larger-than-life face of a cat and holding something transparent in front of her face is combined with various other pictures taking up the relation between the self and images. In one of them we see an old man cleaning a mirror in an open-air landscape setting; in another one a woman holding an enormous mirror on her knees and so confronting the photographer with her own image (and through her also us as spectators with our images); then there is a girl, deep in concentration, almost absorbed in a photo album, beside her a young man sits on his bed, fiddling with something – perhaps another camera – which is flashing up in glaring light. Finally, one of the images shows the colourful façade of an entertainment centre called 'Planet Hollywood' with some passers-by.

In this montage the process of performing the self – setting the self into a picture – is related to private and public image worlds, among them also the cinema. This makes visible that the enthusiasm emerging vis-à-vis these image worlds is not only able to provide a passage towards the other but also towards the self as other. As Dieter Mersch has pointed out, perceiving is never solely constructed in a subjective way but receives a continuous perturbation and confusion from the part of another who is able to throw the certainties with which we view the world into crisis (Mersch 2002: 33). The photographs by Helga Härenstam expose this, but they also show that such processes usually involve mass-media arenas such as the cinema.

The fact that cinema has the capacity to provoke its viewers to the other, which sometimes is also the self as other, also implies that there is not necessarily a contradiction between self-culture and public culture. Nevertheless, and as I have shown above, there is no direct way between perceiving, judging things aesthetically and community building – but there is a need for translation and imagination that bridges the split self and the lack of community that constitute the basis of our being in the world. This is made evident by another artwork, *Community cinema for a quiet intersection (against Oldenburg)* by Rirkrit Tiravanija (1999), which I have already analysed at the beginning of this book. The interruption of everyday procedure through the brusque, montage-like arrangement of four screens directly above a traffic intersection in connection with the notion of 'community cinema' precisely challenges any idea of a linear connection between cinema and community and invites us to imagine various possibilities of translating between them.

These last examples are part of a system of art, in which – similar to consumer practice – adaptations of mass culture have become frequent throughout the twentieth century, but in a more pronounced way since the 1960s. Because of such correlations, cinema activists, especially those who have gained public presence in the last two decades, often pose as artists: for instance, the initiators of A Wall Is A Screen highlight the artistic, creative side of their public deeds and Kumru Uzunkaya, besides organizing the women's film festival, also made a film herself.[23] Yet this does not mean that the borders between the everyday life of the consumers and the system of art are blurred – both remain strictly separated and guided by different procedures (Schober 2009b: 373f.), even if such correlations have been foregrounded by artists as well as consumers or critics, in recent decades.

In taking up – and transforming – a thesis devoloped by Miriam Hansen (1999: 69f.) one can conclude that today it is not so much the classical cinema itself but certain forms of cinema adaptation that seem to correspond particularly well to the contemporary form of experience and the regime of perception that goes with it. This is the cinema as a harbourage, the film festival, combinations of cinemas and pubs or restaurants (adopted also by Multiplex cinemas), mobile cinema events in urban spaces and various forms of translation between cinema and everyday life. In all these forms of appearance, the cinema still shapes not only how but also in which form we see the world. But at the same time – and beyond any dark prophecy of de-politicization – the cinema once again also provides a cultural horizon in which the condition of contemporary society, its changes as well as the fears and desires connected to it, can be reflected, negotiated, rejected, disavowed and transformed. The potential that these forms of cinema emerging today have for civil society still lies in their ability to challenge and renegotiate sense afresh, in a way that addresses the individual as well as allowing for the creation of connectivity. In this setting, spectatorship, an experience of heterogeneity and the enthusiasm and translations linked to them can build contingent and fragile coalitions, which are, however, always threatened by attempts to eliminate ambivalence and to re-establish univocal divisions.

Notes

1 Only after the interview was 'finished', that is, after the recorder was switched off, did Miloš Kukurić tell me that before the wars he lived in France for four years and attended high school there and returned to Belgrade only shortly before the war started. He completed his last year of high school in Belgrade, had to enlist in the military and then the war in Kosovo (1996–1998) started. He described the years between 1991 and 1996–1997 as the most difficult ones, characterized by the complete impoverishment of broad sections of the population, war and collective 'craziness'. Because of this, the encounter with cinema Rex and the onset of Low-Fi Video were so important to him: 'suddenly everything made sense' (I MK).

2 Ljiljana Filipović (2003) mainly foregrounds the psycho-cathartic function of these films.

3 In European and especially northern European countries in the 1980s and 1990s this went along with an explicit re-reading of struggles between men and women, various ethnic groups or hetero- and homosexuals. In former Yugoslavia in the 1990s such struggles often overlapped and merged with battles that were fought in relation to the recent wars. In cities like Belgrade, for example, the *Women in Black*, who also explicitly supported war deserters, were publicly attacked as 'lesbians' and 'non-mothers' (Schober 2005).

4 On this double narrative operation constituting central topoi of nationalisms such as 'the people' or 'the nation', see Bhabha 1990. On the pluralization of 'antagonistic nationalisms',

which replaced the formulation of alternative political conceptions in former Yugoslavia around 1990, see Bieber 2005: 223f.

5   Even readings in which the ambivalence of humour is acknowledged often show an overemphasis on the 'resistance' side of humour and parody. Pamela Downe's article (1999) is an example of this. She points out that prostitutes use playful self-insults and self-accusation in order to ridicule discriminatory attitudes towards themselves, without mentioning also the other side to this that consists in the fact that in this way the insults and the accusation are also kept present, re-enacted in an almost masochistic way by the women themselves.

6   Nevertheless Pavle Levi highlights some important aspects of Kusturica's films: for instance that they internalize and appropriate a series of 'Balkanist' stereotypes that tend to be externally projected onto the region or that the 'national' ascription of leading figures as well as of historic events are such that they can link up with those prominently circulating in Serbia at this time (Levi 2007: 97 and 112).

7   However, as he further explains, non-involved people present at a humorous occurrence or at a humorous representation are also able to laugh with humorous pleasure – then they somehow copy the process happening to the humorist, but their presence does not add anything new (Freud 1992b: 241).

8   'Yugo-nostalgia' and a defiant reference to the 'old Yugoslavia' was articulated by diverse political agents in the various successor states in the 1990s. As already mentioned Low-Fi Video activists for instance called the festival they organized in Subotica the 'First Yugoslav Festival of Cheap Film'. The 'old Yugoslavia' acted as a kind of discursive nodal point that linked various political positions and allowed people to 'wander' between them.

9   This today quite 'frozen' judgement is not a result of some essential qualities of Kusturica's films themselves, as Pavle Levi's reading would suggest, but rather it acquired its dominance from a linking-up of several reading processes that in themselves are often informed by fantasies of purity and attempts of exterminating ambivalence – to which, however, Kusturica's further and sometimes very provocative deeds, for example of having himself baptized as Serbian-Orthodox, have contributed.

10 Today the group has six members: Sabine Horn, Sarah Adam and Sven Schwarz have joined the initiators.

11 The group's members included Thomas Renoldner, Pepi Öttl, Wolfgang Kopper and Florian Flicker. The film discos are also known as ZAK, Zentrale audiovisuelle Konferenz (Central Audiovisual Conference). Like some initiators of A Wall Is A Screen, Florian Flicker also gained his first experience in the art world in the theatre scene in Hamburg. In the 1980s he worked there for three years as an assistant director for theatre and advertising (I FF).

12 The Radio Ballet has been in existence since 2002. See http://ligna.blogspot.com/2009/12/radio-ballet.html (20 December 2011).

13 As in other cinemas, the usual programme is composed of films selected at international festivals – with the Berlinale and the festivals in Rotterdam, Karlovy Vary, Leipzig and Toronto being mentioned as the most important ones – or through existing rental structures and networking with cultural institutions.

14 Usually such negotiations (Esposito 2006; Zerilli 2004; Lyotard 1994; Lyotard 2009) of enthusiasm as aesthetic judgment holding a particular political potential go back to

Immanuel Kant, who in *Der Streit der philosophischen Fakultät mit der juristischen/Conflict of the Philosophy Faculty with the Faculty of Law* (1798) refers to the spectators of the French Revolution as those who engage publicly in a position-taking that is at the same time universal and devoid of personal interest and is linked to the risk that it may turn out disadvantageously for those engaging in it (Kant 1996: 302).

15   This closeness of spectatorship, cinema and political judgment is also reflected upon in the film *Enthusiasm* (1931) by Dziga Vertov.

16   Already the Turkish Women's Film Festival in the Topkino in 2007 screened several films dealing with the issue of migration. In 2009 a follow-up festival was co-organized by Kumru Uzunkaya, this time in the Schikaneder cinema and under the title Blick-Wechsel (alternating gazes), which was solely devoted to screening films by directors with a migrant background. See http://www.blickwechselfilm.at/ (20 December 2011)

17   The programme of the first event of the Identities Queer Film Festival in 1994 was built around questions of ambivalent identities and options in respect to sexual identity. Barbara Reumüller explains this rise of films dealing with these arguments: 'There are strong fantasies, the desire to have options beyond binary solutions' (I BR).

18   In these figurations, a further connective line to contemporary protest movements such as the Alter Globalisation Movement can be found, where these are also used to address 'everybody' (Schober 2013).

19   See http://kadinfilm.devbase.at/festival2007/index.php (12 December 2011).

20   The name Kinoapparatom makes a link to Dziga Vertov and the tradition of politically motivated cinema activism that he represented, since it relates to his films *Man with a Movie Camera* (1929) whose first title was *Chelovek's kinoapparatom*.

21   Werner Schiffauer (2008: 92f.) formulates a similar thesis related to a positioning of the self in urban districts or cities – for instance 'Kreuzbergers' for those living in the Kreuzberg district in Berlin. According to him this differs from a national self-location since it has the capacity to go beyond univocal self-attributions.

22   Kumru Uzunkaya describes how, for her, the feminist discussions she became familiar with during her studies at the University of Vienna 'no longer made any sense, they were only about theory, there was no longer any road contact'. By contrast, she characterizes the women's movement in Turkey and especially the women film-makers collective Filmmor as 'not happening solely on paper', but as a young movement where she could 'lodge into' (IKU).

23   She made the film *Klitoris Viyana da nedir?/What is Clitoris in Vienna?* (2007) together with one of her brothers and adopted a pattern for it used in the Filmmor film on the same subject by Melek Özman, but transferred it to the Viennese context.

Interviews Cited

Babac, Marko, by A. S. and Vera Konjović, February and March 2004 (I MB).

Budde, Kerstin (A Wall Is A Screen), by A. S., 3 May 2009 (I KB).

Can, Ali (Kurdish Film Festival), by A. S., 25 April 2001 (I AC).

Dimitrovski, Duško, by A. S., 24 September 2007 (I DD).

Farocki, Harun, by A. S., 20 June 2008 (I HF).

Feguš, Marko, by A. S., 20 March 2008 (I MF).

Flicker, Florian (film disco), by A. S. and Werner Schwarz, 21 September 2000 (I FF).

Godina, Karpo, by A. S., 18 June 2007 (I KG).

Haubenreisser, Antje (A Wall Is A Screen), by A. S., 3 May 2009 (I AH).

Hein, Birgit, by A. S., 4 December 2004 (I BH).

Hein, Wilhelm, by A. S., 8 December 2004 (I WH).

Hurch, Hans (Film Festival Viennale), by A. S. and Werner Schwarz, 22 August 2000 (I HH).

Jovanović, Jovan, by A. S., 18 March 2008 (I JJ).

Kangwana, Biki (Slum-TV and Ghetto Filmclub), by A. S., 30 April 2009 (I BK).

Karanović, Srđan, by A. S., 28 November 2009 (I SK).

Konstantin, Herta, by A. S., 28 September 2000 (I HK).

Križnar, Naško, by A. S., 17 March 2008 (I NK).

Kukurić, Miloš (Low Fi Video), by A. S., 23 February 2004 (I MK).

Makavejev, Dušan, by A. S., 4 October 2007 (I DM).

Mekas, Jonas, by A. S., 11 February 2008 (I JM).

Reumüller, Barbara (Identities Queer Film Festival), by A. S., 20 January 2010 (I BR).

Schardt, Simone (Kinoapparatom), by A. S., 12 February 2009 (I SS).

Schlemmer, Gottfried, by A. S. and Werner Schwarz, 21 December 2000 (I GS).

Schrage, Dieter (Freies Kino), by A. S., 10 February 2004 (I DS).

Uzunkaya, Kumru (First Turkish Women Film Festival), by A. S., 27 July 2007 (I KU).

Vučićević, Branko, by A. S., 10 October 2007 (I BV).

Wegenstein, Johannes (Schikaneder, Top Kino), by A. S., 21 January 2010 (I JW).

Žilnik, Želimir, by A. S., 25 April 2008 (I ZZ).

References

Alexander, G. (1976), 'Filme wie aus Beton. Western – das internationale Gesellschaftsspiel', *Film*, 12 (December), pp. 14–20.

Arendt, H. (1958), *The Human Condition*, Chicago, University of Chicago Press.

Arthur, P. (1992), 'Routines of Emancipation: Alternative Cinema in the Ideologies and Politics of the Sixties', in D. E. James (ed.), *To Free the Cinema: Jonas Mekas and the New York Underground*, Princeton, Princeton University Press, pp. 17–48.

——— (2001), 'Escape from Freedom: The Films of Dusan Makavejev', *Cineaste*, 27:1, pp. 1–15.

Babac, M. (2001), *Kino-Klub 'Beograd'*, Belgrade, Jugoslovenska kinoteka.

Baer, V. (1970), 'Jagdszenen aus Oberbayern, Rainer Werner Fassbinders Film Katzelmacher', *Tagesspiegel*, July 3.

Balibar, É. (2006), *Der Schauplatz des Anderen. Formen der Gewalt und Grenzen der Zivilität*, Hamburg, Hamburger Edition.

Banes, S. (1993), *Greenwich Village, 1963: Avant-Garde Performance and the Effervescent Body*, Durham, Duke University Press.

Bardon, X. G. (2002), 'Exprmtl. Festival hors normes. Knokke 1963, 1967, 1974', *Revue Belge du Cinéma*, 43 (December).

Barthes, R. (1975), 'En sortant du cinéma', *Communications*, 23:1, pp. 104–108.

Bauman, Z. (1991), *Modernity and Ambivalence*, Cambridge, Polity Press.

Belting, H. (2008), *Florenz und Bagdad: Eine westöstliche Geschichte des Blicks*, Munich, C. H. Beck.

Bensoussan, G. (2004), 'Wir sitzen auf einem Vulkan: Rainer Werner Fassbinder über Deutschland, Antisemitismus und Homosexualität'. in R. Fischer (ed.), *Fassbinder über Fassbinder. Die ungekürzten Interviews*, Frankfurt/Main, Verlag der Autoren, pp. 557–576.

Bertsch, G. K. (1973), 'The Revival of Nationalism', *Problems of Communism*, 22:6, pp. 1–18.

Beyerle, M., Brinckmann, N., Gramann, K., and Sykora, K. (1984), 'Ein Interview mit Birgit Hein', *Frauen und Film*, 37, pp. 95–101.

Bhabha, H. K. (1990), 'DissemiNation: Time, Narrative, and the Margins of the Modern Nation', in H. K. Bhabha (ed.), *Nation and Narration*, London and New York, Routledge, pp. 291–322.

Bieber, F. (2005), *Nationalismus in Serbien vom Tode Titos bis zum Ende der Ära Milosević*, Vienna, LIT Verlag.

Bippus, E. (2009), 'Skizzen und Gekritzel. Relationen zwischen Denken und Handeln in Kunst und Wissenschaft'. in M. Hessler and D. Mersch (eds.), *Logik des Bildlichen. Zur Kritik der ikonischen Vernunft*, Bielefeld, transcript, pp. 76–93.

Bjelić, D. I., and Savić, O. (2005), *Balkan as Metaphor: Between Globalisation and Fragmentation*, Cambridge, MA, and London, The MIT Press.

Bloom, P. (2006), 'Beur Cinema and the Politics of Location: French Immigration Politics and the Naming of a Film Movement', in E. Ezra and T. Rowden (eds.), *Transnational Cinema: The Film Reader,* London and New York, Routledge, pp. 131–141.

Böhler, I., and Gehler, M. (eds.) (2007), *Verschiedene europäische Wege im Vergleich: Österreich und die Bundesrepublik Deutschland 1945/49 bis zur Gegenwart,* Vienna, Bolzano, Innsbruck, Munich, Studien Verlag.

Boglić, M. (1975), 'Radnička klasa i naš film (na marginama jugoslovenskog socijalnog filma)', *Filmska Kultura,* 100 (July), pp. 38–51.

Bontemps, J., and Fieschi, J.-A. (1966), 'Nouveau cinéma en Yougoslavie – Dusan Makavejev: le sens et la fonction dubitative de L'Homme n'est pas un oiseau', *Cahiers du cinéma,* 182 (September), pp. 55–58.

Bovenschen, S. (1979), *Die imaginierte Weiblichkeit. Exemplarische Untersuchungen zu kulturgeschichtlichen und literarischen Präsentationsformen des Weiblichen,* Frankfurt/Main, Suhrkamp.

Braad Thomsen, C. (2004a), 'Es ist besser, Schmerzen zu genießen, als sie nur zu erleiden', in R. Fischer (ed.), *Fassbinder über Fassbinder. Die ungekürzten Interviews,* Frankfurt/Main, Verlag der Autoren, pp. 391–404.

——— (2004b), 'Hollywoods Geschichten sind mir lieber als Kunstfilme', in R. Fischer (ed.), *Fassbinder über Fassbinder. Die ungekürzten Interviews,* Frankfurt/Main, Verlag der Autoren, pp. 233–241.

——— (2004c), 'Meine Filme handeln von der Abhängigkeit', in R. Fischer (ed.), *Fassbinder über Fassbinder. Die ungekürzten Interviews,* Frankfurt/Main, Verlag der Autoren, pp. 221–227.

Braidotti R. and Butler J. (1994), 'Feminism by Any Other Name', *Differences: A Journal of Feminist Cultural Studies,* 6.2+3, pp. 27–61.

Brocher, C. (2004a), 'Die Gruppe, die trotzdem keine war. Rainer Werner Fassbinder über die Entwicklung des antiteaters und die Entstehung seiner ersten fünf Filme', in R. Fischer (ed.), *Fassbinder über Fassbinder. Die ungekürzten Interviews,* Frankfurt/Main, Verlag der Autoren, pp. 17–176.

——— (2004b), 'Nur wer Leier spielt, lernt Leier spielen. Rainer Werner Fassbinder über FONTANE EFFI BRIEST und über das Produzieren fürs Kino und fürs Fernsehen', in R. Fischer (ed.), *Fassbinder über Fassbinder. Die ungekürzten Interviews,* Frankfurt/Main, Verlag der Autoren, pp. 243–255.

Calvino, I. (1978), *Invisible Cities,* Orlando, Harcourt.

Castoriadis, C. (2007), 'Imaginary and Imagination at the Crossroad', in D. A. Curtis (ed.), *World in Fragments: Writings on Politics, Society, Psychoanalysis, and Imagination,* Stanford, Stanford University Press, 2007, pp. 71–90.

Cavarero, A. (2000), *Relating Narratives: Storytelling and Selfhood* (Warwick Studies in European Philosophy), London and New York, Routledge.

Centar Film Beograd, Prizma Kragujevac, Slovenska kinoteka Ljubljana and Zepter International (eds) (2000), *Srđan Karanović,* Kragujevac, Prizma.

Ciment, M. (1968), 'Entretien avec Dusan Makavejev', *Positif. Revue du Cinéma,* 99 (November), pp. 13–27.

Ciment, M., and Cohn, B. (1971), 'Entretien avec Dusan Makavejev sur WR, Les mystères de l'organisme', *Positif. Revue du Cinéma*, 129 (July–August), pp. 48–53.

Codelli, L. (1975), 'An Interview with Dusan Makavejev', *Monogram,* 6 (October), no pagination available.

Čolić, M. (1970), '"Crni film" ili kriza "autorskog" filma', *Filmska Kultura*, 71 (June), pp. 3–25.

Čolović, I. (2000), *The Politics of Symbol in Serbia*, London, Hurst & Company.

Copjec, J. (1994), *Read My Desire: Lacan Against the Historicists*, Cambridge, MA, and London, MIT Press.

Corrigan, T. (1991), *A Cinema Without Walls: Movies and Culture After Vietnam*, New Brunswick and New Jersey, Rutgers University Press.

Coury, D. N. (2004), *The Return of Storytelling in Contemporary German Literature and Film: Peter Handke and Wim Wenders*, Lewiston, Queenston, Lampeter, The Edwin Mellen Press.

Cowie, P. (2004), *Revolution! The Explosion of World Cinema in the 60s*, London, Faber and Faber.

Cozarinsky, E., and Clarens, C. (1975), 'Dušan Makavejev Interview', *Film Comment*, 11:3, pp. 47–51.

Crossley, N. (2006), *Contesting Psychiatry: Social Movements in Mental Health*, London and New York, Routledge.

—— (2007), *Movements, Lifestyles, Identities and Bodies*, unpublished manuscript.

Crowley, D. and Reid, S. E. (eds.) (2002), Socialist Spaces: Sites of Everyday Life in the Eastern Bloc, Oxford and New York, Berg.

Daković, N. (2003), 'The Unfilmable Scenario and Neglected Theory. Yugoslav Avant-garde Film, 1920–1990', in D. Đurić and M. Šuvaković (eds.), *Impossible Histories. Historical Avant-gardes, Neo-avant-gardes, and Post-avant-gardes in Yugoslavia, 1918–1991*, Cambridge, MA, and London, UK, MIT Press, pp. 466–488.

Daney, S. (2000), *Im Verborgenen: Kino–Reisen–Kritik*, Vienna, PVS Verleger.

de Certeau, M. (2002), *The Practice of Everyday Life*, Berkeley, Los Angeles and London, University of California Press.

de Landa, M. (1991), *War in the Age of Intelligent Machines*, New York, Zone Books.

Delany, S. R. (1999), 'Three, Two, One, Contact: Times Square Red', in M. Sorkin and J. Copjec (eds.), *Variations on a Theme Park: The New American City and the End of Public Space*, New York, Hill and Wang, pp. 19–85.

de Valck, M. (2007), *Film Festivals: From European Geopolitics to Global Cinephilia*, Amsterdam, Amsterdam University Press.

Dichter, Ernest International, Ltd. (1971), 'Freizeitbedürfnisse und Präferenzstrukturen' in Dieter Prokop (ed.), *Materialien zur Theorie des Films*, Munich, Hanser, pp. 339–382.

Didi-Huberman, G. (1999), *Was wir sehen, blickt uns an*, Munich, Wilhelm Fink, pp. 11ff.

Dörner, A. (2001), *Politainment: Politik in der medialen Erlebnisgesellschaft*, Frankfurt/Main, Suhrkamp.

Downe, P. J. (1999), 'Laughing When It Hurts: Humor and Violence in the Lives of Costa Rican Prostitutes', *Women's Studies International Forum*, 22:1, pp. 63–78.

Drakulić, S. (1993), *How We Survived Communism and Even Laughed*, New York, Harper Perennial.

——— (1996a), 'Still Stuck in Mud', in S. Drakulić (ed.), *Café Europa: Life After Communism,* London and New York, Penguin Books, pp. 195–203.

——— (1996b), 'The Trouble With Sales', in S. Drakulić (ed.), *Café Europa: Life After Communism,* London and New York, Penguin Books, pp. 69–78.

Duguet, A. M., Klotz, H., and Weibel, P. (eds.) (1997), *Jeffrey Shaw – A User's Manual: From Expanded Cinema to Virtual Reality,* Ostfildern, Hatje Cantz.

Duras, M. (1963), *Un barrage contre le Pacifique,* Paris, Gallimard.

Durgnat, R. (1999), *WR: Mysteries of the Organism,* London: BFI Publishing.

Đurić, D., and Šuvaković, M. (eds.) (2003), *Impossible Histories. Historical Avant-Gardes, Neo-Avant-Gardes, and Post-Avant-Gardes in Yugoslavia, 1918–1991,* Cambridge, MA, and London, UK, MIT Press.

Dyer, R. (1993), 'Entertainment and Utopia', in S. During (ed.), *The Cultural Studies Reader,* London and New York, Routledge, pp. 271–283.

Dyer, R., and Vincendeau, G. (1992), *Popular European Cinema,* London, Routledge.

Elsaesser, T. (1989), *New German Cinema: A History,* New Brunswick and New Jersey, Rutgers University Press, 1989.

——— (2001), *Rainer Werner Fassbinder,* Berlin, Bertz.

——— (2005), *European Cinema: Face to Face with Hollywood,* Amsterdam, Amsterdam University Press, 2005.

Esposito, R. (2006), *Communitas. Origine e destino della comunità,* Torino, Einaudi.

Export, V. (n.d.), *Tapp und Tastfilm,* unpublished manifesto.

Ezli, Ö. (ed.) (2010), *Kultur als Ereignis. Fatih Akins Film, Auf der anderen Seite' als transkulturelle Narration,* Bielefeld, transcript.

Fassbinder, R. W. (1992), 'The Cities of Humanity and the Human Soul: Some Unorganized Thoughts on Alfred Döblin's Novel Berlin Alexanderplatz', in M. Töteberg and L. A. Lensing (eds.), *The Anarchy of the Imagination: Interviews, Essays, and Notes by Rainer Werner Fassbinder,* Baltimore and London, The John Hopkins University Press, pp. 160–167.

Featherstone, M. (1995), *Undoing Culture: Globalization, Postmodernism and Identity,* London and New Delhi, Sage Publications.

Fehrenbach, H. (1995), *Cinema in Democratizing Germany: Reconstructing National Identity After Hitler,* Chapel Hill, University of North Carolina Press.

Filipović, L. (2003), 'Film as an Abreaction of Totalitarianism', in A. Sabbadini (ed.), *The Couch and the Silver Screen: Psychoanalytic Reflections on European Cinema,* New York, Brunner-Routledge, pp. 204–212.

Fischer, W. (2013), 'Ancient Myth Did Not Destroy Yugoslavia. Discourse and Literature in Post-WWII vs. 1989 Yugoslavia', in M. Živković and S. Pavlović (eds.), *Transcending Fratricide: Political Mythologies, Reconciliations, and the Uncertain Future in the Former Yugoslavia,* West Lafayette, Purdue University Press, in print.

Flusser, V. (1994), *Gesten. Versuch einer Phänomenologie,* Frankfurt/Main, Fischer.

Foucault, M. (1986), 'Of Other Spaces', *Diacritics,* 16: 1, pp. 22–27.

——— (1989), *The Order of Things: An Archaeology of the Human Sciences,* London and New York, Routledge.

Freud, S. (1992a), 'Der Witz Und Seine Beziehung zum Unbewußten (1905)', in S. Freud, *Der Witz und Seine Beziehung zum Unbewußten. Der Humor,* Frankfurt/Main, Fischer, pp. 23–249.

――― (1992b), 'Der Humor (1927)', in S. Freud, *Der Witz und Seine Beziehung zum Unbewußten. Der Humor,* Frankfurt/Main, Fischer, pp. 251–258.

――― (2005), *Civilization and its Discontents*, James Strachey (ed.), New York, Norton.

Friedberg, A. (1994), *Window-Shopping, Cinema and the Post-Modern,* Berkeley and Los Angeles, University of California Press.

Friedrichs, J. H. (2010), 'Milieus of Illegality: Representations of Guest Workers, Refugees, and Spaces of Migration in *Der Spiegel*, 1973–1980', in C. Bischoff, F. Falk and S. Kafehsy (eds.), *Images of Illegalized Migration: Towards a Critical Iconology of Politics,* Bielefeld, transcript, pp. 31–45.

Frisch, S. (2007), *Mythos Nouvelle Vague. Wie das Kino in Frankreich neu erfunden wurde,* Marburg, Schueren Verlag.

Garcelon, M. (1997), 'The Shadow of the Leviathan: Public and Private in Communist and Post-Communist Society', in J. Weintraub and K. Kumar (eds.), *Public and Private in Thought and Practice: Perspectives on a Grand Dichotomy,* Chicago and London, The University of Chicago Press, pp. 303–332.

Gauthier, C. (1999), *La passion du cinéma. Cinéphiles, ciné-clubs et salles spécialisées à Paris de 1920 à 1929*, Paris, École des Chartes.

Geertz, C. (2000), 'The World in Pieces: Culture and Politics at the End of the Century', in C. Geertz, *Available Light. Anthropological Reflections on Philosophical Topics,* Princeton and Oxford, Princeton University Press, pp. 218–263.

Genocchio, B. (1995), 'Discourse, Discontinuity, Difference: The Question of Other Spaces', in S. Watson and K. Gibson (eds.), *Postmodern Cities and Spaces,* Oxford, Blackwell, pp. 35–46.

Götürk, D. (2000), 'Migration und Kino – Subnationale Mitleidskultur oder transnationale Rollenspiele?' in C. Chiellino (ed.), *Interkulturelle Literatur in Deutschland. Ein Handbuch,* Stuttgart and Weimar, Metzler, pp. 329–347.

Goulding, D. J. (1994), 'Makavejev', in D. J. Goulding (ed.), *Five Film-makers. Tarkovsky, Forman, Polanski, Szabó, Makavejev,* Bloomington and Indianapolis: Indiana University Press, pp. 209–263.

――― (2002), *Liberated Cinema: The Yugoslav Experience 1945–2001*, Bloomington and Indianapolis, Indiana University Press.

Grafl, F. (1995), 'Reizender Scharm, Französische Filmkultur in Österreich', in T. Angerer and J. Le Rider (eds.), *'Ein Frühling, dem kein Sommer folgte'? Französisch-österreichische Kulturtransfers seit 1945,* Vienna, Cologne, Weimar, Böhlau, pp. 205–215.

Grant, J. (2004), 'Der Sinn der Realität. Rainer Werner Fassbinder über HÄNDLER DER VIER JAHRESZEITEN, DIE BITTEREN TRÄNEN DER PETRA VON KANT und ANGST ESSEN SEELE AUF', in R. Fischer (ed.), *Fassbinder über Fassbinder. Die ungekürzten Interviews,* Frankfurt/Main, Verlag der Autoren (1974), pp. 313–329.

Greenberg, A. C. (1979), *Artists and Revolution: Dada and the Bauhaus. 1917-1925*, Auflage, Michigan, UMI Research Press.

Habermas, J. (1990), *Strukturwandel der Öffentlichkeit*, Frankfurt/Main, Suhrkamp.

Habich, C. (1985), *W + B Hein: Dokumente 1967–1985. Fotos, Briefe, Texte*, Frankfurt/Main, Deutsches Filmmuseum.

Hajek, P. (1968), 'Für McLuhan, Bazooka Joe und die Garbo', *Kurier*, March 25, p. 3.

Hake, S. (2002), *German National Cinema*, London and New York, Routledge.

Hall, S., and du Gay, P. (eds.) (1996), *Questions of Cultural Identity*, London, Thousand Oaks, New Delhi, Sage Publications.

Halter, M. (2006), 'Ethnic and Racial Identity', in R. Ueda (ed.), *A Companion to American Immigration,* Oxford, Blackwell, pp. 161–176.

Hansen, M. (1991), *Babel & Babylon: Spectatorship in American Silent Film*, Cambridge and London, Harvard University Press.

—––– (1993), 'With Skin and Hair: Kracauer's Theory of Film, Marseille 1940', *Critical Inquiry*, 19:3 (Spring), pp. 437–469.

—––– (1999a), 'Benjamin and Cinema: Not a One-Way Street', *Critical Inquiry*, 25: 2 (Winter), pp. 306–343.

—––– (1999b), 'The Mass Production of the Senses: Classical Cinema as Vernacular Modernism', *Modernism/Modernity*, 6:2, pp. 59–77.

Hansen, M. B. (2006), *New Philosophy For New Media*, Cambridge, MA, and London, MIT Press.

Häntzschel, J. (2011), 'Winter in Amerika. Nach der Räumung – die New Yorker Occupy-Bewegung überlegt, wie es weitergeht', Süddeutsche Zeitung, December 13.

Hein, B. (1971), *Film im Underground. Von seinen Anfängen bis zum unabhängigen Kino*, Frankfurt, Berlin, Wien, Ullstein.

Hein, W+B, Michelis, C., and Wiest, R. (eds.) (1971), *XSCREEN. Materialien über den Underground-Film*, Cologne, Phaidon Verlag.

Henley, J. (2004a), In a Secret Paris Cavern, the Real Underground Cinema', *Guardian Unlimited* (8 September) at: www.guardian.co.uk.

—––– (2004b), 'Paris's New Slant on Underground Movies: Clandestine Group Reveals How It Built Its Cinema Beneath the City', *Guardian Unlimited* (11 September) at www.guardian.co.uk.

Hobsbawm, E. (2007), *Globalisation, Democracy, and Terrorism*, London, Little, Brown.

Hofman, A. (2010), 'Kafana Singers: Popular Music, Gender and Subjectivity in the Cultural Space of Socialist Yugoslavia', *Narodna umjetnost: Croatian Journal of Ethnology and Folklore Research*, 47:1, pp. 141–160.

Horton, A. (2002), 'Laughter Dark & Joyous in Recent Films from the Former Yugoslavia', *Film Quarterly*, 56:1, pp. 23–28.

Hughes, J., and McCormick, R. (2004), 'Der Tod der Familie. Rainer Werner Fassbinder über ANGST VOR DER ANGST', in R. Fischer (ed.), *Fassbinder über Fassbinder. Die ungekürzten Interviews,* Frankfurt/Main, Verlag der Autoren (1977), pp. 379–389.

Hutcheon, L. (1994), *Irony's Edge: The Theory and Politics of Irony,* London and New York, Routledge.

Jansen, P. W. (1972), 'Verschiedene Sachen Namens Kino. Unterhaltung, Kunst oder Emanzipation', in H. H. Prinzler and H. Schwarz (eds.), *Über das Kinomachen. Eine Dokumentation kommunaler und privater Initiativen.* Berlin, Deutsche Film- und Fernsehakademie, pp. 9–17.

——— (1975), 'Das Kino der Alternative', in H. H. Prinzler and W. Seidler (eds.), *Kinobuch. Der Katalog Nr. 2. Eine Dokumentation kommunaler und privater Initiativen,* München, Stiftung Deutsche Kinemathek, pp. 9–12.

——— (2004), 'Ich bin in dem Maße ehrlich, in dem mich die Gesellschaft ehrlich sein lässt. Rainer Werner Fassbinders Versuch eines Blicks auf Deutschland, seine Arbeit und sich selbst', in R. Fischer (ed.), *Fassbinder über Fassbinder. Die ungekürzten Interviews,* Frankfurt/Main, Verlag der Autoren(1978), pp. 415–443.

Jenkins, H. (1992), *Textual Poachers: Television Fans & Participatory Cultures,* London and New York, Routledge.

Jovičić, V. (1969), 'Crni talas u našem filmu', *Borba Reflektor,* August 3, pp. 22–29.

Jullien, F. (2008), *De l'universel, de l'uniforme, du commun et du dialogue entre les cultures,* Paris, Fayard.

Jutz, G., and Tscherkassky, P. (eds.) (1995), *Peter Kubelka,* Vienna, PVS Verleger.

Kant, I. (1996), 'The Conflict of the Faculties', in Paul Guyer and Allen W. Wood (eds.), *Religion and Rational Theology: The Cambridge Edition of the Works of Immanuel Kant,* Cambridge, Cambridge University Press, pp. 233–328.

Karanović, S. (1998), *Dnevnik Jednog Filma. Virdžina 1981–1991*, Beograd, Institut Fakulteta dramskih umetnosti.

Keith, M., and Pile, S. (1993), *Place and the Politics of Identity,* London and New York, Routledge.

Klimke, M. (2010), *The Other Alliance: Student Protest in West Germany & The United States in the Global Sixties,* Princeton and Oxford, Princeton University Press.

Koch, G., Spencer, A., and Hansen, M. (1986), 'Torments of the Flesh, Coldness of the Spirit: Jewish Figures in the Films of Rainer Werner Fassbinder', *New German Critique*, 38 (Spring–Summer), pp. 28–38.

Koch, K. (1985), *Die Bedeutung des 'Oberhausener Manifests' für die Filmentwicklung in der BRD,* Frankfurt/Main, Peter Lang.

Kosanović, Dejan (1986), 'L' activité cinématographique en Yougoslavie de 1896 à 1945', in Z. Tasić and J.-L. Passek (eds.), *Le Cinéma yougoslave,* Paris, Centre Georges Pompidou, pp. 43–48.

——— (2004), *A Short History of Cinema in Serbia and Montenegro, Part I, 1896–1945,* Belgrade, Jugoslovenska kinoteka.

Kotek, J. (1996), *Students and the Cold War,* London, Macmillan.

Kramer, R., and Makavejev, D. (1975), 'Conversation sur "milestones"', *Positif. Revue de Cinema,* 176 (December), pp. 18–27.

Kraushaar, W. (ed.) (1998), *Frankfurter Schule und Studentenbewegung. Von der Flaschenpost zum Molotowcocktail 1946–1995*, Vol. 1, Munich, Rogner und Bernhard.

Kristeva, J. (1998), 'The Subject in Process', in P. French and R.-F. Lack (eds.), *The Tel Quel Reader,* London and New York, Routledge, pp. 133–178.

Kritischer Film (1972), 4.

——— (1973), 2.

Kuchler, C. (2006), *Kirche und Kino. Katholische Filmarbeit in Bayern (1945–1965),* Paderborn, Munich, Vienna, Zurich, Ferdinand Schöningh.

Laclau, E. (1996), *Emancipation(s),* London and New York, Verso.

——— (1990), *New Reflections on the Revolution of Our Time,* London and New York, Verso.

Laclau, E., and Mouffe, C. (1985), *Hegemony & Socialist Strategy: Towards a Radical Democratic Politics*, London and New York, Verso.

Laclau, E., and Zac, L. (1994), 'Minding the Gap: The Subject of Politics', in E. Laclau and L. Zac (eds.), *The Making of Political Identities,* London, Verso, pp. 11–39.

Latour, B. (2005), *Reassembling the Social: An Introduction to Actor-Network-Theory*, Oxford and New York, Oxford University Press.

Lefèbvre, H. (1999), *The Production of Space*, Oxford, Blackwell.

—— (2003), *The Urban Revolution*, Minneapolis and Minnesota, University of Minnesota Press.

Lefort, C. (1986), *The Political Forms of Modern Societies: Bureaucracy, Democracy, Totalitarianism*, Cambridge, Polity Press.

Levi, P. (2007), *Disintegration in Frames: Aesthetic and Ideology in the Yugoslav and Post-Yugoslav Cinema*, Stanford, Stanford University Press.

'Lexikon zum Avantgardefilm. Österreich 1950 bis heute (1995)', in A. Horwath, L. Ponger and G. Schlemmer (eds.), *Avantgardefilm. Österreich. 1950 bis heute,* Vienna, Wespennest, pp. 323–338.

Limmer, W., and Rumler, F. (2004), 'Alles Vernünftige interessiert mich nicht. Rainer Werner Fassbinder über sein künstlerisches Selbstverständnis und die Wurzeln seiner Kreativität', in R. Fischer (ed.), *Fassbinder über Fassbinder. Die ungekürzten Interviews,* Frankfurt/Main, Verlag der Autoren, pp. 493–555.

Lydall, H. (1984), *Yugoslav Socialism: Theory and Practice*, Oxford, Oxford University Press.

Lyotard, J.-F. (1994), *Lessons on the Analytic of the Sublime: Kant's Critique of Judgement*, Stanford, Stanford University Press.

—— (2009), *Enthusiasm: The Kantian Critique of History*, Stanford, Stanford University Press.

MacDonald, S. (ed.) (1992), *A Critical Cinema: Interviews with Independent Filmmakers,* Vol. 2, Berkeley and Los Angeles, University of California Press.

Makavejev, D. (1965), *Poljubac za drugaricu parolu*, Belgrade, Nolit, 1965.

—— (1967), 'Dusan Makavejev: Une affaire de coeur', *Cahier Du Cinéma*, 191 (June), pp. 38–41.

—— (1975), 'Eisenstein. Rouge, or, noir', *Positif. Revue Du Cinema*, 176 (December), pp. 7–17.

—— (1977), 'Interview with Dušan Makavejev', in *Ciné-Tracts. A Journal of Film, Communications. Culture, and Politics*, 1 (Summer), pp. 48–53.

—— (1984), 'Let's Put the Life Back in Political Life', in D. Georgakas and L. Rubenstein (eds.), *The Cineaste Interviews, London and Sydney* (Pluto Press, London), pp. 77–86.

—— (2001), 'Parallel Realities', *Afterimage*, 28:4, p. 8.

Markovits, A. S., Benhabib, S., and Postone, M. (1986), 'Rainer Werner Fassbinder's Garbage, the City and Death: Renewed Antagonisms in the Complex Relationships between Jews and Germans in the Federal Republic of Germany', *New German Critique*, 38 (Spring–Summer), pp. 3–27.

Marks, L. U. (2000), *The Skin of the Film: Intercultural Cinema, Embodiment, And the Senses*, Durham and London, Duke University Press.

Massey, D. (2005), *For Space, London, Thousand Oaks*, New Delhi, Sage Publications.

Maule, R. (2008), *Beyond Auteurism: New Directions in Authorial Film Practices in France, Italy and Spain since the 1980s*, Bristol and Chicago, Intellect Books.

Mekas, J. (1972), 'Movie Journal, Part 3 of an Interview with Dusan Makavejev', *Village Voice*, February 3, p. 65.

Merleau-Ponty, M. (1964a), 'Eye and Mind', in J. M. Edie (ed.), *The Primacy of Perception, and Other Essays on Phenomenological Psychology, the Philosophy of Art, History and Politics,* Evanston, Illinois, Northwestern University Press, pp. 159–190.

——— (1964b), 'Film and the New Psychology', in M. Merleau-Ponty and P. Allen Dreyfus (eds.), *Sense and Non-Sense,* Evanston, Illinois, Northwestern University Press, pp. 48–59.

Mersch, D. (2002), *Ereignis und Aura. Untersuchungen zu einer Ästhetik des Performativen,* Frankfurt/Main, Suhrkamp.

Miles, M. (2009), 'Public Spheres', in A. Harutyunyan, K. Hörschelmann and M. Miles (eds.), *Public Spheres After Socialism,* Bristol, UK, and Chicago, Intellect Books, pp. 133–150.

Moderna galerija (ed.) (1994), *OHO. Retrospektiva,* Ljubljana and Frankfurt/Main, Revolver.

Morrison, T. (1992), *Playing in the Dark: Whiteness and the Literary Imagination,* Cambridge, MA, Harvard University Press.

Mortimer, L. (2009), *Terror and Joy: The Films of Dušan Makavejev,* Minneapolis: University of Minnesota Press.

Mueller, C., and Segeberg, H. (2008), 'Öffentlichkeit und Kinoöffentlichkeit. Zum Hamburger Forschungsprogramm', in C. Mueller and H. Segeberg (eds.), *Kinoöffentlichkeit (1895–1920). Entstehung, Etablierung, Differenzierung,* Marburg, Schüren, pp. 7–31.

Naica-Loebell, A. (1996), 'Das totale Kino. Die Arbeit der Gaufilmstellen der NSDAP und die Jugendfilmstunde, konkretisiert am Beispiel München-Oberbayern', in M. Schaudig (ed.), *Positionen deutscher Filmgeschichte. 100 Jahre Kinematographie: Strukturen, Diskurse, Kontexte,* Munich, Diskurs Film Verlag, pp. 179–196.

Nancy, J. L. (1986), *L'oubli de la philosophie,* Paris, Galilée.

Negt, O., and Kluge, A. (1972), *Öffentlichkeit und Erfahrung,* Frankfurt/Main, Suhrkamp.

Novaković, S. (1969), 'Naša decenija: 1960–1969/Ili: Teze za razgovor o jugoslovenskom filmu danas', *Filmska Kultura,* 68–69 (December), pp. 42–50.

Obrdlik, A. J. (1942), 'Gallows Humor – A Sociological Phenomenon', *American Journal of Sociology,* 47 (March), pp. 709–719.

Orton, F. (1996), 'Footnote One: The Idea of the Cold War', in F. Orton and G. Pollock (eds.), *Avant-Gardes and Partisans Reviewed,* Manchester, Manchester University, pp. 205–218.

Oumano, E. (1985), *Film Forum: Thirty-five Top Filmmakers Discuss their Craft,* New York, St. Martin's Press.

Palm, M. (1996), 'Which way? Drei Pfade durchs Bild-Gebüsch von Kurt Kren', in Hans Scheugl (ed.), *Ex Underground Kurt Kren. Seine Filme,* Vienna, PVS Verleger, pp. 114–129.

Pamuk, O. (2008), 'Entre-acte oder: Ah! Cleopatra!' in O. Parmuk (ed.), *Der Blick aus meinem Fenster. Betrachtungen,* Frankfurt/Main: Fischer, pp. 179–183.

Paul, W. (1994), 'The K-Mart Audience at the Mall Movies', *Film History,* 6:4, pp. 487–501.

Pavlović, Z. (1969), *Đavolji film. Ogledi i razgovori,* Belgrade, Institut za film.

Pechriggl, A. (2000), *Corps Transfigurés. Stratifications de l'imaginaire des sexes/genres,* Vol. I (Du corps à l'imaginaire civique), Paris, l'Harmattan.

Pelinka, A. (1993), 'Die Studentenbewegung der 60er Jahre in Österreich. 8 Thesen aus politikwissenschaftlicher Sicht', *Schriftenreihe zur Lehrerbildung im berufsbildenden Schulwesen,* 146, pp. 87–104.

Pomian, K. (1990), 'Religion and Politics in a Time of Glasnost', in R. J. Hill and J. Zielonka (eds.), *Restructuring Eastern Europe: Towards a New European Order,* Brookfield, VT, Edward Elgar Publishing Company, pp. 113–129.

Prinzler, H. H., and Rentschler, E. (2001), *Der alte Film war tot. 100 Texte zum westdeutschen Film 1962-1987*, Frankfurt/Main, Verlag der Autoren.

Prinzler, H. H., and Schwarz, H. (eds.) (1972), *Über das Kinomachen. Eine Dokumentation kommunaler und privater Initiativen*, Berlin, Deutsche Film- und Fernsehakademie.

Prinzler, H. H., and Seidler, W. (eds.) (1975), *Kinobuch. Der Katalog Nr. 2. Eine Dokumentation kommunaler und privater Initiativen*, Munich, Stiftung Deutsche Kinemathek.

Privett, R. (2000), 'The Country of Movies: An Interview with Dusan Makavejev' in senses of Cinema, http://www.sensesofcinema.com/2000/11/makavejev/, pp. 1–11.

Rancière, J. (1999), *Dis-agreement: Politics and Philosophy*, Minneapolis, University of Minnesota Press.

Rayns, T. (2004), 'Das Publikum muss zufrieden sein. Rainer Werner Fassbinder über seine Themen und seine Arbeitsweise', in R. Fischer (ed.), *Fassbinder über Fassbinder. Die ungekürzten Interviews,* Frankfurt/Main, Verlag der Autoren, pp. 331–339.

Reichert, R. (2007), *Im Kino der Humanwissenschaften. Studien zur Medialisierung wissenschaftlichen Wissens*, Bielefeld, transcript.

Reimer, B., and Gibbins, J. R. (1999), *The Politics of Postmodernity: An Introduction to Contemporary Politics and Culture*, London, Thousand Oaks, New Delhi, Sage Publications.

Reitz, E. (1968), 'Parolen, Proteste, Pornographie. Ein Brief von Edgar Reitz', *Film*, 2 (February), pp. 17–18.

Robinson, D. (1971), 'Joie de Vivre at the Barricades', *Sight and Sound*, 40:4, pp. 177–180.

Rouvillois, F. (1984), *Utopia: The Search for the Ideal Society in the Western World*, New York and Oxford, Oxford University Press.

Rupieper, H.-J. (1993), *Die Wurzeln der westdeutschen Nachkriegsdemokratie. Der amerikanische Beitrag*, Opladen. Westdeutscher Verlag.

Rushdie, S. (2008), *The Satanic Verses: A Novel*, New York and London, Random House.

Sakai, N. (2005), 'Introduction. Nationality and the Politics of the Mother Tongue', in N. Sakai, B. de Bary and T. Iyotani (eds.), *Deconstructing Nationality,* New York, Cornell East Asia Series, pp. 1–38.

Savković, M. (1994), *Kinematografija u srbiji tokom Drugog svetskog rata 1941–1945*, Belgrade, Fakultet Dramskih umetnosti.

Scheugl, H. (2002), *Erweitertes Kino. Die Wiener Filme der 60er Jahre*, Vienna, Triton Verlag.

Schidor, D. (2004), 'Ich musste mein Leben gelebt haben, um diesen Film machen zu können. Rainer Werner Fassbinder über QUERELLE', in R. Fischer (ed.), *Fassbinder über Fassbinder. Die ungekürzten Interviews,* Frankfurt/Main, Verlag der Autoren (1982), pp. 617–623.

Schiffauer, W. (2008), *Parallelgesellschaften. Wie viel Wertekonsens braucht unsere Gesellschaft? Für eine kluge Politik der Differenz*, Bielefeld, transcript.

Schlemmer, G. (ed.) (1993), *Avantgardistischer Film 1951–1971: Theorie*, Munich, Carl Hanser Verlag.

Schlemmer, T. (1999), 'McCloys Botschafter in der Provinz. Die Demokratisierungsbemühungen der amerikanischen Kreis Resident Officers 1949–1952', *Vierteljahresschrift für Zeitgeschichte*, 47, pp. 265–297.

Schober, A. (2001), *Blue Jeans. Vom Leben in Stoffen und Bildern*, Frankfurt/Main und New York, Campus.

——— (2002), 'Kairos im Kino. Über die angebliche Unvereinbarkeit von Subversion und Bejahung', in I. Nierhaus and F. Konecny (eds.), *räumen. Baupläne zwischen Architektur, Raum, Visualität und Geschlecht,* Vienna, edition selene, pp. 241–267.

——— (2003), 'Close-ups in der Kinostadt', in P. Mörtenböck and H. Mooshammer (eds.), *Visuelle Kultur. Körper, Räume, Medien,* Vienna, Böhlau Verlag, pp. 231–253.

——— (2004), 'Hollywood-Movies and the Alteration of Styles and World-Views', *Contemporary Austrian Studies, The Americanization/Westernization of Austria*, Vol. XII, New Brunswick, London, Transaction Publishers, pp. 122–138.

——— (2005), 'Lumpen Design, Penis Fashion and Body-Part Amplifiers: Artistic Responses to the New Image-Environments in Former Socialist Countries since 1989', *Performance Research, 'On Form'*, 10:2, pp. 25–37.

——— (2007), 'City-Squats: The Cinema-Space as a Cave for Politics', *International Journal of Media and Cultural Politics*, 3:1, pp. 25–46.

——— (2009a), 'Irony, Montage, Alienation: Aesthetic Tactics and the Invention of an Avant-Garde Tradition', *Afterimage, The journal of media arts and cultural criticism*, 37:4, pp. 15–19.

——— (2009b), *Ironie, Montage, Verfremdung. Ästhetische Taktiken und die politische Gestalt der Demokratie*, Munich, Wilhelm Fink.

——— (2011), 'Gender und (A-)Symmetrie', *Zeitschrift für Kulturphilosophie, special issue on 'Kulturalisierung'*, 5:2, pp. 377–400.

——— (2012), 'Die bestechenden Anderen (und das Bestechen der Anderen). Subversion, Massenkultur und das (politische) Subjekt im Werden', in N. Bandi, M. G. Kraft and S. Lasinger (eds.), *Kunst, Krise, Subversion: Zur Politik der Ästhetik,* Bielefeld, transcript, 63–103.

——— (2013), 'Picturing gender: Iconic figuration, popularization, and the contestation of a key discourse in the New Europe', in D. Zuev and R. Nathanson (eds.), *Sociology of the Visual Sphere,* London und New York, Routledge, 57–80.

Schütte, W. (1974), 'Lakonische Parabel. Rainer Werner Fassbinders Film Angst essen Seele auf', *Frankfurter Rundschau*, 27 June.

Schwanebeck, A. (1990), *Evangelische Kirche und Massenmedien. Eine historische Analyse der Intentionen und Realisationen evangelischer Publizistik*, Munich, Fischer.

Sennett, R. (2003), *The Fall of Public Man*, London and New York, Penguin Books.

Shigeno, R. (2004), *From the Dialectics of the Universal to the Politics of Exclusion: The Philosophy, Politics and Nationalism of the Praxis Group from the 1950s to the 1990*, PhD thesis, Essex University, Colchester.

Simmel, G. (1992), *Soziologie. Untersuchungen über die Formen der Vergesellschaftung*, Gesamtausgabe, Vol. 11, Frankfurt/Main, Suhrkamp.

——— (1997), 'The Sociology of Space', in D. Frisby and M. Featherstone (eds.), *Simmel. On Culture,* London, Thousand Oaks, New Delhi, Sage Publications, pp. 137–170.

Sitton, R., MacBean, J. R., and Callenbach, E. (1971/1972), 'Fight Power with Spontaneity and Humor', in *Film Quarterly*, 25:2, pp. 3–9.

Sorkin, M. (1992), 'Introduction: Variations on a Theme Park', in M. Sorkin and J. Copjec (eds.), *Variations on a Theme Park: The New American City and the End of Public Space,* Hill and Wang, New York, xi–xv.

Sparrow, N. (2004), 'Ich lasse die Zuschauer fühlen und denken', in R. Fischer (ed.), *Fassbinder über Fassbinder. Die ungekürzten Interviews,* Frankfurt/Main, Verlag der Autoren (1977), pp. 405–414.

Steinborn, B., and von Naso, R. (2004), 'Ich bin das Glück dieser Erde. Rainer Werner Fassbinder über QUERELLE', in R. Fischer (ed.), *Fassbinder über Fassbinder. Die ungekürzten Interviews,* Frankfurt/Main, Verlag der Autoren (1982), pp. 589–616.

Suárez, J. A. (2007), *Pop Modernism: Noise and the Reinvention of the Everyday,* Urbana and Chicago, University of Illinois Press.

Ugrešić, D. (1998), *The Culture of Lies,* London, Phoenix.

Unser Arbeiterbund. Information in Bildung und Unterhaltung (1954), 1 (September).

van de Port, M. (1998), *Gypsies, Wars & Other Instances of the Wild: Civilization and its Discontents in a Serbian Town,* Amsterdam, Amsterdam University Press.

—––— (2004), 'Registers of Incontestability: The Quest for Authenticity in Academia and Beyond', *Etnofoor,* 17:1–2, pp. 7–22.

Veith, U. (1974), *Gewerkschaftliche Medienpolitik und Filmarbeit. Am Beispiel des DGB und der IG Metall,* Cologne, Pahl-Rugenstein.

Veselinović, S. (ed.) (1996), *Ovo je Studentski Kulturni Centar. This is the Student Cultural Center,* Belgrade, Studentski kulturni centar.

von Mengershausen, J. (2004), 'Unsere Vorstellungen von Anarchie haben nichts mit Chaos zu tun. Rainer Werner Fassbinder über LIEBE IST KÄLTER ALS DER TOD und das antiteater', in R. Fischer (ed.), *Fassbinder über Fassbinder. Die ungekürzten Interviews,* Frankfurt/Main, Verlag der Autoren, pp. 179–203.

Vučo, A. (1946), 'Naša mlada filmska proizvodnja', *Film,* 1 (December), pp. 1–4.

Wasson, H. (2005), *Museum Movies: The Museum of Modern Art and the Birth of Art Cinema,* Berkeley and Los Angeles, The University of California Press.

Weibel, P. (1972), 'Aktion statt Theater', *Neues Forum. Österreichische Monatsblätter für kulturelle Freiheit,* 221 (May), pp. 48–52.

—––— (1973), *Kritik der Kunst. Kunst der Kritik,* Munich, Jugend & Volk.

Wenders, W. (1968), 'Keine "exprmte". Filme in einer Einstellung – Gedanken zur "exprmtl 4"', *Film,* 2 (February), p. 16.

—––— (2004), 'Auf der Suche nach Bildern – Orte sind meine stärksten Bildgeber', in C. Maar and H. Burda, *Iconic Turn. Die neue Macht der Bilder,* Cologne, Du Mont, pp. 283–302.

Wiegand, W. (2004), 'Ich weiß über nichts als über den Menschen Bescheid', in R. Fischer (ed.), *Fassbinder über Fassbinder. Die ungekürzten Interviews,* Frankfurt/Main, Verlag der Autoren, pp. 273–300.

Wieviorka, M. (2001), *La différence,* Paris, Balland.

Williams, R. (1988), *Keywords: A Vocabulary of Culture and Society,* London, Fontana Press.

Willemen, P., in conversation with N. King (1993), 'Through the Glass Darkly: Cinephilia Reconsidered', in P. Willemen (ed.), *Looks and Frictions: Essays in Cultural Studies and*

Film Theory, Bloomington, Indianapolis and London, Indiana University Press and BFI Publishing, pp. 223–257.

Wolfe, A. (1997), 'Public and Private in Theory and Practice: Some Implications of an Uncertain Boundary', in J. Weintraub and K. Kumar (eds.), *Public and Private in Thought and Practices: Perspectives on a Grand Dichotomy*, Chicago and London, The University of Chicago Press, pp. 182–203.

Yanitskii, O. (1993), *Russian Environmentalism: Figures, Facts, Opinions*, Moscow, Mezhdunarodnye otnoshenija Publishing.

Young, A. (2001), *Women Who Become Man*, Albanian Sworn Virgins, Oxford, Berg.

Zerilli, L. (2004), 'Aesthetic Judgement and the Public Sphere in the Thought of Hannah Arendt', *ÖZG (Österreichische Zeitschrift für Geschichtswissenschaften)*, *Ästhetik des Politischen*, 3, pp. 67–94.

Zimmermann, C. (2007), *Medien im Nationalsozialismus. Deutschland, Italien und Spanien in den 1930er und 1940er Jahren*, Cologne and Weimar, Böhlau UTB.